DATE DUE

D1367761

Praise for *Upstarts!*

"One of the richest veins in startup gold is GenY entrepreneurs. Fenn deconstructs the DNA of this collaborative, tech-savvy generation to illuminate the future of entrepreneurship."

—Guy Kawasaki, Cofounder of Alltop and author of *Reality Check*

"If your business is stuck in old school ways of thinking, this book will bring new perspective and insight on how a whole new class of upstarts are thinking!"

—Tony Hsieh, CEO, Zappos

"This book will make you feel confident. Confident in the fact Generation Y has the tools, creativity, desire, passion, energy, and smarts to keep this great nation in a position of leadership economically for decades to come."

—Harry Paul, Coauthor, *FISH! A Remarkable Way to Boost Morale and Improve Results* and *Instant Turnaround! Getting People Excited About Coming to Work and Working Hard*

"In this smart, timely book, Donna Fenn shows us how Generation Y— probably the most entrepreneurial generation ever—is radically remaking the business world in its own image, one innovative startup company at a time."

—Jane Berentson, Editor, *Inc.*

"With *Upstarts!* Donna Fenn has given us the most colorful and complete picture yet of the entrepreneurial generation creating our future: who they are, how they think, and why they are going to change the world. She captures and categorizes them with the eye of a scientist and the words of a poet. There are only two choices: Buy this book or get left behind."

—Billy Shore, Founder, Share our Strength

"I'm convinced we're seeing the rise of a new generation of entrepreneurs, and *Upstarts!* is a storm warning. Fuelled by their initial experiences in the workforce, and empowered by their digital skills and culture of innovation, many of today's youth are setting a new course. This book nails the trend— a rich and thoroughly enjoyable insight into the future."

—Don Tapscott, author of 13 books about new
technologies in business and society, including
Wikinomics and most recently *Grown Up Digital*

"In *Upstarts!* Donna Fenn has navigated the millennial entrepreneurship generation, exposing thorough research and compelling stories. This book will change your perception of millennials, and by the time you're finished reading it, you'll either want to work for one, partner with one, or be that age again. Donna is onto a major trend with *Upstarts!* and it will change the business world in the coming years."

—Dan Schawbel, author of *Me 2.0: Build a Powerful
Brand to Achieve Career Success*

"Upstarts is a rallying cry for the next generation of entrepreneurs, and a wakeup call for everyone who hopes to compete with them."

—Steve Mariotti, Founder, The Network
for Teaching Entrepreneurship (NFTE)

"A compelling analysis of Generation Y–NOT. With the world predicting the death of capitalism, Donna Fenn persuasively makes the case for a coming entrepreneurial boom—led by a cadre of street-smart young people who are reshaping the business world from the bottom up with their collaborative, tech-savvy, and workplace renegade ways. If you want to understand what most entrepreneurial businesses will look like ten years from now, read this book."

—Keith McFarland, author of *The Breakthrough
Company* and *Bounce*

UPSTARTS

DONNA
FENN

UPSTARTS

How GenY
Entrepreneurs
Are Rocking
the World of
Business and
8 Ways
You Can
Profit from
Their Success

 New York   Chicago   San Francisco   Lisbon
London   Madrid   Mexico City   Milan   New Delhi
San Juan   Seoul   Singapore   Sydney   Toronto

The *McGraw·Hill* Companies

1 2 3 4 5 6 7 8 9 0   DOC/DOC 1 0 9 8 7 6 5 4 3 2 1 0

ISBN: 978-0-07-160188-7
MHID: 0-07-160188-0

McGraw-Hill books are available at special quantity discounts to use as premiums and sales promotions, or for use in corporate training programs. To contact a representative please e-mail us at bulksales@mcgraw-hill.com.

For Guian, Ariana, and Erich, with joyful anticipation of the adventures ahead!

CONTENTS

ACKNOWLEDGMENTS

Every book is a collaborative effort, but none so much as this one. My biggest debt of gratitude goes to the 150+ GenY entrepreneurs (known from here on in as Upstarts!) who shared their stories, responded to multiple e-mail and Facebook messages with generosity and good cheer, introduced me to their entrepreneurial pals, mentioned me in their blog posts, and taught me more about what it means to be a young entrepreneur than I could ever fit into one book. And they did it all without promises of being mentioned or featured in the book. You'll meet many of them in these pages, but I also want to single out the following, who don't appear in the book, but who helped me generously and faithfully and who you should look for in future postings on the Upstarts blog: Ada Polla, Adam Witty, Alan Blake, Alex Lindhal, Ashleigh Hansberger, Brandi Daniels, Brett Jackson, Bunmi Zalob, Corey Kossack, David Mullings, Jason Duff, Ken Carnesi, Michael Mothner, Morgan First, Philip Krim, Ryan Allis, Sunny Bonnell, Tom Wollmann, Vinicio Otto Montes, and Zach Hurst.

As always, my work as a contributing editor at *Inc.* magazine informs almost everything I write about entrepreneurs. I'm immensely grateful for the support of John Koten and the incredibly talented staff of writers, editors, and designers at *Inc.* Jane Berentson and Mike Hofman gave me the opportunity to work on features for the magazine that were related to book content and offered wise editorial counsel. Many, many thanks to Rod Kurtz for making Inc.com's "30 Under 30" feature the go-to list for everyone who wants to know who's hot in the vast community of promising, young entrepreneurs. The list, which I'm always champing at the bit to work on, provided great fodder for this book. Loren Feldman gets my heartfelt thanks for encouraging and supporting my blog on Inc.com, "The Entrepreneurial Generation." Jim Melloan, *Inc.*'s amazing project manager for the Inc. 5000, generously shared data so that I could find and contact young CEOs on the list.

George Gendron, *Inc.*'s former editor-in-chief, has been a trusted friend and advisor for more than 20 years. This time around, his wisdom was particularly priceless, given his current position as founder and director of the Innovation and Entrepreneurship Program at Clark University in Worcester, MA. George also put me in touch with Ashley Emerson Gilbert, then one of his students at Clark, who signed on as my intern during a critical stage of the book's research. Thanks Ashley!

Aislinn Raedy formerly of EO (Entrepreneurs' Organization), David Cohen at TechStars, Michael Simmons at Extreme Entrepreneurship Tour, and Jennifer Kushell at YSN.com, gave great advice and recommended some fantastic entrepreneurs for me to interview. Dan Schawbel has been a faithful and generous supporter, and Anastasia Goodstein at YPulse gave me a forum to speak about *Upstarts!* before it even hit the bookstores—a leap of faith that's greatly appreciated.

Every author thinks she has the best agent in the world, but I really do. Hands down. Esmond Harmsworth at Zachary Shuster Harmsworth has been my most trusted and valued advisor since I started writing books seven years ago. He's been my editor, my advocate, my critic and, yes, sometimes my psychotherapist. Plus he loves dogs and laughs at my jokes, which makes him as close to perfect as a guy can get.

It's a lucky author who starts and finishes a book with the same editor. I've had this privilege not just once, but twice with—miracle of miracles— the same fabulous editor. McGraw-Hill's Leah Spiro edited *Upstarts!* as well as my first book, *Alpha Dogs: How Your Small Business Can Become a Leader of the Pack* (Collins, 2005). An author has no better friend than a highly skilled editor who manages to be tough, honest, and compassionate all at once. That is Leah to a tee, and I could not have asked for a better navigator on the challenging but thrilling journey from first draft to bound book. Leah's colleagues at McGraw-Hill—Heather Cooper, Ann Pryor, Keith Pfeffer, Morgan Ertel, Ron Martirano, Chuck Yuen, Maureen Harper, and Ty Nowicki—employed every resource available to them to expertly support the writing, design, and launch of *Upstarts!*. Thanks for the great teamwork!

To Buddy, Bailey, and Indie: thanks not only for your unconditional love but also for the wet snouts on my keyboard and the slobbery tennis balls dropped at my feet. Everyone needs to be reminded to take a break once in a while.

Finally, I can never be grateful enough to my family. My husband, Guian Heintzen, and my children, Ariana and Erich, remind me every day that, especially in tumultuous times, there is no better anchor than the steadfast love of a happy family. My parents, Donald and Virginia Fenn, and my in-laws, Harry and Ilse Heintzen—with over 100 years of marriage among them—are living proof of that. I am indebted to them immeasurably, and blessed by the richness they bring to our lives.

The Upstarts Are Coming!

Joel Erb slid into the black limousine and settled in for the long road trip from Richmond, VA, to Manhattan. Wearing a somewhat oversized suit coat that he hoped made him look older than he was, he clutched the portfolio of website designs that he planned to present to executives at Calvin Klein, Armani, and Hugo Boss. He was a little nervous but also confident in the way that people with very little to lose typically are. Using a trial download of Flash, he had created the designs on the computer in his bedroom (aka "Suite 101"). It was 1998, and Web design was still an emerging profession; back then, a smooth-talking neophyte like Erb could generate enough interest in his mockups to cajole his way into appointments at those prestigious fashion houses. "I'll be in New York in two weeks," he told them, "and I'd love to meet with you." He was 14 years old, and it would be his first trip outside the state of Virginia.

Erb's previous Web design experience consisted of creating a website for his middle school and doing a bit of work for a local carpet-cleaning service and for some companies in the heating, ventilation, and air-conditioning (HVAC) industry. The son of working-class parents with limited financial resources, he had a passion for art and design and an impressive toolbox of self-taught technology skills. He also had a family friend with a limo company who was willing to make the drive to New York, open doors for him, and call him "Mr. Erb" whenever anyone was listening. "He pulled out all the stops for me," says Erb. "I felt like Richie Rich." The friend's parents lived in Brooklyn, and they fed Erb a good dinner, put him up for a night, and helped him iron his clothes so that he'd look fresh for his Manhattan meetings.

> "Suite 101 was my bedroom."
>
> —Joel Erb, INM United

Reality hit home the next day. The marketing director at one firm took a look at him and asked if his father was coming to the meeting, too. "Have you even reached puberty?" he sneered. Erb was given short shrift at the second meeting as well. But at the third, they asked him the magic question: "How much?" Erb can't say which company it was because of a nondisclosure agreement, but he went back to Richmond, wrote a proposal, and ended up landing a $30,000 contract to create banner ads. It wasn't a website design project, but it was a good start. "When the checks came to my house, my parents were completely stunned," Erb says.

The next few years were a whirlwind. Erb became the first high school student in Virginia to earn his diploma by taking classes on the Web, and he grew his company, now called INM United, to $1 million in revenue, only to be wiped out after 9/11. "We lost every single project in New York and a lot near Richmond," he recalls. "I had to let all my employees go except two. And then I started getting panic attacks. I was an 18-year-old with the stress level of 40-year-old businessman." With 80 percent of his business gone, he enrolled at the University of Richmond and built his company back up from his dorm room, drawing on advice from professors and local businesspeople. He reconceived INM, transforming it from a Web design firm into an integrated marketing company, and that would double his revenue.

Since then, Erb has been honored as a rising start by the Greater Richmond Technology Council, won a Small Business Administration (SBA) regional "Entrepreneur of the Year" award, and has been recognized as one of Virginia's top "40 Under 40" entrepreneurs. He houses his staff of 12 in a leased 3,000-square-foot office situated in renovated warehouse space in the trendy Shockoe Bottom section of Richmond, where "we have mood lighting, a drum set and a little helicopter that we fly around the office," he says proudly. Revenues in 2008 were in excess of $1 million.

At age 26, Erb has already been in business for longer than he's been able to order a drink in a restaurant or attend an R-rated movie without sneaking in. Precocious? Sure. An anomaly? Well, not really. Over the course of more than 25 years of studying and writing about entrepreneurship, I can't ever recall talking to so many business owners who started bona fide companies in their twenties or earlier. "I've got my own business" has not only replaced "I'm in a band" as the ultimate boast; it also has replaced "I've got a lemonade stand."

The Upstarts Are Coming!

Erb is a member of the generation we've come to call "Y" (or "Generation Why?" the "Me Generation," the "Net Generation," the "iPod Generation," "Echo Boomers," and most recently, "Generation O," for the enormous role they played in President Obama's election). They were born between 1977 and 1997, and you can call them what you like; I call them the *entrepreneurial generation*. There are approximately 77 million of them, and their sheer numbers, combined with the rate at which they're starting businesses, will make them a force to be reckoned with. And because their approach to entrepreneurship is so different from that of previous generations, these "Upstarts" are destined to have a profound effect on the economy and specifically on the small-business landscape. It's the purpose of this book to document this revolution and to paint a narrative portrait of this entrepreneurial generation.

Upstarts! began to take shape three years ago, after the publication of my first book, *Alpha Dogs: How Your Small Business Can Become a Leader of the Pack* (Collins, 2005). *Alpha Dogs* chronicled the success of eight extraordinary companies that had achieved entrepreneurial greatness not by virtue

> "Starting your own business is the most creative thing you can do. It's a living, breathing work of art."
>
> —Shazi Visram,
> Happy Baby Food

of what they make or sell, but because they were masters at setting themselves apart from the pack through their sophisticated business strategies—strategies that all small businesses must master if they want to survive and thrive in an increasingly cutthroat economy. In *Alpha Dogs*, I mentioned four compelling competitive challenges that are forcing small businesses to become more strategic: the growing number of demanding and fickle consumers; industry consolidation, which breeds huge competitors; advances in technology, which allow big competitors to look small and intimate and small ones to look formidable; and market saturation by a burgeoning number of products and services.

But shortly after I began to speak to audiences about *Alpha Dogs*, I realized that something huge and exciting was happening in the world of small-business creation and that I needed to add a fifth challenge: An emerging group of young, brash, and highly educated "upstart" entrepreneurs was beginning to raise the bar for mature companies in every industry. Everywhere I looked, I saw Joel Erbs.

 ## An Entrepreneurial Revolution

Technology, it seemed, was helping entrepreneurial dreams come true for a whole new demographic. Company founders were getting younger and smarter, and they appeared to be undaunted by—or naively unaware of—the challenges that make small-business survival such a risky proposition. If a young person was inspired and inclined, he or she might dip a toe into the world of commerce with a mere click of the mouse. Fifteen-year-olds could make a killing on eBay or, like Joel Erb, pass themselves off as seasoned Web developers not by means of deceit, but simply by cloaking themselves in the anonymity of the Internet.

> "When I started the company, I had to go to customer dinners with a fake ID."
>
> —Rachel Hennig,
> Catalyst Search

Like previous generations of entrepreneurs, they're driven by the desire for financial independence, motivated by the sudden perception of an unmet market need, eager to sell a newly conceived product or service, or convinced that they can improve on something that already exists in the marketplace. Or maybe they're just having fun. To them, the decision to start a business is not particularly intimidating; for better or worse, it's often not thoroughly planned out. It may start out with a tiny germ of idea like, "Hey,

I really like design, and I'm good with computers, so let me take a crack at mocking up some websites for clothing designers." Startup costs? Nil. Risk? Nonexistent. Support? Abundant. Parents, teachers, and mentors provide everything from words of encouragement to advice to financial backing, sending a "can-do" message that may have seemed imprudent or indulgent 10 years ago. Welcome to the new lemonade stand.

Some of these young CEOs approached me directly; others made their way onto my radar screen via a great number of breathless public relations pitches, which I typically ignore unless I begin to discern a trend. In this case, I most certainly did. But I was captivated by more than just anecdotal tidbits about "baby" CEOs.

A study by Intuit and the Institute for the Future predicts that "Generation Y will emerge as the most entrepreneurial generation ever." Sean Rush, Junior Achievement Worldwide (JA) CEO and president, says that JA's curriculum is now being taught to more than 4 million U.S. students, some as young as five years of age; that represents a 50 percent increase over 10 years. The organization, which teaches kids workforce skills, the basics of entrepreneurship, and financial literacy, also polled 1,155 teenagers and found that 69 percent of them wanted to start a business. The SBA recently started partnering with

> "Generation Y will emerge as the most entrepreneurial generation ever."
> —Report by Intuit and the Institute for the Future

JA to launch a business portal for teens and reported that nearly two-thirds of college students want to start their own businesses. According to the Kauffman Foundation, a Kansas City not-for-profit that tracks and funds entrepreneurship initiatives, there are more university-based programs than ever to help them do just that—a phenomenon that's a direct result of exploding demand among student populations and one that's helping foment a new kind of entrepreneurial revolution.

Never in our country's history have so many young adults wanted to become entrepreneurs or have so many colleges and universities been committed to helping them realize their entrepreneurial dreams. Approximately 2,100 U.S. colleges and universities offer courses in entrepreneurship (compared with 400 only 10 years ago), and according to the Kauffman

Foundation, there are now more than 400 endowed chairs in graduate *and* undergraduate entrepreneurship programs that have over 200,000 enrolled students; this represents a 70 percent increase in the past seven years.

More telling is that the curriculum in these programs has changed radically over the past several years to accommodate a more demanding student population. "Forty percent or more of students who come into our undergraduate entrepreneurship program as freshmen already have a business," says Jeff Cornwall, the Massey Chair in Entrepreneurship at Belmont University in Nashville. "It's a whole new world." And so Belmont not only teaches entrepreneurship but also houses three incubators for college business owners and has helped to launch six student-operated businesses on campus. Five of them are profitable, ongoing concerns that serve both their fellow students and the surrounding Nashville community. "Serving the needs of this generation has caused us to change how we teach entrepreneurship," says Cornwall. "The old model was, go off and do liberal arts, and when you're a junior, we'll give you an entrepreneurship course. Now, if I wait until junior year, I'll lose them. Everything has to be tied to experience."

> "Forty percent or more of students who come into our undergraduate entrepreneurship program as freshmen already have a business. It's a whole new world."
>
> —Jeff Cornwall,
> Belmont University

 ## A Different Mind-set

So what is it about this particular generation that draws them to the entrepreneurial life? Why are they starting companies, and what industries are they attracted to? Are they growing and running their companies in ways that are fundamentally different from previous generations? What impact will they have on the economy, and how are their triumphs—and their failures—instructive to all small-business owners? These are the questions that inspired me to write this book, and my journey gave me a fascinating glimpse into what I believe is our entrepreneurial future. After more than 150 in-depth interviews and 18 months of research, I found myself with a mental snapshot of a generation that looked altogether more complex than the self-absorbed, impatient, unfocused, and materialistic young adults that the media would have us believe comprise Generation Y.

Yes, many of the young CEOs I spoke to seemed to possess those traits, just like a good number of the older entrepreneurs I've written about over the past 25 years. But these Upstarts also were extraordinarily collaborative and team-oriented individuals who were technologically precocious, agile, and flexible, quick to recognize emerging trends, hell-bent on creating innovative and balanced workplaces, determined to change the world, and dismissive of the industry conventions that they felt had kept their competitors treading water.

It's tempting to call them risk-takers, and indeed, some might even refer to themselves that way. But risk implies that you have something to lose. The fact remains that when you start a company in your teens or 20s, there is far less to lose than when you are in your 30s, 40s, or 50s, when career options narrow and financial and personal responsibilities factor into your decision to make the entrepreneurial leap. So what sometimes feels and looks like risk-taking to GenY entrepreneurs is really more youthful exuberance—a willingness to experiment, to jump into an idea feet first without that gut-wrenching sensation that you are betting the farm. You might fail miserably, you might find that your original idea morphs into something altogether different, or you might just find yourself with a multimillion-dollar company on your hands. Whatever the outcome, it is highly unlikely that you will default to a corporate career. This is a generation of serial entrepreneurs.

> "Our business is the best résumé builder we could shoot for."
>
> —Jon Levi, Jlevi StreetWerks

What's driving this startup fever?

There are two critical distinctions that define the startup mentality of Upstart entrepreneurs. Most importantly, they are the first "grown up digital" generation. We all know now that the Internet, cloud computing, mobile devices, and social media can make starting and running a business infinitely cheaper, less risky, and more efficient than it's been in the past. But knowing it and jumping on it are two different things. While older entrepreneurs may struggle with getting up to speed or even resist the call of Web 2.0, new technology is like the air that Upstarts breath—there's no learning curve at all. Secondly, GenY is the first generation to come of age with entrepreneurship as a highly attractive life path. Remember that both GenY and their Baby Boomer parents witnessed the preeminence of established entrepreneurial heroes. First, we had Bill Gates, Steve Jobs, Oprah Winfrey, Richard Branson, Jeff Bezos, and the late Anita Roddick, and then, younger high-profile innovators like Larry Page and Sergey Brin (Google), Jerry Yang (Yahoo!), Chad Hurley and Steve Chen (YouTube), and Mark Zuckerberg (Facebook) attracted the kind of media attention and public adoration typically reserved for rock stars and athletes. They made business seem cool to kids as well as to their parents, who were often victims of corporate bloodletting.

But it wasn't just the celebrity factor that was compelling. Starting roughly in the 1980s, we heard over and over again that it was small, entrepreneurial companies that truly drove economic growth, job creation, and innovation in our country. Suddenly, the unsung heroes were getting the recognition they richly deserved, and entrepreneurship was not just cool, it was also noble—worthy of a spot in grade school curriculum. Junior Achievement Worldwide's biggest area of growth is in kindergarten through fifth grade.

A host of other social, economic, and political events also plays a huge role in GenY's fascination with entrepreneurship. It begins with their birth to Baby Boomer parents—arguably the most child-centric generation in history. Sometimes called "helicopter parents," they devoured parenting books (between 1975 and 2005, the number of parenting books published increased from 57 to 684!), coached their kids' sports teams, volunteered at their schools, enrolled them in countless "enrichment" activities, and generally instilled in their progeny the notion that they were capable of doing just about anything they set their minds to. Praise was frequent ("You're special"); criticism was meted out sparingly.

A Gallup poll reveals strong parent-child relationships among GenY. Ninety percent said they were very close to their parents, whereas back in 1974, 40 percent of Baby Boomers said they'd be better off without theirs. Clearly, this is a reflection of the times we live in; the Vietnam War, combined with revolutionary changes in music, fashion, and culture gave Baby Boomers and their parents plenty to disagree about. While teens and young adults are perennially rebellious, the "generation gap" is no longer the chasm it was in the 1960s and 1970s. And that's evident in plenty of GenY companies where young CEOs are partnering directly with parents, hiring them as employees, or taking over responsibility for family-owned companies at increasingly young ages.

Several young entrepreneurs who I interviewed claimed that their parents encouraged their entrepreneurial pursuits from a strikingly young age. "Our parents had us create a business plan and pitch them every Christmas," says David Mullings, 28, who owns a Caribbean music company, RealVibez, with his brother, Robert. "And every year they said no until we came up with RealVibez. Dad is a lecturer at university and a doctor, and mom is a nurse, but they wanted us to be in business." Alana Millstein, the 24-year-old founder of *College Affair* magazine in Phoenix, AZ, says that when she was 12, her mother tore up little pieces of paper to explain the concept of buying shares in the stock market. "Then she gave me $1,000 and said, 'start researching companies, and I'll invest for you,'" recalls Millstein. "The one that made me a lot of money was Apple. I used $120,000 from my sale of stock to start my company." Casey Golden, now 29 and the CEO of new venture called Golden Rule Technology, has started five companies. "The first was when I was 13, and I founded it with my Dad," recalls Golden. "We invented a biodegradable golf tee." His dad raised the initial capital, and his mom worked on the recipe, which initially consisted of water, flour, peat moss, and applesauce. Golden won a national K-mart–sponsored competition called "Invent America," and before you could yell "fore!" his bio tees were in every K-mart in the United States, he was traveling to Japan to meet with patent attorneys, and the U.S. media was calling him "Mr. Tee."

Parents of GenY children are typically more supportive of their children's company-building dreams than their own parents may have been under similar circumstances. Back then, starting a business had all the cachet of hawking watches on a street corner; if you were serious about making a living, you landed a job in a big corporation, where you'd be taken care of until the gold watch came your way at age 65. But the implicit employment-for-life contract ended in the 1980s when global competition, downsizing, and consolidation forced big companies to reduce their workforces. Since 1984, more than 30 million Americans have lost their jobs; only 40 percent of us now work for corporations with more than 1,000 employees. Parents who lost their jobs and the children who watched them work hard only to come home with a pink slip are far less inclined to have faith in a future linked to large corporations. If corporate scandals involving once-trusted companies like Enron and WorldCom weren't enough to reinforce the distrust, the events of 2008 sealed the deal: Companies "too big to fail" did exactly that. In January 2009, the Bureau of Labor Statistics reported that "payroll employment has declined by 3.6 million since the start of the recession in December 2007; about one half of this decline occurred in the past three months." At this writing, there has been no clear end to the recession in sight.

If corporate employment looks more and more fragile, so does the world in general. GenY grew up with Amber Alerts, HIV, the Columbine shootings, the dot-com boom and its spectacular bust, the 9/11 tragedy, and the subsequent invasions of Afghanistan and Iraq. At the same time, they were far more independent than previous generations: Three out of four grew up with working mothers, and one-quarter lived with a single parent. Throughout their young lives, the subtle and not so subtle message was clear: You're unlikely to be taken care of by institutions that were once trusted and cherished by previous generations; better look out for yourself. Armed with the self-confidence instilled in them by their parents, they have sought to do just that. And if that sometimes makes them difficult and demanding employees, it often makes them extraordinary entrepreneurs.

> "Generation Y is changing the face of global business, possibly the most dramatic upheaval in business culture since women entered the workplace during World War II."
>
> —Randstad USA, 2008 World of Work

I started my research by casting a very wide net. Over the past few years, the burgeoning number of young entrepreneurs has spawned lists such as *Inc.* magazine's "30 Under 30: America's Coolest Young Entrepreneurs" and *Business Week*'s "America's Best Young Entrepreneurs." I drew from these compilations, as well from the Inc. 500 and Inc. 5000 lists of fastest-growing companies (my colleagues at *Inc.* magazine generously shared database information with me so that I could find CEOs in the GenY demographic, which I define as people born between 1977 and 1997). I also contacted such groups as The Network for Teaching Entrepreneurship (NFTE), Young and Successful, the Extreme Entrepreneurship Tour, Entrepreneurs' Organization (EO), the William J. Clinton Foundation, and two organizations—YCombinator and TechStars—that mentor and fund young entrepreneurs. The Athena Foundation and Count Me In for Economic Independence put me in touch with young female entrepreneurs.

I also spread the word among my colleagues and my extensive professional network that I was looking for successful GenY CEOs to interview. And I made it clear to everyone I spoke with that I wasn't interested in people who had merely managed to get obscenely rich at strikingly young ages. While that may be impressive to some, it does very little to pique my curiosity. I wanted company builders—people whose financial success was the by-product of creating something of greater economic value than a healthy bank account. I also should note here that I deliberately chose not to focus the book primarily on the superstars of the GenY entrepreneurial world. Stories about Facebook, YouTube, Digg, and other familiar brands are truly awe inspiring, but they've been told many times, and I wanted fresh material.

In no time I had a list of entrepreneurs longer than I could ever manage to make my way through in the months I had to write this book. With each interview, I inevitably added more names to the list because young entrepreneurs tend to know other young entrepreneurs—typically lots of them—and they are eager to draw others into projects that they find relevant and exciting. It wasn't just their sheer numbers that struck me, but their incredible diversity: I found more women and minority business owners in this generation than I've ever seen in my career.

My Excellent Social Media Adventure

I wanted to reach out to these young entrepreneurs in a way that was meaningful, relevant, and practical to them. So I dove into the world of social media by creating a Facebook page. This probably doesn't seem like such a big deal now, but when I did it a year and a half ago, joining Facebook was something that no mother of teenaged children should do without a very good explanation. That just goes to show you how quickly things change. I added my interviewees to my page as friends and then also invited them to join a private group on Facebook where I could ask them follow-up questions collectively and where they could meet and network with each other.

I can say unequivocally now that this would be a different book without Facebook. My private group grew to 80 or so people, and every time I sent out a message to them (e.g., "I'm working on a section about partnerships; give me a shout if you've got good stories"), at least a few responded with lightening speed. I got better and quicker responses from my Facebook messages than from e-mail, and I came to know my interviewees a little more intimately from the links they posted and the messages that appeared on my newsfeed. In some instances, I watched their entrepreneurial struggles evolve in a very public way as they shared with their Facebook friends the details of company launches, searches for capital, and partnerships gone bad. And yes, I also saw a few things that that I wish I hadn't and that gave me pause. (How much Grey Goose vodka can you drink and still be able to function well enough to run a business?)

To further get the word out about the project and to connect with others who might have been able to help, I started a blog on Inc.com called "The Entrepreneurial Generation." I got multiple comments on most of the posts, some of which helped to shape my thinking for the book. My LinkedIn contacts were helpful as well. And lastly, I started tweeting on Twitter, the micro-blogging site that's become mind-bogglingly popular over the past year or so.

My goal was to speak with as many successful young CEOs as possible so that I could get at the heart of their entrepreneurial motivations, their success strategies and how they manage their companies. I've organized this book around the themes that emerged—themes that I believe not only help to characterize an important and influential segment of this generation but also provide a roadmap to the future for all of us who are engaged in and care about the entrepreneurial economy. This is a highly collaborative generation whose proficiency with technology, brand awareness, and impatience with outmoded business models will give us a new crop of companies that will look altogether different from the one we've admired in the past. And that goes for how those companies operate as well. In Upstart companies, there's often a clear social mission, rejection of traditional hierarchy, and the desire to make work meaningful and fun. So who exactly are these Upstarts? They are:

Extreme Collaborators

Forget the lone-wolf entrepreneur. Young entrepreneurs rarely go down the startup road alone but frequently team up with a partner or partners. They often start companies with friends, college classmates, professors, parents, or spouses. Upstarts know their limitations and seek out cofounders and investment partners who can compensate for their weaknesses and complement their strengths. Frequently, they also learn the pitfalls of partnerships. As they grow their companies, they continue to be highly collaborative, often drawing in teams of employees, their social networks, and groups of customers through community-based innovation tools that help them to develop new products and services.

Technology Mavens

According to the Pew Internet and American Life Project, GenY spends significantly more time than its older counterparts on the Internet and comprises 30 percent of all Internet users. However, while technology is the big differentiating factor for this generation of digital natives, don't assume that they're all starting Web-based companies. Some of them, of course, *are* in industries that didn't exist a couple of years ago. Witness, for example, the large number of small companies whose primary business is creating applications for Facebook or the iPhone. But Upstarts are just as likely to put their own tech-savvy stamp on more traditional businesses as well. Technology is not only the catalyst for innovative new products and services but also the key factor in the ability of Upstarts to distinguish their companies in crowded marketplaces.

Game Changers

Upstarts change the game by finding chinks in conventional or outmoded business models and the assumptions that go along with them. They might steamroll the competition by introducing cutting-edge technology to established industries, demanding that their business partners adapt new systems of information sharing or best practices. A healthy disrespect for the status quo leads them to experiment fearlessly. They disrupt and revitalize old economy businesses by reimagining the supply chain, reinventing mature family businesses, and finding new ways to deliver traditional products and services to new niche markets.

Market Insiders

Upstarts are in the catbird seat when it comes to serving the needs of a very large and wealthy market segment—their 77 million peers in GenY. They already have annual incomes of $211 billion, and they spend $172 billion of it. Their buying habits are vastly different from those of previous generations. Upstart companies target college students with services such as moving and storage and laundry and cleaning; they create new social networking communities; they build brands that appeal to youth; and they put their own spin on traditional business concepts, such as personal finance and online dating. And increasingly, they even set up shop with the intention of selling their own GenY savvy to the companies that want to learn how to reach this important market segment.

Brand Builders

Upstarts know how to build brands. From how they name their companies to how they market, sell, and produce their goods and services, GenY entrepreneurs embrace brand building as the key to setting themselves apart from the competition. Their distinctive brand personalities drive faster and broader market penetration, which helps them to generate national public relations and marketing buzz. Many attract attention from large companies that may want to partner with them or even acquire their companies. Branding also gives them an edge when it comes to appealing to an enormously critical market segment—their own brand-conscious peers in GenY.

Social Capitalists

GenY has a keen sense of social justice. A study by Cone, Inc., and Amp Insights of 1,800 young people shows that 61 percent of 13- to 25-year-olds feel responsible for making a difference in the world, and 79 percent of them want to work for a company that feels the same way. In 2005, a report by the Higher Education Research at the University of California at Los Angeles found that entering freshmen were the most civically minded class in 25 years—86 percent were engaged in some sort of volunteer activity. While it's true that a good number of people in GenY have felt compelled to volunteer, either by socially conscience parents, high school graduation requirements, or simply the desire to build a résumé, the spirit of volunteerism seems to have worked its way into the ethos of this generation. GenY companies very often make the commitment to give back right from the start, not just when the profits start pouring in. They consistently blur the dividing line between for-profit and not-for-profit endeavors, a characteristic that helps them to attract and retain younger workers.

Workplace Renegades

Upstart companies tend to be flexible, mission-driven, employee-centric meritocracies; it's tough to find a traditional hierarchical, clock-punching workplace among them. These CEOs saw their parents forfeit huge chunks of their lives to the office for precious little thanks; they flatly refuse to do the same. And so they build companies where work-life balance, flexibility, and fun are core values. Upstarts create work environments where employees who excel are promoted quickly, where everyone has the opportunity to contribute to the idea pool, and where decision making is transparent. They're more likely to think of themselves as "servant leaders"—company founders whose jobs are not only to build successful companies but also to create work environments that are democratic and autonomous. "Work hard, play hard" is their mantra. While you're highly likely to find a Foosball table and Wii in the break room, you'll also find employees who are checking e-mail or working on projects at night and on weekends.

Morph Masters

GenY entrepreneurs are fabulous improvisers—they're more likely to take a "just do it approach" to business than they are to spend huge chunks of time on business plans. Failure doesn't faze them; they adapt and reinvent as necessary, very often changing business strategies as rapidly changing markets demand. To them, part of the excitement of business is that it's dynamic, and they're always prepared to pounce on unexpected opportunities. When they fail, they tend to "fail fast" and then quickly move on to the next big thing.

In every generation, some entrepreneurs successfully make that transition from startup to mature company, and others fail to meet the demands of the companies that outgrow them. It's potentially a bigger problem for GenY than for their older counterparts because so many lack the traditional management experience that entrepreneurs often draw on when faced with the challenges of scaling their companies. So what happens to GenY companies as they grow, become more sophisticated, and place more demands on their young owners? Often, adult supervision is in order, and young founders hire older, more experienced CEOs to take their companies to the next level. They also may find that managing a growing company isn't nearly as fun as starting a new one and decide that selling doesn't necessarily mean selling out. Or they stick to their knitting, put their own stamp on the art and science of management, and remain firmly at the helm as they grow their companies.

In the chapters that follow, I'll introduce you to a number of young CEOs who are in the process of starting and growing their companies. I've chosen some of them because they are industry leaders and innovators; others seemed to me to have cornered niches that their competitors had not even heard of; a great number are breaking the mold by disregarding conventional wisdom and creating their own business models in companies that may seem traditional and are anything but. Some have had tremendous revenue growth, whereas others are still very much in the startup phase. And I fully expect that some of them may not exist by the time this book is published. But I promise you this: GenY is at the very center of an entrepreneurial revolution that's being driven by demographics and technology; its members are highly motivated, nimble, and intuitive, and there are lots of them. Yes, they are Upstarts with far less experience than their more seasoned counterparts, but they come hard-wired with an impressive—and, to some, threatening—set of competitive tools. To ignore them is perilous; an inside look at their playbook is priceless. So get ready because the Upstarts are coming!

CHAPTER

Extreme
Collaborators

Building Cooperative
Tribes to Compete

Welcome to the collaborative economy. Today, an increasingly complex, competitive, and global business environment makes it virtually impossible, not to mention foolish, for any entrepreneur to cultivate a lone-wolf mentality. Even simple business models ultimately require a scope of knowledge rarely contained within the confines of a single cerebral cortex. Great minds still conceive innovative ideas, but those ideas are incubated more successfully by the collective intelligence of a team. Perhaps that's always been the case. Thomas Edison, for instance, may have a posthumous reputation as a brilliant inventor, but most of his 1,000-plus patents were for ideas generated at his "invention factory" in West Orange, NJ, where he employed teams of chemists, engineers, and machinists who all worked together to get the lights turned on. Today, we'd call it "team-based innovation."

Working in teams is second nature to members of GenY, and they are changing and refining the very definition of collaborative teamwork. They have, after all, been at it virtually since birth. All those baby play dates, pee-wee soccer tournaments, and team-base science projects nurtured the notion that working and playing in groups is fun, productive, and, well, expected. Not that they don't value individual achievement; they just expect their success to come as a result of team effort. "My students don't respond well to the whole notion of 'the brand called me,'" says George Gendron, referring to the slogan made popular by management guru Tom Peters. Gendron is director of the Innovation and Entrepreneurship Program at Clark University in Worcester, MA. "They're very team-oriented. I never worked on a team in college; everything I did was solo. Now, half of what is done in liberal arts education is team-based. The mentality is you have to have partners."

But what exactly is a team? A subset of people within the same organization assigned to solve a thorny problem or achieve a lofty goal? In Edison's day, that was an accurate definition of *team*. Today, it's far too narrow, and no one knows that better than Upstarts. For them, a team is virtual and flexible, and consists not only of people within their own companies but also of friends, family, professors, experts they find on the Web, and even people halfway around the globe whom they've never met. They are relentless

> "My students don't respond well to the whole notion of 'the brand called me.' They're very team-oriented."
>
> —George Gendron, Clark University in Worcester, MA

and fearless and, yes, shameless about asking for help and advice. From the time the idea is hatched, the entrepreneurial conversation is not a founder's monologue but a constant dialogue among a diverse and often dispersed group of people assembled for the sole purpose of achieving a specific goal. Upstarts are not just starting companies, they are building tribes.

The Campus as Incubator

What better place is there to build a tribe than a college campus? There was a time, not so long ago, when starting a business meant that you put just about everything else on hold. Remember the old version of the Game of Life, the popular board game published by Milton Bradley? At the beginning of Life's winding road, players steered their pink and blue plastic cars down one of two paths: "college" or "business." The choice pretty much mirrored the options at that time. Now, business and college, even at the undergraduate level, are a powerful combination. The resources available on campus for budding entrepreneurs are almost irresistible: Friends become partners and employees, professors become advisors, and school business plan competitions provide the startup capital. The risks are minimal, there are no families to support and no mortgages to pay, and the dorm room and the meal plan provide the ultimate safety net. College is the new incubator.

Andrew Zacharakis, the John H. Muller, Jr. Chair in Entrepreneurship at Babson College in Wellesley, MA, notes that "out of an incoming freshman class of 400 kids, there are always 20 to 30 who have already done something amazing in the entrepreneurial area before they even enter college, and that wasn't the case 10 years ago." Back then, students came to Babson to learn how to be entrepreneurs; today, they're increasingly likely to be looking for ways to refine their skills and to grow existing companies. "They're much more worldly than I remember being at age 18," says Zacharakis. "They know the language of business, and they're not afraid to approach people for advice."

Business plan competitions, now ubiquitous on college campus, have become an extraordinarily popular way for young entrepreneurs to test their ideas. Siamak Taghaddos, age 27, won Babson's competition in 2003 when he and classmate David Hauser, age 26, came up with an idea for a company that would provide virtual phone systems for entrepreneurs and small businesses. Both Taghaddos and Hauser knew from experience how difficult it was for startups to purchase professional-sounding, affordable telecommunications systems. So they developed a software-based tool that, for as little as $10 a month, gives entrepreneurs the ability to set up (via the Web) voicemail and mailbox systems, to receive voice mail as an MP3 file within an e-mail, and to integrate different phone lines into one voice-mail system and one inbound number. For startups and virtual companies that often employ staff in different geographic locations, it was a communications tool that allowed small companies to look big and professional without spending $10,000 on a phone system. "Both David and I wanted to start a service like this," recalls Taghaddos. "And when we met at Babson, we decided that given our strengths, we'd be better off as partners than as competitors."

Both young men had startup experience. Taghaddos had founded an online pager distribution company and worked at an educational consulting startup, and Hauser had cofounded ReturnPath, an e-mail management company, as well as WebAds 360, an ad-serving technology provider. But they hit pay dirt with the company they started together, GotVMail. With help from classmates, Taghaddos wrote a business plan for the company, entered it in Babson's 2003 Business Plan Competition, and walked away a winner, with $5,000 in cash. But the bigger benefit, says Taghaddos, was "the confirmation from many business leaders that the plan was solid, a great motivation for me to pursue it after class." So Taghaddos and Hauser officially launched Needham, MA–based GotVMail in 2003, with the former focusing on business development and the latter building out the technology infrastructure.

But winning the competition was just the beginning of the support they got from Babson. Professor Heidi Neck helped the founders understand the business development side of their marketing plan and stressed the importance of segmentation. "A Realtor using GotVMail is different than a consultant is different from a dot-com," says Taghaddos. That advice helped him to develop a marketing strategy so effective that GotVMail grew to $8.8 million in revenue by 2006, landing it the number 66 spot on the 2007 Inc. 500 list of fastest-growing privately held companies.

Also a key factor in the company's financial health: involvement from Babson's Dr. Joel Shulman, who advised the founders on financial modeling. "We used negative cash conversion cycle financing," says Taghaddos. "We made money; then we spent it and were therefore profitable since month two. Ninety-nine percent of companies do it the other way—they invest, start sales, and then wait to become profitable. Our technology didn't look too pretty in the first few months, but it allowed us to grow without outside funding. We spent what we had and grew at our own pace. Shulman, being the financial guru that he is, was a tremendous help."

In May 2009, Taghaddos and Hauser rebranded GotVMail and changed its name to Grasshopper in order to position the company as "a global brand for entrepreneurs," says Taghaddos. While the company will continue to offer virtual phone systems, the cofounders plan to offer a full suite of services to startups, including Internet-based hiring, recruiting, and time-management tools. Taghaddos is predicting increased demand for those kinds of services; he says that he's already noticed a significant uptick in business during the recession because "so many people have been laid off, and they're starting their own companies." The cofounders won't reveal the company's current revenues, except to say that they are "upwards of $10 million." With 30,000 customers and 50 employees, the company continues to grow organically with no outside venture capital. And Shulman, say the founders, remains a close advisor.

Incubators Everywhere

Grasshopper's story is a classic and dramatic tale of entrepreneurial success at a college whose primary mission it is to foster and nurture entrepreneurship. But all across the United States, students are starting and growing companies at colleges and universities that, while not widely known for their emphasis on business creation, are nonetheless helping to jump-start their students' entrepreneurial aspirations.

Josh Kowitt, age 27, and Scott Neuberger, age 28, started College Boxes, a company that handles moving and storage for college students, at an entrepreneurship class at Washington University in St. Louis. "We wouldn't be as far along as we are if we hadn't started this in college," says Neuberger. "We learned how to execute a business." The company grew to between $3 and $5 million before the founders sold it in January 2008.

> "We wouldn't be as far along as we are if we hadn't started this in college. We learned how to execute a business."
>
> — Scott Neuberger,
> College Boxes

Luke Skurman, founder of College Prowler, started developing his college-guide publishing company at Carnegie Mellon University when he was a junior. It was the university's president, Jared Cohon, who introduced Skurman to the investor who ultimately would play a major role in helping him to grow his company to $900,000 in revenue. And Duke University served as a springboard for Will Pearson and Mangesh Hattikudur, both age 29, whose highly successful trivia magazine and website, $2 million *Mental Floss*, got its start on campus.

It's the burgeoning interest in entrepreneurship among college students that's driving the growth of 27-year-old Michael Simmons' business, Extreme Entrepreneurship Education Tour in Manhattan. Simmons started his first company, Princeton Web Solutions, when he was 16 and then founded his current company with Sheena Lindahl, now his wife, when the two were juniors at New York University. The idea was to spread the entrepreneurial gospel to students via a nationwide series of college- and university-sponsored half-day programs in entrepreneurship education. The programs include networking, workshops, and inspirational keynote speeches by young and successful entrepreneurs. Since 2006, when Simmons and Lindahl first took their tour on the road, they've held over 60 conferences on campuses; the events typically attract at least 200 attendees. "I've noticed an increasing interest by campus departments and outside organizations in entrepreneurship," says Simmons. "For example, economic development organizations are now focusing more and more on building local entrepreneurs rather than attracting large companies. And career services offices on campus are starting to expose students to entrepreneurship rather than just getting a job."

Buddy Up

You'll find that many of the companies featured in this book were started on college campuses; you'll also notice that more than half of them were founded by one or more partners. That should come as little surprise where campus startups are concerned, considering the increasing number of college entrepreneurship programs combined with the constant presence of peers with common interests, passions, and fields of study. For instance, Brad Weinberg and Rajiv Kumar, Brown University Medical School students, started an innovative online wellness company called Shape Up The Nation (see Chapter 2); John Vechey and Brian Fiete began developing multiplayer video games together at Purdue, and their collaboration ultimately evolved into PopCap Games (see Chapter 8); and the three co-founders of Higher One, Miles Lasater, Mark Volchek, and Sean Glass, who you'll meet later in this chapter, drew upon their own experiences at Yale when launching their student banking and funds disbursement company.

GenY thrives on group dynamic, and it very often happens that the companies they start are simply the result of groups of friends asking one another questions that start with "what if ..." A question is posed, a discussion follows, the entrepreneurial seed is planted and, somewhere down the line, a company begins to emerge. But those conversations clearly don't end at graduation. Lists like *Inc.* magazine's "30-Under-30: America's Coolest Young Entrepreneurs," and *Business Week*'s "America's Best Young Entrepreneurs" are dominated by companies started by partners. Often, they're just trying to earn a little extra money, like brothers Aaron and Evan Steed at Meathead Movers (see Chapter 5) and Omar Soliman and Nick Friedman at College Hunks Hauling Junk (see Chapter 3). Neither pair of founders ever imagined that ventures started so casually would one day be multi-million-dollar, uniquely branded companies. For Rachael Krantz Herrscher and Stephanie Petersen, the "aha" moment came when they were pushing double strollers through a mall and lamenting the lack of local activities guides for moms. So they met that need by starting TodaysMama (see Chapter 7).

Increasingly, those "what if" conversations take place much earlier and much closer to home. As I mentioned in the introduction, GenYers tend to be much closer to their parents than previous generations, so it makes perfect sense that they'd be eager to draw their folks into their entrepreneurial pursuits. Mom may take a stake in the company in exchange for answering the phone and shipping orders; or Dad may agree to wine and dine potential clients if the CEO is too young to order a scotch. These arrangements turn the family business dynamic upside down and can pose their own unique set of challenges, but I believe multigenerational partnerships can be powerful: Combine tech-savvy, innovative youth with their operational-savvy and worldly elders and you've got a great recipe for success.

My Parent, My Partner

Sean Belnick would agree with that. Belnick started BizChair.com with his stepfather, Gary Glazer, when he was just 14 years old. "He was an independent sales rep for a furniture company," recalls Belnick, now 22 and a recent graduate of Emory College in Atlanta. "I was big into computers, and I would see how he placed his orders and end up helping him with his company." A bright and curious kid, Belnick had designed a website devoted to the Comedy Central series *South Park* when he was in fifth grade. And when his Pokémon cards lost their allure, he sold them on eBay, earning more than $1,000.

So Belnick's mom and stepfather were not all that surprised when he locked himself in his bedroom for three days to build a website that combined his technology skills with what he had learned from Glazer about the furniture industry. BizChair.com, one of the first online retailers of office chairs, was born in Belnick's bedroom in 2001—an endeavor that so impressed Gary Glazer that he used his industry connections to serve as a liaison between young Sean and manufacturers who were skittish about new distributors, particularly Web-based ones. "They didn't know my age at the time," concedes Belnick. "When I started BizChairs, I was basically a customer of Gary's. I would buy the product through him from the manufacturers and drop ship the chairs to customers." Belnick quickly become one of Glazer's biggest customers, and Glazer, convinced of the high growth potential of his stepson's Internet-based business model, eventually folded his own business and joined BizChairs as an equal partner.

Between Glazer's industry experience and connections and Belnick's Web savvy, it's been an ideal partnership. Glazer ran the company on a day-to-day basis while Belnick attended Emory's Goizueta Business School, where he typically fielded 50 to 100 e-mails a day from the company. Belnick recently stepped into the CEO's seat at BizChair, which now has over 100 employees, sells 30,000 to 40,000 items, and has a 327,000-square-foot warehouse that stocks products purchased directly from Asia. Those direct ties with factories in Asia helped Belnick and Glazer create their own branded product line called Office Furniture in a Flash. "We're able to offer our own personal brand with better pricing," says Belnick. The company's customer roster now includes Microsoft, Google, and the Pentagon, and it posted a whopping $40 million in sales for 2008. Having expanded into other office furniture, home furniture, and medical equipment, Belnick's goal is as simple as it is ambitious: "We'd like to be the biggest retailer of office furniture online," he says.

When Good Partnerships Go Bad

Not all partnerships are happy ones, of course. And no one knows this better than Casey Golden. Now 29, Golden started his third company in Washington, DC, at the age of 21 with three classmates from Cornell University. The company, which was venture capital backed, offered post-purchase online customer support for software such as Salesforce.com.

(*Note:* Golden prefers not to name the company, which is still in business.) His best piece of advice for entrepreneurs going into business with one or more partners: "Get it in writing from the beginning."

Golden and his three original partners brought in three additional equity partners who worked part time in the company's early days. They all came to a tentative agreement on ownership but did not put the details in writing. Nine months down the road, when the company had landed its first round of angel financing and needed a formal shareholder agreement, the seven partners met at a Starbucks in Georgetown to put it all in writing. "At the beginning of the meeting, things were joyous and friendly, but as soon as the 'any final concerns or requests' questions came up, it was like the sky turned deathly dark, and the ominous clouds of greed rolled on in," recalls Golden. One of the part-time partners felt that he deserved more equity, and then "the sparks erupted and everyone was standing, yelling, and a poor, innocent bystander and his laptop got drenched at the next table with a café latte as it got backhanded across the room by one of the partners." It took several more painful sessions to work out the agreement—pain that might have been avoided, says Golden, if a written agreement had been created before there was angel money on the table. As it tuned out, though, the fracas at Starbucks was a foreshadowing event.

"The company was very team oriented, but as it grew, it became very myopic," says Golden. "One of the biggest holdups for young entrepreneurs is accepting that they don't know everything. For example, my partners couldn't take customers' feedback that the product they had created wasn't working well. It was a pride issue." Golden also suggested personal coaching to his partners, but says they flatly refused. The partners had been in perfect sync when the company was founded, but as it grew to $3 million and 90 employees in 2006, tensions were running high. "It's very difficult to know who you're going into business with when your feet aren't up against the fire yet," says Golden, who ultimately left the company. While he's since started another company, called Golden Rule Technologies, his failed partnership "still puts a knot in my stomach."

Mentor Me

When Golden's unhappy partnership ended, one of the first things he did was to join Entrepreneurs' Organization (EO, formerly YEO) "because I wanted to learn more from experienced entrepreneurs." One of the smartest things any entrepreneur can do is to seek out mentors and advisors who can help shorten the learning curve and provide perspective that often comes only with experience and age. In fact, veteran Baby Boomer enterprenuers and Upstarts are very often a powerful combination: The latter are brimming with new ideas; the former supply the managerial and operational know-how to turn those ideas into sustainable businesses.

Mangesh Hattikudur and Will Pearson, both age 29, scoured the Internet for expert advice when they were first starting their trivia magazine, *Mental Floss*. The two Duke University students found Samir Husni, also known as "Mr. Magazine," a University of Mississippi professor who wrote a book called *Launch Your Own Magazine*. "We pestered him with e-mails, and he finally agreed to waive his consulting fee to meet with us," recalls Pearson. "So we traveled to Mississippi, and he sliced through the magazine with unbelievable speed, letting us know where it was boring, that we had to punch things up, how we had to rethink how we were looking at magazines," adds Hattikudur. "He told us to look at it like a fancy meal, with appetizers and courses and deserts, and keeping the readers' mouths watering the whole way through. His critique made us set our ambitions so much higher." After the first issue of *Mental Floss*, the two partners immediately recruited a board of advisors that included former editors from *Time* and *Newsweek*. "They gave us advice, they opened doors, and they lent a lot of credibility to the venture," says Hattikudur. Today, *Mental Floss* has national newsstand distribution, a website that attracts over 2 million unique visitors a month, a multibook contract with HarperCollins, and $2 million in revenue. Hattikudur and Pearson, still partners, now work in different parts of the country, and you can read more about how they grew *Mental Floss* as a virtual company in Chapter 7.

Talia Mashiach, age 32, also relied heavily on a mentor—Ed Chen, director of catering for Hilton Chicago—when she first started her Chicago-based company, Eved Services. Eved, now a $9 million company, works with hotels to provide their corporate clients with event-management services, such as transportation, videography, chair rental, and entertainment. "I met Ed because initially I was trying to get a booking for my husband's band," says Mashiach. "And he suggested that I start a business that would handle all event services for corporate groups."

Hotels typically provide linens and flowers for big events and then contract with a variety of vendors for other services. Mashiach's concept was to work with hotels as the conduit between their corporate clients and the plethora of vendors that provide event services. But she knew very little about the hotel industry. "I used to sit outside Ed's office waiting to talk to him for advice, and he saw that I was very persistent. So he said to me, 'Call me at 8:15 in the morning when I'm driving to work.' I knew that was my time slot, and I called him every morning to talk through my ideas and have him teach me about the hospitality industry."

> "My mentor believed in me and was willing to put his name on the line to help me get my first contracts."
>
> —Talia Mashiach, Eved Services

Chen coached Mashiach, but he also "put his name on the line to help get me my first contracts," she says. "He saved at least two years [of work] for us because we learned from him before making the mistakes." Eved Services now works with 35 hotels in the Chicago area and has expanded to Milwaukee and Indianapolis. Mashiach is also a "Game Changer" and a "Workplace Renegade," so you can learn more about her in Chapters 3 and 7.

Peer Group Power

Sometimes one mentor just isn't enough. To accelerate his learning curve, 28-year-old Brian Adams called on not just one advisor, but 12. When he first started Restoration Cleaners six years ago in Houston, he knew absolutely nothing about the dry-cleaning industry. What he did know was that mold, fire, and water-damage restoration was big business in Texas because insurance companies were covering those losses. "The industry was very fragmented," says Adams. "I saw that there was an opportunity for someone to do an old service with enhanced quality."

But Adams knew he needed expert assistance. So he hired a consultant to help him assemble an industry peer group—12 noncompetitive restoration cleaners in different parts of the country who take turns hosting quarterly meetings. They discuss industry trends, management issues, new technology, and any challenges they may be facing in their companies. "The closest in age is 15 years older than me," says Adams. "Some of them are third-generation business owners. So I surrounded myself with these people, and I just listen. I learned about percentages, and I learned about regulations. At first, they thought I was really crazy," he says with a Texas drawl.

> "My goal is to shove myself under the wings of some very successful people."
>
> — Brian Adams,
> Restoration Cleaners

"But now they don't think I'm so crazy." In 2008, Restoration Cleaners' revenues were $5.6 million. "We're the largest hotel cleaner in Houston," says Adams, who is now in the process of buying other service-based companies, such as a furniture refinishing firm, an electronics restoration business, and other dry cleaners. "My goal is to shove myself under the wings of very successful people, and I want to have my own collection of companies than I can buy and sell."

Strategic Partnerships for Fun and Profit

Advice from industry experts is invaluable, but the right strategic partnership can put you on the fast track to revenue growth. This most certainly was the case for 25-year old Bryan Sims, the CEO of Corvallis, OR–based Brass Media, which has $3 to $5 million in revenue. Sims was financially precocious; he had worked since he was 15 years old, and he invested his paychecks in the stock market. "I made money, so I ended up creating an investment club at my high school," he recalls. "We had 40 to 50 teenagers—everyone from football team captains to the band and the chess club—investing their McDonald's paychecks in companies like Pfizer. The emphasis of the club was on education, so to make an investment recommendation, everyone had to do research. It was pretty cool; we had $25,000 invested in the club."

When Sims was a senior, money management took on a whole new meaning for him. It was 2001, and the financial reverberations of 9/11 hit very close to home: His father, a vice president of business development for a builder of sports complexes, lost his job when investors pulled the plug on the company. And then a car accident further hindered his dad's ability to work. "I was working 80 hours a week busing tables to make money," recalls Sims. The following fall, he enrolled as a scholarship student at the University of Oregon. He was, however, more charged up than ever about teaching money management and investment strategy to his peers.

He wrote a business plan for a financial magazine called *Brass*—a publication that targeted young people—and entered it in a university-sponsored business plan competition where one of the judges, Gene Pelham, was the CEO of Rogue Federal Credit Union. Sims's idea was intriguing to Pelham, but he suggested that Sims shift his focus away from newsstands and instead think about creating a custom publication that would be sold to existing financial institutions to help them reach the growing but elusive youth market. "It shifted our whole focus," says Sims. "And if we hadn't done that, we'd be out of business right now."

Pelham became Sims's mentor, introducing him to several local companies and then eventually becoming a customer himself when Sims finally launched his venture in early 2004. His dad, Steve, signed on as chief operating officer (COO) of the company, which Sims called Brass Media. "My dad told me that if *Brass* didn't get off the ground, he might have to declare personal bankruptcy," recalls Sims. "So I gave up the scholarships, the full ride, and my dad and I went at it full force." The two approached over 200 potential investors and eventually raised "in the low six figures" from two stockbrokers, a retired teacher, a former doctor, a real estate developer, a bus driver who had won a lawsuit, and two Japanese onion farmers from eastern Oregon.

When the prototype went to press, Brass Media had 10 financial institutions committed to distributing the magazine to 30,000 readers. Today, the company has 200 financial partners, half a million readers, and 37 employees. Sims also has expanded his strategic partnerships to include schools, which distribute a special edition for students through local credit unions. "We have teachers in economics, entrepreneurship, math, and social studies using the magazine to teach kids about money and other real-world stuff," says Sims. Every public school in New York and Wisconsin now distributes the magazine, and Sims says that several other states have expressed interest in partnering. "People partner with us because they don't really know how to reach Generation Y," says Sims.

The Wisconsin Credit Union League, for example, has been sponsoring the distribution of *Brass* to all 603 public high schools in Wisconsin for over a year. "I heard Bryan speak at a seminar for credit unions to teach them how to reach the GenY market, and I was really impressed with his story and his passion," says Jill Weber, director of member solutions at the Wisconsin Credit Union League, which acts as a trade association for Wisconsin credit unions. For teachers who use the magazine in their classrooms, *Brass* has an online resource center with lesson plans and additional resources. Weber says that almost 300 teachers have registered on the site, and many are incorporating *Brass* content into their curriculum. "We're hearing that the material resonates with the kids because it's not a hard-core lesson," says Weber. "They might read about a young entrepreneur or an athlete talking about doing what they love, making money, and what they're learned." Ninety-seven percent of the teachers surveyed say that they want to continue receiving the magazine, says Weber.

For their part, the credit unions are hoping the relationship helps to win the loyalty of a new, younger customer base. The magazine contains inserts that list all the credit unions in Wisconsin and explains the difference between credit unions and banks. But Weber also hopes that early financial education will give those credit unions young customers who are better informed than their elders. "So many of the issues we have going on in the economy right now are due to lack of education about 'Can I really afford this?'" she says. "The younger we can reach out to people to help them understand how to use credit wisely, the better."

Without its strategic partnerships, *Brass* may well be just another struggling startup magazine. By partnering with large financial institutions that act as a distribution channel, Sims is able to reach young readers more efficiently and much more economically.

Synergistic Startups

Bryan Sims used strategic partnerships to shift his revenue model away from his end users (GenY) to the people who wanted to reach them (financial institutions). Anderson Schoenrock, age 29, is using strategic partnerships to grow his company by differentiating it from others in the marketplace and by offering his customers additional services without incurring extra costs.

Schoenrock is the CEO of El Segundo, CA–based ScanDigital, a $500,000 Web-based service that allows customers to preserve old photos, slides, videos, and reel-to-reel film by converting them to digital format. Photos are scanned, restored, and color-corrected, and all digitized images are put on a CD or DVD and returned with the original materials. ScanDigital also gives customers' images a permanent—and free—online home on the company's photo-sharing site, where customers also can upload additional images.

In June of 2008, Schoenrock forged a strategic partnership with Capzles, an online social media company where users can upload their photos and other media and use the company's Flash-based interface to create multimedia timelines with custom backgrounds and music. Think of it as Flickr on steroids. "It's a new approach to photo sharing—the idea of tracking people's lives over time," says Schoenrock. "But no one has anything in digital format older than 10 years. So they approached us about a partnership, and now our site is integrated with theirs." Now, ScanDigital is Capzles' exclusive partner for scanning.

"As a relatively young startup, one of the challenges we face is consumer awareness," says Schoenrock. "Most people need our service but do not know it exists. Advertising and PR are a great way for us to grow our customer base. Word of mouth has been very important for our growth, but the final piece is really strong strategic partnerships. These allow you to tap into entirely new customer bases and in the case of Capzles, a customer base that is focused on social story telling and heritage preservation through photography—these individuals are ideal customers for us." Likewise, by offering ScanDigital's scanning services to its customers, Capzles makes its own services more attractive and gains a way to distinguish the company from potential competitors.

The Money Tribe

The right partners, advisors, and strategic alliances are essential to a company's growth, but nothing ever gets off the ground without adequate funding. For a young entrepreneur with a great idea and a small bank account, a deep-pocketed investor who also becomes a trusted advisor can be a dream come true. Luke Skurman started his company, College Prowler, when he was an undergraduate at Carnegie Mellon University, and his progress was painfully slow the first couple of years. The company publishes college guidebooks written by students who have the inside skinny on the schools they attend. By commissioning students to write the guides for $100, Skurman was able to produce his first books quickly and cheaply; by the fall of 2002, just a few months after he launched in earnest, he had nine books to showcase at the National Association for College Admission Counselors national conference in Salt Lake City. "We had our first two orders from that show," says Skurman. "We made $240, but we felt like we had validated our idea." It took more than a year, however, before College Prowler got recognition beyond the local Pittsburgh press. First came a mention in *Publishers Weekly*'s issue on test prep; CNN, the *Boston Globe*, the *New York Times*, and the *Washington Post* followed. Still, Skurman was frustrated by the company's slow growth; in 2003, revenues were just $37,000.

But that would all change after a fateful meeting with Carnegie Mellon's president, Jared Cohon, who Skurman went to for advice in the spring of 2004. Cohon was a fan of College Prowler and admired Skurman's determination, so he offered to introduce him to a member of the university's board of trustees, venture capitalist Glen Meakem. "Six weeks later, I met him, and we hit if off," recalls Skurman. "Glen led a $550,000 round of financing, and suddenly we were able to put our five employees on full salary and give them health insurance." Skurman also was able to beef up his college guides, making them longer and upgrading the binding to make them more attractive to bookstores. Meakem, who is now the company's largest shareholder, says that he "saw a business that I thought was innovative and unique in their approach to getting student-created content about colleges. And Luke was very compelling—he's passionate about the business, he's smart and hard-working, and he's a good leader."

> "What differentiates young founders is who they can connect with early on."
>
> —David Cohen, TechStars

As important as the money was the advice that came with it. "The first thing I told him to do was raise prices," says Meakem. "New entrepreneurs often don't have the confidence to get full value for their products, and Luke was in that boat. But if you undervalue your product, others will undervalue it as well. So we increased the price from $5.95 to $14.95 almost overnight, and we got no objections and a lot more volume." Meakem, who put another $500,000 into the company in December of 2005, also encouraged Skurman to digitize College Prowler's content. The company now publishes guides for more than 250 schools, has approximately $900,000 in revenue, and has made its digitized content available on its website through an annual subscription fee. With continuing counsel from Meakem, Skurman is in the process of shifting his business model once again, as you'll read about in Chapter 8.

Casting a Wide Net

The cofounders of Higher One took a slightly different but highly effective approach to fund-raising. The New Haven, CT–based company, which provides colleges and universities and their students with online banking and disbursement services, was started by three Yale classmates in 2000. Miles Lasater and Mark Volchek, both age 31, and Sean Glass, age 30, noticed a number of inefficiencies in the way their university handled financial services for students. To get financial aid disbursements, for instance, students stood in line waiting for paper checks that they then needed to deposit in a bank account. What if, the young partners asked, you could develop technology that would help to manage and disburse funds to students via a card-based system that was linked to student IDs?

"The first stage was that we talked to people at the universities for advice, and then the students told us what they wanted," says Volchek. As it turned out, many state universities and community colleges were bearing a huge administrative burden when it came to disbursing funds but did not have the resources to invest in the technology that would make the process more efficient. As for the students, their needs were simple: They wanted their money faster.

Convinced that they had identified an unmet need, the partners were faced with a huge challenge: raising money in 2000, in the wake of the dot-com bust. "We sent out about 100 letters to Yale alums and told them about the business we wanted to start and asking for advice," recalls Lasater. Even though there was no overt mention of fund-raising, the letter captured the interest of about half its recipients, and the partners had about 50 meetings or phone calls with those early advisors, some of whom were eager to invest. In the summer of 2000, Higher One raised $600,000, giving up about 30 percent of the company. The original advisors and investors helped Higher One's founders expand their fund-raising network, and the three sent out more letters updating their newly assembled tribe on their progress, asking for more advice, and reeling in more investors.

Wasn't it risky for Volchek, Lasater, and Glass to be so utterly transparent about their startup plans with a highly educated and well-resourced community of people? Weren't they concerned that their letter might serve as a tempting blueprint for a potential competitor who might beat them to market? "If it's that easy to steal an idea, someone will probably steal it as soon as you launch it anyway," says Volchek. "You've got to have the confidence to go out and talk to people; it's the only way to raise money and get good advice."

In Higher One's case, the initial $600,000 allowed them not only to build a robust technology platform but also to hire an older and more experienced vice president of sales, Walter Hinckfoot, to help them reach the college market. The following year, 2002, they also would hire a CEO, Dean Hatton, who came with an impressive corporate résumé. "We always had the intention of building a management team around us to grow the business to scale," says Volchek. "We value success over control." As it turns out, that was an effective strategy. Revenues were $29 million in 2007, when the company ranked number 87 on the Inc. 500 list. And in 2008, revenues spiked to $44 million. According to Lasater, Higher One is still growing at a rate of 60 to 80 percent a year and now serves 250 campuses. The founders continue to expand their tribe, drawing not only the advice of experts but also the collective intelligence of their student customers.

> "If it's that easy to steal an idea, someone will probably steal it as soon as you launch it anyway. You've got to have the confidence to go out and talk to people; it's the only way to raise money and get good advice."
>
> —Mark Volchek,
> Higher One

 ## Mass Collaboration

The term "collective intelligence" has worked its way into our lexicon through popular books like *The Wisdom of Crowds: Why the Many Are*

Smarter Than the Few and How Collective Wisdom Shapes Business, Economies, Societies and Nations by James Surowiecki (Doubleday, 2004), and *Wikinomics: How Mass Collaboration Changes Everything* by Don Tapscott and Anthony D. Williams (Portfolio, 2006). The same year that *Wikinomics* was published, *Time* magazine's Person of the Year was "You." The magazine declared that in 2006, we saw "community and collaboration on a scale never seen before. ... It's about the many wresting power from the few and helping one another for nothing and how that will not only change the world, but also change the way the world changes." It sounded breathless back then, but in the past three years, our increasingly networked culture has indeed begun to facilitate exactly the kind of transforation that *Time* predicted. *Wikinomics* coauthors Tapscott and Williams also observed that "a new kind of business is emerging—one that opens doors to the world, co-innovates with everyone (especially customers), shares resources that were previously closely guarded, harnesses the power of mass collaboration, and behaves not as a multinational but as something new: a truly global firm."

That description could apply to several companies in this book, but none so much as Threadless. The Chicago-based T-shirt company (that's right, T-shirts) was recognized as "the most innovative small company in America" by *Inc.* magazine in June 2008. Like so many great entrepreneurial companies, the secret sauce of Threadless's success lies not in its products, but in its process. And that process is all about ceding product development—not to mention its associated costs—to absolutely anyone who cares to participate.

The company was founded as a hobby in 2000 by Jake Nickell and Jacob DeHart, who started running online T-shirt design contests in which designers submitted their best work and then voted for their favorites among the entire entrant pool. Nickell was at the Illinois Institute of Art, and DeHart was attending Purdue, and neither ever dreamed that their hobby, called "Threadless," would one day become the anchor brand in a multimillion-dollar company called skinnyCorp, let alone the subject of a Harvard Business School case study. By 2002, though, when Threadless racked up $100,000 in sales, the two knew that they had created something unique. And it wasn't merely a T-shirt company.

The engine that drives Threadless's growth is a social network of 700,000 members, many of whom are simultaneously designers and customers. They chat online with one another on the company's online forum, post and comment on designs in progress, and also get feedback and help from Threadless staff members who monitor and post on the forum. Hundreds of users submit T-shirt designs every week and vote on the best ideas, which are then manufactured for Threadless by American Apparel and Fruit of the Loom. Winning designers get $2,000 in cash, plus a $500 gift certificate from Threadless; Threadless gets T-shirt designs that sell out consistently because its community has voted for their production. Margins are tremendous (around 30 percent) because there's little overhead; the company did $18 million in revenue and posted $6 million in profits in 2006. While Nickell, who scored some venture money from Insight Venture Partners in late 2006, is reluctant to reveal current revenue figures, he concedes that Threadless now has "over $20 million" in sales.

So is the success of this quirky Chicago-based company, where employees can play Ping-Pong, Guitar Hero, and Xbox Live and drive go-carts in the office, just a fluke? Karim Lakhani, the assistant professor at Harvard Business School who coauthored the case study of Threadless thinks not. "The progenitors for this type of business are Linux, Apache, and Firefox, which were also developed in community-like settings," he says. "So in my generation, the geeks have been doing this for a long time. The mental switch is that we can leverage communities for a range of economic opportunities, and that's what's new with this new generation. They've grown up with Facebook and IM and MySpace, so it's natural for them to think about business models that involve community."

> "Threadless is a platform for community involvement that happens to sell T-shirts."
>
> —Karim Lakhani, Harvard University

The Business of Community

Ben Kaufman, age 22, would agree. The Long Island native was a student at Champlain College in Burlington, VT, when he started his first company, Mophie (named after his two golden retrievers, Molly and Sophie), a maker of iPod accessories. Mophie's first product was an iPod case with retractable headphones; its second creation, a case that was compatible with an armband, a belt clip, and an audio splitter, won a "Best of Show" award for innovation at MacWorld in January 2006. Kaufman was on a roll, but he knew that he was playing a commodity game: Companies that make iPod accessories are a dime a dozen, so he put a GenY spin on his fledgling company.

When it was time for MacWorld 2007, Kaufman bought a booth but decided that instead of displaying his existing product line, he would turn his display into a live "creation lab," where conference attendees were invited to submit ideas for new gizmos to enhance Apple products. "We handed out pens and pads, and said 'doodle,'" Kaufman recalls. "In four hours, we collected 120 legitimate product ideas. That night, we scanned everything into the computer and asked people to vote online." The top three ideas made their way to the company's industrial designer, and three months later, the first product—an iPod shuffle case that's also a bottle opener and key chain called "Bevy"—went into production. Kaufman blogged regularly about the product's progress, making the innovation and design process entirely transparent.

Kaufman's approach to innovation places enormous value on the wisdom of communities rather than restricting idea generation to the confines of the company. And he also understood that his community approach would differentiate Mophie in the marketplace, giving him a unique brand identity and a loyal following of users. This kind of brand loyalty is priceless in a crowded marketplace where good ideas that generate revenue and profit are often easily replicated. Jake Nickell says that consumer loyalty is a huge part of Threadless's success. "People have tried to copy our idea, but our customers get angry because they have a sense of ownership," he says.

Kaufman was so taken with the concept of community-based innovation that he decided to make the process the core of his business. He sold the Mophie brand of iPod accessories in the fall of 2007 and used the cash to transform his company into a pure product-development lab using the community-based approach. The company, which he named Kluster, was launched in a very public and prestigious venue: TED, the über-exclusive annual business conference in Monterey, CA, that claims to assemble the 1,000 smartest people in the world (admission fee: $10,000). A TED organizer had seen Kaufman in action at MacWorld and had invited him to the conference to further demonstrate the power of his community-based innovation concept. The goal: Guide TED attendees in the process of developing an entirely new product in 72 hours. Kaufman did exactly that. Using the Kluster technology platform, which allows a community of participants to suggest product ideas, collaborate on design, and reap financial reward for their efforts, TED attendees created an educational board game called *Over There*, designed to promote cross-cultural awareness. Kaufman says the game will be in production sometime next year.

Since the TED conference, Kaufman has refined the Kluster concept, fiddling with a way to sell the platform to companies that will use it for their own internal idea generation. And he's also pledged to launch several of his own businesses (called *Kluster Labs*) using the Kluster platform. The first, a community-driven online newspaper called *Knewsroom*, was closed down after just 37 days. "We watched it, we tweaked it, [and] then we made the decision that it was not for us," says Kaufman. "It became too complicated." The second, NameThis.com, is a Web-based business that enlists the help of the Kluster community to name new products or services. Customers pay $99, and the community (now 11,000 strong) suggests names and invests Kluster currency, called watts, in their favorite names. After 48 hours, and with help from some fancy logarithms, Kluster chooses the winners and distributes $80 among the members who created and influenced the selections. The money is loaded on a MasterCard-branded debit card. As of this writing, NameThis.com had run over 1,000 projects, generating 140,000 names submitted by 45,000 participants—enough volume for Kaufman to declare a success. In 2008, Kluster had just under $1 million in revenue.

Kaufman knows, however, that his company is a work in progress, and he's quite comfortable—some would say disarmingly comfortable—with allowing the world to watch it evolve in real time (you can learn more about how Kluster has evolved in Chapter 8). It is, after all, a collaborative experiment, and he's committed to making the company—and its errors—transparent. In fact, Kaufman and the Kluster staff regularly post on their company blog, "Klusterfck" (the *fck* stands for "fostering community knowledge"), where they interact with users who have comments or concerns about NameThis.com and Kluster. It's like Threadless but on a much smaller scale.

Can every company benefit from the lessons of Threadless and Kluster? Karim Lakhani thinks so. "There's a general trend in the economy for these types of companies to take hold," he says. "If you look at the business models and the energy behind MySpace and Facebook, they're harbingers of the community ethos."

At first blush, what he's suggesting requires a radical new approach to innovation and business development, but it's one that few businesses can afford to discount. If you could tap into the collective intelligence of your own customer base to produce products or services with minimal overhead and no sales force, promotional, or distribution costs, why on earth wouldn't you do exactly that?

UPSTARTS PLAYLIST

Track 1 : Get into the Collaborative Spirit

1. **Manage partnerships wisely.** Choose partners who compliment your strengths and compensate for your weaknesses. Define everyone's role at the outset and agree upon the breakdown of ownership and responsibility; put it all in writing with the help of an attorney. Remember that partnerships can be fragile and that your college roommate or the guy in the next cubicle over may seem like the perfect partner now, but it's not unlikely that you'll go your separate ways as your company grows. Plan for that possibility in the early startup days to minimize future pain. Breaking up is hard to do, but if you can't repair it, end it. The lack of a formal written agreement can result in nasty disputes or even may mean that both/all of you end up walking away from the venture.

2. **Expand your definition of "team."** Your partners and your staff are critically important, but a growing business also needs a tribe, especially in the start phase when you frequently can't afford to pay for top talent. Assemble a group of trusted advisors who fill in your own knowledge gaps. Know what you don't know, and don't be afraid to ask for advice. The founders of GotVMail (rebranded as Grasshopper) were coached on marketing and financial modeling by their Babson professors; the founders of Higher One drew upon 100 member of the Yale alumni community for advice; Ben Kaufman used ideas from complete strangers to come up with an innovative design for a new iPod accessory.

3. **Find a mentor.** You're never too young or too old for a mentor. Whether you're just starting up or you've been around the entrepreneurial block a few times, there's always someone out there who knows more than you do. The founders of *Mental Floss* found their mentor, magazine expert Samir Husni, through a Google search; after a good bit of badgering, they convinced him to waive his consulting fee. Talia Mashiach of Eved Services stalked an older hotel industry contact and convinced him to show her the ropes. Bryan

Sims of Brass Media says he doubts he'd still be in business were it not for distribution advice from his mentor, Gene Pelham.

4. **Join or start a peer group.** National groups such as Entrepreneurs' Organization (EO) have local chapters where business owners in various industries help one another to solve thorny business problems and grow their companies. But you also may want to consider a group like the one Brian Adams started. It consists solely of companies in the same industry (in this case, dry cleaning) that are situated in noncompeting geographic locations. Adams's group, filled with people who had been in the business for years, helped him get up to speed quickly and grow his fledgling company to over $5 million in revenue.

5. **Forge smart strategic partnerships.** Seek out, but carefully evaluate, potential strategic partners who not only can help to expand your market but also can offer your existing customers value-added products or services. ScanDigital's Anderson Schoenrock recently partnered with Capzles, a photo and video social networking/archiving site. It's a business that perfectly complements the photo-scanning services he offers his customers; the partnership makes good sense for Capzles as well because it can now offer customers an additional service without making a capital investment. Brass Media's partnerships with credit unions and schools give the company access to its key demographic—young people interested in learning about personal finance.

6. **Create deep community ties.** Your very best source of information about your product or service is your community of customers. You don't need a business model like Threadless or Kluster to tap into their collective intelligence. Use your company's blog to encourage open discussion about your company and to solicit advice on new products or services. But be prepared to step up to the plate and show customers that you take their input seriously enough to implement the changes they suggest.

Technology Mavens

Technology Is the Great Enabler and the Best Differentiator

The ability to master, develop, modify, and employ new technology quickly and efficiently is a significant factor in the entrepreneurial success equation. For Upstarts, these skills are virtually second nature. It all starts with the Internet, where members of GenY spend an average of 12.2 hours per week. They participate in social networks at twice the rate of all U.S. adults, and they are voracious consumers (and frequently creators) of streaming videos and blogs. And when they do all this, they are often taking advantage of technologies created by the superstar entrepreneurs of their own generation. Mark Zuckerburg gave them Facebook; Chad Hurley and Steve Chen founded YouTube; Kevin Rose created Digg, the popular social bookmarking site; and Matt Mullenweg, the CEO of WordPress, and Mena and Ben Trott, cofounders of Six Apart (the company behind Movable Type), built the two most popular blogging platforms on the Web. These companies and others like them send the message that the Internet and the world of technology are not just a playground, but a playing field for highly successful businesses that change the way in which we interact with one another and the world around us.

Moreover, this message is being conveyed loud and clear at a time when starting a technology-based company is far less expensive and intimidating than it was in the dot-com days. "Barriers to entry are low now, so the idea of starting a business doesn't seem daunting," says Bruce Tulgan, CEO of Rainmaker Thinking and author of *Not Everyone Gets a Trophy: How to Manage Generation Y* (Jossey-Bass, 2009). "I think that GenYers have an acute sense that it's much less expensive to start a business than it used to be." But there's something else going on here as well. GenY understands the obsolescence curve because, says Tulgan, they're intimately familiar with how quickly today's cool new tech toy loses its novelty. "Knowledge becomes obsolete very quickly," says Tulgan, "and that diminishes the strategic disadvantages of being young and inexperienced."

> "Knowledge becomes obsolete very quickly, and that diminishes the strategic disadvantages of being young and inexperienced."
>
> —Bruce Tulgan, Rainmaker Thinking

In fact, being young and inexperienced is now often a strategic advantage, and that's borne out by the huge number of GenY entrepreneurs who get started on very high-growth companies simply by fiddling around on their computers. In their teens, they build websites for local businesses and launch cottage information technology (IT) support companies (translation: setting up your elderly neighbor's computer for a few bucks). They cut their teeth on the world of e-commerce by trading on eBay, and then they use what they've learned to create their own online marketplaces. They tinker with existing technology, such as Outlook or Photoshop, find it lacking, and set about perfecting it. Some are even brave enough to take on Facebook. The result: businesses that would never have been conceived in a life lived largely off the grid—businesses that are largely products of their founders' need to tinker, perfect, customize, and revolutionize.

 ## Turning Passion into Profit

Brendan Ciecko is tall and lanky with Elvis Costello glasses, a mop of dark hair that tends to fall in his face, and an unassuming demeanor that you wouldn't expect from someone who does business with guys like Mick Jagger. Ciecko is the 21-year-old CEO of Ten Minute Media, a website developer and marketing company in Holyoke, MA. But not so long ago he was the quintessential nerdy kid who spent hours in his room with his computer. He also had a passion for music, and when he wasn't playing guitar in local rock bands, he was designing websites for them. He had little or no desire to start a business; he was simply acting like a typical teenaged boy, stealing as much time as he could to do the things that he loved. But Ciecko was anything but typical.

When he was just 13, his favorite band, Slick Shoes, held a contest that gave fans an opportunity to design a Flash introduction for the band's website. Ciecko won the contest and scored a free CD and T-shirt; then he convinced the band's manager to let him redesign the entire website for free. "They were just emerging on the music scene, so a lot of people from the industry were going to their site," says Ciecko. Among the admirers were executives from Vagrant Records, one of the largest independent record labels in the world. The execs, based in Los Angeles, were impressed with Ciecko's work and invited him to meet them for a drink in New York. "Uh, I'm younger than you think," Ciecko demurred. "I'm still in high school." But his youth worked to his advantage. "They referred to me as their wonder boy," says Ciecko. He was a just a kid, but he understood the technology and the youth market better than any music industry executive twice his age.

Throughout high school, he continued to work for record labels, earning the kind of money that delighted but somewhat shocked his parents, a plumber and a school bus driver. "They never really understood how big it was until I asked them if I really needed to go to school," says Ciecko. He graduated from high school and applied only to nearby Hampshire College, known for its highly unstructured learning environment. He was accepted but continued to run his business, taking on clients such as Natalie Cole and Clear Channel, which hired him to revamp the Web presence of its biggest R&B/hip-hop station. And then came his *really* big break.

Ciecko had worked with the vice president of strategic marketing at Capitol Records and had impressed the fellow with his creativity and technical know-how. So the vice president called Ciecko one day with an offer that left the young Web developer virtually speechless: "I was on the road with Mick Jagger and I showed him your work, and he's really interested," said the exec. "He needs a new site for his new solo album, so could you come to New York and meet him?"

So in October 2007, Ciecko drove his BMW to Manhattan for what was probably the most memorable meeting of his life. Jagger, dressed in tight white jeans and a suit coat, sat down with Ciecko and explained exactly how he wanted his site to look. "It was a huge, huge event for me," says Ciecko. "He was very energetic and very eloquent. At the end of the meeting, I was in the elevator with Mick Jagger, his manager, and his bodyguard, and I just laughed. I realized I had so much potential to grow my business." And that's exactly what he did, although he did take a leave of absence from Hampshire to do it. Ciecko added to his impressive roster of clients: Van Morrison, Lenny Kravitz, New Kids on the Block, Katy Perry, and Taylor Hicks have hired him, helping him to boost revenue to $450,000 in 2008.

> "I was in the elevator with Mick Jagger, his manager, and his bodyguard, and I just laughed. I realized I had so much potential to grow my business."
>
> —Brendan Ciecko, Ten Minute Media

That's not bad for a guy who invested nothing but his own brainpower in his business and who spent precious little time consciously deciding if he really did want to start a company. Ten Minute Media just seemed to be a natural extension of his skills, his passions, and his tinkering. You can read more about the evolution of Ciecko's business in Chapter 8.

 ## Pimp My Technology

When this kind of tinkering evolves into a big idea that's scalable and marketable, it's very frequently because technology is being used in one of three ways:

- To forge social connections, share ideas, or expand networks
- To build on, perfect, or customize existing technology applications or platforms
- To improve on traditional ways of producing, marketing, and selling products

Businesses such as Facebook and YouTube have had a profound impact on GenY. Their detractors explain them away as mere sources of online entertainment, but they signal much deeper trends. They mobilize the power of virtual communities, democratize the creation of content, and show us how entrepreneurial endeavors profit handsomely when they are less a CEO's monologue than an ongoing conversation with customers. The young entrepreneurs who actively participated in the evolution of nascent social technologies are now using their skills and their market intelligence to build the next generation of disruptive, game-changing companies.

In *Grown Up Digital: How the Net Generation Is Changing the World* (McGraw-Hill, 2008), author Don Tapscott talks about eight "norms" or characteristics of GenY or, as he refers to them, the "Net Generation." One of those norms is love of customization. "The *potential* to personalize a product is important to the Net Gen," writes Tapscott, "even if the individual decides not to make any changes. The desire is about personalizing and accessorizing." The obvious example is personalized Facebook and MySpace pages, but GenY's love of customization goes beyond aesthetic sensibilities and is now moving into the realm of functionality. GenY entrepreneurs are great at tweaking existing technology to make it their own.

Take Adam Smith, age 24, and Matt Brezina, age 28, the cofounders of San Francisco–based Xobni (*inbox* spelled backward), who have developed a free, downloadable Microsoft Outlook plug-in that helps to organize your inbox. Xobni, which appears as a vertical panel to the right of your Outlook screen (think of it as a sidebar), adds social networking capability to Outlook by indexing mail and organizing it by people, making it much easier to keep track of your conversations. Click on any e-mail in your inbox, and the Xobni panel automatically creates a profile for the sender, showing the history of your conversations, the files you've exchanged, and the contacts you have in common. It also extracts phone numbers (click on the number, and you'll be taken directly to Skype) and tells you if your contact has a LinkedIn profile and if you're friends on Facebook. The program is also integrated with Hoovers and Yahoo! e-mail.

"This kind of innovation wouldn't come from a 40-year-old veteran of the software industry or from someone who had been using Outlook for a long time because those people have become desensitized to the pain," offers Brezina. "We're from the Facebook generation, and we're users of all these other communications and networking tools—IM, LinkedIn, and Facebook. It was like e-mail had been around for 15 years and no one got the memo that the world had changed." So Xobni's mission is to integrate those tools into Outlook, making the world's most popular e-mail application less about dates and timelines than about people and their relationships.

The two started the company in the summer of 2006 with $12,000 in seed funding from YCombinator, a Cambridge, MA, organization that funds and mentors young high-tech startups. That stamp of approval helped them to raise an additional $4.26 million in venture capital several months later from Khosla Ventures. And in September 2007, Brezina and Smith were chosen to introduce their software at TechCrunch40, a highly selective annual conference where promising startups demo their products. Within 12 hours, 10,000 new users had downloaded Xobni, and the company shut down registration.

"It was like e-mail had been around for 15 years and no one got the memo that the world had changed."

— Matt Brezina, Xobni

"We spent nine months working with those users and fixing their problems," says Brezina. He and Smith had plenty of help. They had hired a new CEO, Jeff Bonforte, who had headed up Yahoo!'s social search initiatives and grew Yahoo! Messenger to overtake AIM. And they had piqued the interest of Don Dodge, director of business development at Microsoft. Dodge invited them into the company's Start-Up Accelerator Program, which nurtures high-potential startups with products that operate on the Microsoft platform. They soon found themselves in tech-startup nirvana when Bill Gates demoed the Xobni software at the Microsoft Office Developers Conference in February of 2008 and called it "very, very cool" and "the next generation of social networking."

Two months later, the "TechCrunch" blog reported that Microsoft had made a $20 million offer to acquire Xobni. Brezina and Smith won't comment on the offer. They reportedly turned it down even though they have yet to make a penny on Xobni. That, however, did not deter Cisco from investing in Xobni. In January 2009, the company took the lead in a $7 million round of financing, joined by Xobni's previous investors. In the works: customized versions of Xobni for large organizations, now in trial with a handful of Fortune 500 companies. That, of course, is where the big money is.

In addition to the highly lucrative enterprise market, the founders and their 19 employees are developing a premium product that users will pay for and are exploring various other creative ways to monetize free users. To date, there are 1.5 million downloads of Xobni already on individual desktops. But with a total of 400 million Outlook users to tap, there's plenty of market potential. "Right now, we're just hoping to make a product that millions and millions of people will use," says Brezina. "We sit on top of the number one communications device in the world, but e-mail is also a well-known pain point." If Xobni can ease the pain by helping users customize their inboxes, it's highly likely that the company's founders and investors will be sitting pretty.

Mobile Technology Meets Social Networking

If Xobni wants to customize your inbox, then Loopt hopes to do the same with your smartphone. Sam Altman, age 23, cofounded the Mountain View, CA company, which develops cell phone software that allows users to keep track of their friends' whereabouts via Global Positioning System (GPS)-like technology loaded on their phones. Why, you may ask? Mobile devices are now a ubiquitous part of our lives, and we seem to be demanding more and more of them. It's not enough that they deliver our e-mail, play our music, give us directions, and keep track of our schedules. Now, it's virtually a forgone conclusion that we'll ultimately manage all our human interactions on our smartphones, so why not use them to keep physical track of our pals?

Altman came up with the idea for Loopt in the spring of 2005 while he was a sophomore at Stanford; the spark for his inspiration was his desire to know where his friends were—to be able to glance at his phone and know immediately who was close enough to hang out with him. It's yet another great example of using technology to customize an experience.

Altman and a classmate, Nick Sivo, wrote a rough business plan and, like the Xobni partners, submitted it to the incubator YCominbator. "I didn't need the money," says Altman. "I did it totally for the advice. The biggest challenge for young tech entrepreneurs is that we have a deep understanding of the technology but little or no understanding of anything else. It all seems very intimidating." YCombinator accepted Altman and Sivo into the program, and a year later, the organization's cofounder, Paul Graham, described Loopt as "one of the most promising of the startups we've funded so far." His impression of Altman, which he shared in an October 2006 essay derived from a talk at MIT: "Within about three minutes of meeting him, I remember thinking 'Ah, so this is what Bill Gates must have been like when he was 19.'"

Altman did not disappoint. He landed a total funding commitment of $17 million from heavy-hitting venture firms Sequoia Capital and New Enterprise Associates (NEA). And by the end of 2006, he had convinced Boost, the youth brand of Sprint, to offer his software to subscribers. It was by no means an easy sell. "Boost had put out an RFP [request for proposal] for companies that do exactly what we did, but we didn't hear about it until the last minute," recalls Altman. "Twenty other companies were in discussion with them for three months, and we hadn't even incorporated." But Altman and his six-person team were not deterred. They flew to Los Angeles, turned on the charm, and gave the folks at Boost the hard sell.

"We really hit it off," says Altman. "We told them, 'We're the target demographic; we're building this for ourselves.' We knew this was going to be a major deal because Sprint owns Boost and whoever got Boost would also get Sprint." The Boost execs were impressed enough to request a visit to Loopt's headquarters, which Altman and Sivo quickly populated with their friends to make the young company look much bigger than it was. It worked; through sheer persistence and by playing the youth card to their advantage, the Loopt team wrangled the deal away from a competitor at the last minute. In early 2007, Loopt launched to 100,000 subscribers on the Boost network, and by the end of that summer, Sprint had signed on as well.

> "The biggest challenge for young tech entrepreneurs is that we have a deep understanding of the technology but little or no understanding of anything else."
>
> —Sam Altman, Loopt

Loopt has come a long way since then. The company is moving from a subscription-based revenue model, where users pay $3 a month for the service, to an advertising-supported model that allows Loopt to give away the service for free to subscribers willing to tolerate local pop-up ads on their phones. By the end of 2008, the application was available on all carriers and on approximately 100 models of

GPS-enabled handsets. Loopt is available as a free application for the iPhone, and Apple featured it on a television commercial in late November 2008. That exposure helped make Loopt the twentieth most popular downloaded iPhone application—more popular than Facebook and MySpace at one time.

Altman is also partnering with the online local review site Yelp, founded by Upstarts Jeremy Stoppelman, age 31, and Russell Simmons, age 30. Loopt will tell you where your friends are, and Yelp then will give you recommendations for, say, the closest and most highly rated restaurants. Another Loopt feature, called Mix, allows iPhone users to find new people with common interests who may be near them—at a club, conference, or other event, for example—and arrange to meet them in person. Mix actually resulted in a patent-infringement lawsuit against Loopt by a small Chicago-based company called Earthcomber. Altman says the suit has been dismissed, but it's an indication of just how ruthlessly competitive the mobile applications business has become. Case in point: The Silicon Valley venture capital firm Kleiner Perkins Caufiled & Byers has a $100 million "iFund™" created specifically to finance the development of iPhone applications; in their portfolio is Whrrl, a Loopt competitor. There are also rumblings that Facebook and MySpace could enter the location-based social networking industry, which would be akin to Wal-Mart moving in next to the local grocery store.

So Altman will not have this space to himself, and it's clear that he's preparing to duke it out with his current and future competitors. While he's tight-lipped about Loopt's revenues, he did confirm that he's hired the investment bank Allen & Co. to help him raise more capital.

A Photoshop Alternative

If there's a bigger GenY watchword than *customization*, it's probably *democratization*. "We're democratizing the art world by creating Web-based tools and education to the masses," says Avi Muchnick, age 29, the cofounder of Aviary, a website that offers a suite of free browser-based software that visitors can use for digital photo editing. It's the online alternative to Adobe's Photoshop, but without the hefty price tag.

The idea evolved from a hobby website known as Worth1000.com that Muchnick started eight years ago when he was still in law school in

Manhattan. The site, one of the first of its kind, ran online contests for photographs doctored with Adobe's Photoshop digital editing software. It was a venture that kept Muchnick amused but generated little or no revenue.

Then, right after the U.S. invasion of Iraq in 2002, Muchnick announced a new contest called "Where's Saddam?" The idea, says Muchnick, was to use digital editing to show Saddam Hussein hiding in plain sight. The Worth1000 community of artists went crazy, producing photos of Saddam as Elvis, a UPS man, Santa, a Mardi Gras drag queen, a belly dancer, and thousands of other mildly offensive images. While Muchnick's growing community of artists was quietly chuckling, however, a group of U.S. soldiers stationed in Iraq found the images online, downloaded them, printed them, and plastered them all over Baghdad. The press soon got wind of the impromptu propaganda campaign, and the Pentagon issued a statement that it had nothing to do with the pictures. Worth1000 was catapulted out of obscurity into the limelight, with coverage on CNN, *Good Morning America*, and almost every major mainstream newspaper in the country.

> "We're democratizing the art world by creating Web-based tools and education to the masses."
>
> —Avi Muchnick, Aviary

The site continued to grow, and Muchnick monetized it by running custom contests for corporations. Universal Studios, for instance, sponsored a contest to promote the release of *King Kong*. The company had reached approximately $1 million in revenue when Muchnick got lucky again. At the end of 2006, he received an e-mail out of the blue on behalf of an anonymous "high-profile individual" who wanted to know if he was looking for investors. Muchnick traced the e-mail address to a highly secretive privately owned space-exploration company named Blue Origin, and he instantly knew the identity of his secret admirer: Amazon founder Jeff Bezos, who also founded Blue Origin.

As it turned out, Bezos was a big fan of Worth1000 and wanted to know what other ideas Muchnick had on deck. Muchnick, in fact, had noticed something on Worth1000 that gave him insight into what he thought was a potentially lucrative marketplace need. Thousands of people visited the site, but only 100 or so participated in the Photoshop contests. The reason: Full versions of Photoshop start at $600 to $700, making the software far too expensive for most hobbyists. Munchnick's idea was to develop Web-based software and online tutorials that would make digital photo editing accessible to everyone. Bezos thought the idea was promising, so he invested an undisclosed sum and took 10 percent of the new company, called Aviary.

By that time, Muchnick had brought on his friend Michael Galpert, age 25, as an equal partner, and the two flew out to Seattle to meet Bezos. As they sat in a conference room at Amazon, waiting nervously for Bezos, Galpert says that they were both struck by the same observation. "The large table we sat at, in the most important room of a publicly traded company worth billions of dollars, was actually made up of a dozen cheap plastic tables laid out side by side," says Galpert. "They were the same type of tables we bought in Costco for $50 a piece to serve as our office desks. We knew then that Jeff's vision for success fit in line exactly with ours. Even at the advanced stage of his company: Always shun excess."

Aviary, based on Long Island, now has 11 employees, including "the best and the brightest software developers," says Galpert. Five of them are in Atlanta, Italy, Germany, and Canada. Aviary has been up and running in public beta since November 2008 and has 100,000 registered users who can use a basic version of the software for free or pay $9.99 a month for a more advanced version. The software is also now imbedded into the Worth1000 site, where it's available to that site's 600,000 members, as well as to companies who pay $10,000 to $50,000 to use it in viral media campaigns. The investment community clearly thinks Aviary is onto something. A second, "more significant" round of financing was completed in August 2008, with heavy hitters Joi Ito of Creative Commons and Reid Hoffman of LinkedIn joining Bezos as shareholders.

A Social Networking Niche

MySpace and Facebook dominate the world of social networking in terms of number of members and Web traffic, and their staggering success has helped to create a new industry and pave the way for other entrants. Niche social networks seem to proliferate like wire hangers in a closet, but one of the fastest growing and most successful is myYearbook.com. Founded by the Cook siblings, Catherine, age 19, Dave, age 21, and their older brother, Geoff, age 31, the site is essentially Facebook for younger high school students. Catherine and Dave started it in 2005, when they found themselves, at 15 and 16, trying to make friends at a new school in Skillman, NJ. Back then, Facebook membership still was limited to college students, and the Cooks thought that MySpace was "a little creepy." A social networking site geared toward high schoolers would help them to make new friends, but also, the younger Cooks predicted that it also might be a pretty good idea for a business. Like many of their Upstart peers, the Cooks founded a business that was largely a reaction to an established company that wasn't quite meeting their needs.

Their enthusiasm was fueled by their big brother, Geoff, who had started a highly successful college essay editing company when his younger siblings were just eight and nine years old. "We watched him build the company, and we visited him in his really cool office in California," says Catherine. Geoff sold his company, CollegeGate, to Thompson & Peterson's, a test prep and book company, in 2002 and walked away with a very fat wallet. And so, when his younger siblings pitched their business idea to him at the dinner table one night, he did what any devoted, wealthy, and savvy older brother would do. "He wrote us a check for $250,000 right there at the table," recalls Catherine, who became copresident of myYearbook.com with her brother Dave.

With help from programmers hired in Mumbai, India, Catherine and Dave launched myYearbook.com in April 2005 with 300 members from their high school. "We wore really cool T-shirts to launch it," says Catherine. "On the front, they said 'myYearbook.com,' and on the back was 'Who are your friends and are they hot?'" Five months later, they expanded to other high schools and were adding 3,000 new members a day.

The Cooks attribute their success to listening to their users' suggestions, such as allowing members to link to others with the same interests and making it easy to customize pages. They also made the decision to differentiate themselves from Facebook by creating their own applications rather than allowing outside developers access to their platform. "Instead of having thousands of applications, our goal is to have 200 incredibly good ones," says Catherine, who reports that revenues, earned from advertisers, are "in the eight figures."

As for brother Geoff, it was hands off his investment until his two younger sibs decided they needed outside financing to grow the company. "We were nervous about going in and saying, 'Hey, we're 16 and 17, do you want to throw a few million our way,'" recalls Catherine. So they brought Geoff on as CEO and landed $4.1 million in venture capital in late 2006 from U.S. Venture Partners and First Round Capital. Less than two years later, in July 2008, they raised an additional $13 million from Norwest Venture Partners with participation from the original investors.

myYearbook.com now adds 20,000 new users a day, has more than 11 million members, and is the third largest and the fastest-growing social networking site on the Web. It's still dwarfed by Facebook and MySpace, each of which attracts well over 100 million unique monthly visitors at this writing, compared with myYearbook.com's 12 million. But myYearbook.com's tiny market share is increasing exponentially (384 percent from May 2007 to July 2008). It's a great example of a young upstart taking on the 800-pound gorillas in the industry by offering a very specific segment of the market (teens aged 13 to 19) a service that's better suited to their needs. Cook notes that her members spend an average of 30 minutes per visit, compared with Facebook's 20 minutes.

> "Our long-term goal is still to be the largest social media site on the Web, and monetize it."
>
> —Catherine Cook, myYearbook.com

Advertisers love that kind of attention span from an audience that's affluent and impressionable but not particularly well known for its ability to focus. And unlike Facebook, which now attracts a huge number of foreign users, myYearbook.com's constituency is largely U.S.-based, which makes the site a more targeted buy for advertisers.

But the Cook siblings are not content to rest on their laurels. Catherine is now a junior at Georgetown University, where she juggles school with approximately 40 hours a week on the myYearbook.com website. Typically, she heads home on the weekends to put in more time at the office. It's a full plate, but she has big plans. "Our long-term goal is still to be the largest social media site on the Web, and monetize it," she says.

Facebook as Incubator

Facebook may be in myYearbook.com's crosshairs, but the former is currently the undisputed default social network. According to comScore, which tracks online consumer behavior, Facebook had approximately 222 million unique visitors in December 2008,which means that it attracted 22 percent of the global Internet audience. Facebook's popularity is due in part to the huge number of applications that members use to customize their pages. At the end of May 2007, CEO Mark Zuckerberg announced that he was opening up the company's platform to third-party developers who were free to build their own applications and drop them into the Facebook framework. And that spawned a vast community of young entrepreneurs hell-bent on creating popular applications for their favorite social networking site. Jesse Tevelow, age 25, and Joseph Aigboboh, age 23, were among them. They developed a Facebook application called Sticky Notes that allows users to put virtual Post-it notes on their friends' Facebook pages. The partners met in the summer of 2006 at a Manhattan-based Internet startup where Tevelow was an associate consultant and Aigboboh was a summer intern. They became friends and talked about starting a company together but never really crystallized their idea until they attended a Boulder, CO–based entrepreneurial bootcamp called TechStars in the summer of 2007.

"We look for great founders and great teams, and we don't really care so much about ideas," says David Cohen, a serial entrepreneur and cofounder of TechStars, which provides seed capital and mentorship for young startup entrepreneurs in exchange for a 5 percent equity stake. Every year, TechStars runs a summer program for 10 companies (last year, over 300 applied), most of them promising technology-related startups that need help and support to get the ball rolling.

Tevelow and Aigboboh had a vague idea that their company would focus on digital content sharing. "We looked at how people sent links online via e-mail, and we thought we could create a better system," says Tevelow. But TechStars' group of mentors was not impressed. "The idea was derivative," says Cohen. "So they abandoned it when they were halfway through the program." While the other TechStars' entrepreneurs seemed to be well into the development stage of their ideas, Tevelow and Aigboboh were still stuck on their concept. "It was a tense two to three weeks," remembers Aigboboh. "We felt like lame ducks for a while." But that didn't last for long.

Mark Zuckerberg had just announced that third-party developers would be permitted to build applications for Facebook, so Tevelow and Aigboboh decided to jump on the opportunity. Was it desperation? Well, maybe.

Tevelow recalls a stormy night in Boulder when the power went out, and he and Tevelow were forced into some serious soul searching by mentors who kept asking, "What the hell are you two doing?" It was then that they decided to take the leap and develop an application for Facebook. They built Sticky Notes in two days, put it into the Facebook application directory, and launched it with a few friends on the site. By the first week, 30,000 users had installed the application. Advertisers, noting Sticky Notes' growing popularity, came calling, and the two founders soon found themselves monetizing

> "We look for great founders and great teams, and we don't really care so much about ideas."
>
> — David Cohen, TechStars

their application with clients such as Video Egg and Google AdSense. By the time they left Denver in August, Tevelow and Aigboboh, who christened their company J-Squared Media, were the only team in their TechStars class that had developed a revenue-generating product. "One thing they said a lot at TechStars was to fail fast, and we took that to heart," says Aigboboh.

At the end of that summer, they went back home and set up an office in the basement of a grungy West Philadelphia row house, where they quickly began earning $45,000 a month on advertising. By that time, Sticky Notes had been installed 3.5 million times, putting it in the top 1 percent of all Facebook applications. And when the company was just a few months old, the founders received an offer that many entrepreneurs would find difficult to refuse: A private media company wanted to acquire them for $3 million, on the condition that the founders continue to work for the company. Tevelow and Aigboboh refused, much to the chagrin of their friends and family. But the two were not willing to give up their entrepreneurial freedom, and they felt strongly about their ability to grow the company significantly without giving up ownership.

Since then, Sticky Notes has waned in popularity, but that's fine with Tevelow and Aigboboh, who report that they are now involved in "a pretty serious project that's taken us into a development cycle of 10 to 12 months." Revenue from their previous Facebook applications has given them the luxury of that research-and-development time, which they say will yield a new social media–related product in the third quarter of 2009.

If you're tempted to think that the Facebook application business model is just a fad, consider that two California-based venture capital firms, Bay Partners in Menlo Park and Altura Ventures in Monterey, have launched investment funds exclusively for Facebook platforms. And in the fall of 2007, Facebook founder Mark Zuckerburg announced the creation of his own $10 million fund called fbFund. Along with venture capital firms Accel Partners and Founders Fund, Facebook will make 25 cash grants of $25,000 to $250,000 annually to promising developers. The cash comes without strings, but the venture capital firms get first dibs on investments in the finalists. There were about 600 companies in the first pool of applicants, and the 25 winners were announced in the fall of 2008. Another 50 grants were made in May 2009.

Marketing in the Virtual World

You may not be setting the world on fire with game-changing mobile technology or launching your own social network, but if you aren't somehow using online communities to market your business, you're missing the boat. Blogs, forums, and virtual communities of customers play an increasingly significant role not only in the creation and growth of new companies but also in how all companies market their brands, innovate, and serve customers.

According to Ed Moran, director of new-product development at Deloitte Services LP, though, companies frequently don't understand how to leverage those communities properly. In July 2008, Deloitte conducted a "Tribalization of Business Survey" of Fortune 100 companies and startups that had created online communities. "We wanted to take what's happening with the Millennials and show large companies and big enterprises that this is a tremendous business opportunity," says Moran. Too often, he says, companies use a blog or a sponsored online community as a place to publish press releases, to advertise new products, or to tell consumers how they should perceive a brand. It's the wrong approach, says Moran. "There's a subtle shift that a lot of companies have missed," he says. "Branding is not in your control anymore. People will assemble around a product or service, and they've got a much stronger affinity for your product than they do for your company. They create a tremendous amount of buzz."

The real value of an online community lies in a company's willingness to listen to what users have to say and to use their collective intelligence either to create new products or to improve existing ones. A few big companies get it. Dell, for instance, carefully monitors its online community to discern where customers are having trouble with its products and to alert its helpdesk accordingly. The company's community, known as IdeaStorm.com, also suggested that the company offer computers with the Linux operating system instead of Windows. Dell complied. Starbucks' Howard Schultz followed Dell's lead with MyStarbucksIdea.com, where customers make suggestions that are then rated by other customers. One idea that was implemented: a splash stick that customers use to plug the opening in the lid so that coffee doesn't spill as they walk.

Dell and Starbucks are still the exception. "It's my sense that many companies dismiss online communities and social networks as purely social," Moran says. "Generation Y entrepreneurs understand that social networking shifts from a social framework to a market framework very quickly." In other words, people may connect online for social purposes, but the discussion evolves rapidly into a forum for consumers—particularly young ones—to communicate their wants and needs. Upstarts know how to leverage this, and they do it so effectively that they're frequently able to use online communities to launch businesses and gain competitive traction in very traditional or commoditized industries.

Community First, Business Second

This is exactly what Jonathan Levi, age 22, and Nick Palefsky, age 23, have accomplished with their $1.8 million Santa Clara, CA–based company, Jlevi StreetWerks, a Web-based company that sells aftermarket auto parts.

Back in 2004, Levi was a car enthusiast who, at age 16, decided to jazz up the preowned BMW 328Ci that his parents had bought him for his birthday. When his folks refused to pay for the product he wanted—a headlight enhancement called Angel Eyes—because, says Levi, "they thought it was the silliest thing they'd ever seen," the resourceful teen found another way to get what he wanted. He approached an Angel Eyes vendor whom he had met on an online BMW enthusiasts' forum and proposed a partnership: He'd promote Angel Eyes at his high school in exchange for a discount. The vendor had a different arrangement in mind: He suggested that Levi buy five of the products, resell them, and set up shop as his installer in the Bay Area, for which Levi would earn a commission. Levi tapped into his bar mitzvah money to purchase the inventory, and a cottage business was born.

One of his first customers was Nick Palefsky, a 17-year-old whom he had met at a BMW enthusiasts' event; he found other customers on the online car forum where he frequently posted. "But I started getting too much attention on the forum," says Levi, "and the owner wanted me to start paying for advertising." Levi agreed, realizing that he would have to extend his product line and build his own e-commerce website to afford the sponsorship dues. There, he'd sell Angel Eyes and a few other products from the distributor who helped get him started. By August 2005, the business was doing $275,000 in revenue, and Levi, who was getting ready to start his freshman year at UC Berkeley, knew that he needed help. So he brought on Palefsky as a partner and recruited his mom, a substitute teacher, to help with orders and shipping. The following year, sales more than doubled, and the two partners, who always assumed their venture was "a side thing," realized that they had a bona fide money-maker on their hands.

While the company also has opened up a retail location with warehouse space, Palefsky and Levi remain committed to growing it organically and without outside financing. And they're staying true to the marketing strategy they used to launch their business. They tried print advertising and were disappointed with the results, and Google AdWords didn't work terribly well because their products were so niche-oriented. Online forums continue to pay off, however. "Something about our corporate culture just clicks better by directly marketing to customers, by dialoging, answering questions, and posting information," says Levi. Perhaps that's because as long-time members and active participants in those online communities, Levi and Palefsky have built reputations not just as Internet marketers, but also as knowledgeable and passionate car enthusiasts whose advice is as valuable as the products they sell. There's an implicit contract: If the advice is bad, and if the products are shoddy, the community will take them to task. It's not a risk that every company wants to take, but Levi and Palefsky have found it to be their most valuable and authentic path to growth.

Captive Audience

Marcus Adolfsson, age 29, also profited handsomely from his expertise with online communities—a skill that helped to land him the number 37 spot on the 2007 Inc. 500 list. It was a quite a coup for a guy who ran his Gainsville, FL, company, $15.4 million Smartphone Experts, out of a shed in his first employee's backyard for its first three years.

Adolfsson unwittingly planted the seeds for his business back in 1999, when he was a freshman at the University of Florida. He had started an online forum called VisorCentral, where users of the newly launched Handspring Visor could talk about and get information on the product. It was a side project that he did for fun, but he also was able to monetize the site with paid advertising. When Handspring came out with the Treo, the first popular smartphone, Adolfsson launched Treo Central. After graduation, he landed a job as chief technology officer (CTO) at a company called Legendary Marketing, but he continued to run the forums. They had evolved from mere discussion groups into e-commerce sites, where Adolfsson actually sold phones and accessories. He took customer service calls at lunchtime in the company's break room. "I got a license to sell Sprint phones, and I worked out of our spare bedroom at home," he recalls. "At that time, no one was selling the new Treo 600 or accessories online, and I had the perfect marketing machine with the forums." The forum that he had started for fun had turned into a captive audience.

He ordered $500 worth of accessories—cases and phone chargers—from China and coded the online store himself. On the first day, he sold over 200 Treo 600s; in two days, he had sold out the accessory inventory from China. With $200 per activation from Sprint and significant markup on the accessories, Adolfsson found himself going from "making $4,000 a month with $20,000 in credit-card debt to making a $50,000 profit after the first week."

In the fall of 2003, he quit his job and devoted himself full time to his company, which he called Smartphone Experts. For six months, he worked out of a spare bedroom, and when he hired his first employee, Diana Kingree, a former coworker, he moved the company to a shed in her back yard. When the company grew and needed more space for employees and inventory, Adolfsson and Kingree put up more sheds until there were six. "We had six to eight employees, and they were parked in Diana's driveway," says Adolfsson. "We got nervous about zoning regulations, and it was rather embarrassing bringing suppliers to Diana's backyard." By the time Adolfsson moved the company to a 5,000-square-foot warehouse, it was 2005, and Smartphone Experts was racking up $10 million in annual sales. The following year, revenues climbed to over $16 million, which landed the company on the Inc. 500 list. But that success didn't come simply from selling phones and accessories.

> **"I went from making $4,000 a month with $20,000 in credit-card debt to making a $50,000 profit after the first week."**
>
> — Marcus Adolfsson,
> Smartphone Experts

U.S. carriers got Web savvy and ultimately decided that they'd rather sell phones through their own sites, activation fees went way down, and accessories, which still offered great margins, were quickly becoming commoditized. Luckily, the company "was never just a store," says Adolfsson. "First, we started a community; then we added a store. We had a two-tier system." To differentiate the company, Adolfsson created or acquired more community sites, branching out to BlackBerry and iPhone, incorporating reviews and user-generated content that was indexed by search engines. On those sites, he continued to sell accessories, but he knew that it was the strength of the community that was driving the e-commerce. "We're close to the market, so we can tweak products according to what we hear from customers," says Adolfsson. That tweaking was possible because he also took a huge leap and began contract manufacturing his own accessories in South America and China, which not only gave him greater control over product design but also significantly improved his margins. It was a path he could have scarcely imagined when he first started VisorCentral in 1999. Adolfsson's use of communities has evolved even further; you can read more about him in Chapter 8.

There's very little that's special about the products sold by Jlevi StreetWerks or Smartphone Experts; they are, in fact, purveyors of commodity goods. What gives these companies mojo in the marketplace is their CEOs' expertise at making connections with large online communities, providing those communities with valuable information, and then leveraging their reputations as knowledgeable and service-oriented participants to become trusted vendors. It's almost as if they're putting a sophisticated brick-and-mortar spin on their online companies, and that gives them a tremendous edge not only over their Internet competitors but also over traditional retailers.

Exiting the Commodity Game

Joel Holland is also very quick to tell you that there's nothing terribly special about what he sells—stock video footage. "Stock footage is almost a commodity," he says. "My stuff is probably not any better than other companies' but the way I differentiate is that I constantly change out the technology processes." The 24-year-old founder of Footage Firm, in Reston, VA, got his start as a high school sophomore when he was working on a television project that involved interviewing celebrities and CEOs about their advice for young people. After a Hollywood interview with Arnold Schwarzenegger, Holland retuned home to Virginia to edit the film but found himself wishing that he had also shot some footage of the Hollywood sign or the walk of fame so that he could add some visual variety to the interview. He had two choices: Return to California, or pay someone else to shoot the footage for him. Both options were prohibitively expensive, so he did neither, and his production suffered. "I said to myself, 'Why isn't there a company that does this?' If I have a need for something, I always assume someone else does as well."

> "If you look at the business models and the energy behind MySpace and Facebook, they're harbingers of this community ethos. . . . With many of these businesses, the commercial value is established after the community is established."
>
> —Karim Lakhani,
> Harvard University

With money he had earned designing websites, Holland bought a high-quality video camera to shoot some stock footage around Washington, DC. He then sold it on eBay, listing it as B-roll footage for video editing. "I'd list the same footage in 30 different auctions, but each auction would have a different title," he recalls. "And then I'd do Excel spreadsheets to find out what variable made each unit sell." It was pretty resourceful for a 16-year-old, and it was the beginning of Footage Firm, a business name that he chose because he discovered that *footage* was his most successful keyword.

Success on eBay convinced him that he had found an underserved niche, and he began to film stock footage of more U.S. cities. At the same time, he moved the business off eBay and onto his own website. When he was in his senior year in high school, a large production company bought some New York City footage for a Discovery Channel show on the mafia, and Footage Firm was mentioned in the credits. That exposure gave the company credibility and momentum.

Holland says that there was very little competition when he started out. "There were big dogs like MGM, and they'd have all this footage, but it was very expensive. I created a digital video resolution stock that I could charge much less for." And he offered everything for sale in an easily searchable online inventory, a service that wasn't available anywhere else when he first started out.

Footage Firm now has more than 60 freelance videographers who provide footage of 100 U.S. cities and 80 countries to a customer list of 50,000 individuals and production companies. Footage Firm pays its freelancers for the footage, plus a commission on each sale. The average transaction is a mere $149, but Holland describes it as a "high-volume, high-margin business." Because he was a first mover and now has a reputation for quality and reliability, new entrants to the market have trouble stealing clients from him. Besides, Footage Firm's products account for such a small percentage of customers' budgets that they are typically unwilling to trouble themselves with changing vendors. So Holland watches the competition, figures out who's spending a lot of money on Google advertising, and then offers to sell their clips on his website for a 50–50 revenue split. He screens everything he sells to ensure quality and insists that these strategic partners ship everything to him so that he can ship directly to his customers.

Footage Firm's revenues are approximately $1 million, and Holland has an impressive list of clients, including ABC, Disney, Jay Leno, the History Channel, and Comedy Central. His stock footage of Washington, DC, even appeared on NBC's *30 Rock* last year. He's moving into new markets as well, targeting news agencies by offering on-demand video from a newly created online community of videographers called DVprofessionals.com. Holland started the site as a place where video editors could showcase their work to potential clients, communicate with one another, and create groups within the site. Thus, while the main purpose is to provide a marketplace where news agencies can find and hire videographers to shoot footage, there's also a social networking component. "Video production is a line of work, but also a passion and a hobby," says Holland. "Video editors love finding like-minded people." There's no fee to be on the network, and Holland doesn't take a commission from work sold there. But he does use it to advertise Footage Firm's services. "It's a real estate property on the Web that gives us a lot of window space to shop our product," he says. He's also launched another site called stockfootageforfree.com, where hobbyists (such as people who upload their videos on YouTube) can download clips for free. Free? The rationale: Hobbyists grow up and eventually want more and better footage, so the site is really a customer-acquisition tool for Footage Firm.

> "I never wanted to start another eBay business. I wanted to start another eBay."
>
> —Joel Holland, Footage Firm

Holland essentially started a business in a commodity industry and put a GenY spin on it by making it Web-based and virtual. He's been able to grow the company with a stable of freelancers and just two full-time employees. "I would say that I was able to take an old media business and apply a new media technology model that provides a one-stop shopping venue," he says. "I never wanted to start another eBay business. I wanted to start another eBay."

A Tech Spin on Fitness

Holland added a new media model to an old media business, but good things also happen when you apply a new media model to an industry that's never had a technology or community component. Shape Up the Nation, a Providence, RI, company founded by two Brown University medical school students, sells team-oriented, Web-based wellness programs to large organizations that want to help their employees get into shape. As medical students, both Rajiv Kumar, age 26, and Brad Weinberg, age 28, were interested in the U.S. obesity epidemic. "Over 58 diseases are linked to obesity," says Kumar. "I was fascinated with it as a public health challenge, and I began to look at how you could use teams to motivate people to change their lifestyles."

So, in January 2006, Kumar created a nonprofit called Shape Up Rhode Island (see Chapter 6), where statewide community teams compete over a 12-week period to see who can lose the most weight, log the most pedometer steps, or rack up the highest number of minutes exercised. Teams create their own fitness plans, log onto a Web-based program called "TeamTracker" to report their progress, and receive motivational e-newsletters and fitness tips throughout the competition. The program, supported by local companies, community groups, and politicians, culminates in a wellness fair where the winning team is honored. In the first year, says Kumar, there were 2,000 participants; the number more than tripled to 7,000 in 2007, and outcomes were so good that local companies began asking for their own programs.

That's when Kumar brought Weinberg on board. Before medical school, Weinberg had run a company called Event E-Management, which provided an online event registration and management application for universities. He had the technology background to build a robust application that could serve participants nationwide. The two started a separate for-profit called Shape Up The Nation to serve private clients; the idea won a Rhode Island state business-plan competition as well as a Brown University competition. The two students raised approximately $300,000 from angel investors and got their venture rolling in the midst of studying for their second-year medical boards. But the thrill of starting a company ultimately got the best of them, and both Kumar and Weinberg took a leave of absence from Brown to work on the company.

Shape Up The Nation provides turnkey wellness programs to corporations that pay approximately $50 per employee participant. Each participant receives a pedometer, a reminder wrist band, and access to the online system. The Web element is key for two reasons: It takes the administrative burden off a company's human resources department, so there's no management cost involved; and it gives employee teams a place to track their progress and to create community. "A big buzz word in wellness now is *incentive*," says Weinberg. "But we think it's a misconception that you need to pay people to stay healthy. The two major excuses for not exercising are 'I don't have the time' and "I don't have anyone pushing me,' so we created a system where people can find others to help them. We can generate participation rates of 50 percent in large companies, and that's unheard of." For the companies, the payoff is well documented: The average Shape Up The Nation participant loses a full body mass index (BMI) point. According to Weinberg, "research shows that for every BMI point lost, you save $202 in medical and pharmaceutical costs."

With high-profile clients like CVS, Polaroid, and UPS, the company posted almost $1 million in revenue for 2008 and is on track for $2.5 million in 2009. Despite the recession, the partners have also managed to raise an additional $500,000 in angel capital since the end of 2008. "At a time when morale isn't at its highest, it's a perfect time for companies to invest in something that's team-based," says Weinberg. "We're in the right place at the right time."

UPSTARTS PLAYLIST

Track 2: Use Technology to Innovate and Differentiate

1. **Look for the pain in existing technology.** What are the trouble spots—the points of pain—in the technology that you or your customers use every day? For Matt Brezina and Adam Smith, the founders of Xobni, it was the frustration of organizing an Outlook mailbox that led to the creation of software that Bill Gates calls "the next generation of social networking." At Aviary, partners Avi Muchnick and Michael Galpert devised a way to bring innovative browser-based digital photo editing tools to a creative community that could not readily afford pricey Photoshop software. Both companies looked at existing technologies, found their points of pain, and addressed them with original solutions.

2. **Launch fast and imperfectly.** You can never be sure how customers will interact with a new product until you put it their hands. It's best to launch quickly then use customer feedback to perfect and tweak. The founders of Xobni cut off registration for their Outlook plug-in software at 10,000 users, and then spent nine months fixing their problems to create a better product. At Loopt, the company's all-male startup team was taken to task by female users of its smartphone personal GPS software. Women wanted more security features—a need that Loopt addressed in subsequent versions of the software, but never would have discovered through research and development. The lesson: Launch early, and let your customers help you to develop your product to their specifications. You'll save money up front, and you'll end up producing a better product that customers feel invested in.

3. **Apply new technologies to low-tech industries.** Look at traditional, low-tech business models, and ask yourself how they can be made better and more competitive through the use of technology. The founders of Shape Up The Nation built a robust platform for companies and their employees to track fitness goals and accomplishments online. That makes the program far easier and more cost

effective to administer than most traditional wellness programs, giving the company an advantage in a tough economy. Threadless (see Chapter 1) has zero design costs for its t-shirts because a virtual community of users, empowered by an online voting system, does all the work. And Talia Mashiach (see Chapters 1, 3, and 7), built her own proprietary technology platform to vastly simplify corporate events planning for hotels.

4. **Capitalize on social networking.** The founders of MySpace and Facebook gave birth to an industry and now everyone is invited to the party. The Cook siblings, who founded myYearbook.com, capitalized on the success of the big players but tailored their own site to a very specific demographic: the teen/high school market. They now have one of the fastest growing social networking sites on the web. The founders of J-Squared hitched their star to Facebook by creating highly popular applications for the site, earning them ad revenue up to $45,000 a month. And Joel Holland of Footage Firm sells stock video footage to news agencies, but added a free niche social network for videographers to his website. By hosting that community, he creates deeper ties to the people whose work he distributes.

5. **Use online forums to establish expertise.** But take off your sales hat! Your goal here is to establish yourself as a trusted and knowledgeable source of information. First and foremost, be a generous contributor. Marcus Adolfsson created a smartphone forum before he launched his company, Smartphone Experts. When he finally had something to sell, he already had a solid reputation and a captive audience. Jonathan Levi and Nick Palefsky, the founders of Jlevi StreetWerks, still use online forums at their primary marketing vehicle, even though they've added a brick-and-mortar storefront to their online auto parts business.

6. **Find new opportunities in existing businesses.** Avi Muchnick got the idea for Aviary, a website that offers a suite of free browser-based photo editing software, from his previous business, Worth1000. The latter is a website that runs contest for photos that are doctored with Adobe Photoshop. When Muchnick noticed that the number of visitors on Worth1000 far exceeded the number of

contest participants, he attributed the difference to Photoshop's high price tag. That observation led him to cofound Aviary, which democratizes digital editing by offering free software to users. The lesson: Your next startup may be lurking within the glitches of a business you're already working on.

Game
Changers

Disrupting the Status Quo
and Altering the Playing Field

U pstarts demand new exceptions to old rules, ferret out inefficiencies or deficiencies in traditional business models, devise new ways to do business, and convince others to go along for the ride. In just about every industry you can find them stirring things up and raising the bar in ways that have more established players scratching their heads and scrambling to keep up. They follow in the footsteps of such companies as Craigslist, the free online classified advertising website; Zipcar, which rents cars on demand by the hour; and Zappos, which sells shoes online.

A healthy disrespect for the status quo keeps Upstarts constantly questioning how things are done and why, and this restlessness often leads to the kind of experimentation that breathes new life into tired industries. Tweak the business model, and you change the game, throw everyone a little off balance, and stake a claim where your competitors fear to tread. The Upstarts you'll meet in this chapter are loaded with chutzpah—like Jake Sasseville, who badgered big companies into sponsoring his self-syndicated late-night talk show. They find new ways to start businesses in industries that have been locked up by very large companies for years—like Justin

Brown's First Global Xpress, which competes in the world of Federal Express and DHL. Or like the founders of College Hunks Hauling Junk, they professionalize fragmented industries. They are also supply-chain mavericks and family business reinventors. In all cases, these Upstarts are great examples of what happens when youthful ingenuity and the spirit of innovation collide with business as usual.

Who Needs the Status Quo?

That sentiment could be 22-year-old Jake Sasseville's mantra. Five years ago, when he was a high school senior in Lewiston, ME, he started a local-access cable talk show called *The Edge* because he was bored with the same old television shows. "I thought I'd do some crazy stuff with my friends in the studio and have some fun," says Sasseville. "I didn't expect it to go anywhere." Then in 2004 he finagled his way onto the set of *Will & Grace*, where he was allowed to tape interviews with the cast for his show. "I found out that the producer, Adam Barr, was from Lewiston, so I wrote to his mother," says Sasseville, who also had written to Billy Crystal's brother and called Ashton Kutcher's mother in a desperate back-door quest for celebrity guests. Barr's mom took pity on Sasseville and introduced him to her son. Two months later, the teen was on his way to Los Angeles, having convinced a local Maine radio station to foot the travel bill for him and his crew in exchange for a listener giveaway provided by Barr: two tickets to Los Angeles and admission to a *Will & Grace* taping. The *Will & Grace* coup moved Sasseville off local access and onto a Fox affiliate in Maine.

That was just the beginning of Sasseville's chutzpah-driven wheeling and dealing. When he moved to Manhattan to attend the New York Institute of Technology in September of 2004, he launched an aggressive grass-roots campaign to get his show on ABC affiliates at 1 a.m., right after *Jimmy Kimmel Live!* He built a website with the URL JakeAfterJimmy.com, optimized it, and included a link that visitors could click to find out if the show was pending in their particular market. "It wasn't in most markets, of course," says Sasseville, "but people could enter their e-mail addresses in the comment box, and when they clicked "Submit," we had "I Want My Jake After Jimmy" form letters going blindly to executives at Disney, ABC, Jimmy Kimmel's folks, and the local programming executives in the states where senders were located. Over six months, we got 9,000 to 10,000 responses." Disney, by the way, was not amused, says Sasseville.

The campaign gave Sasseville a bit of traction, and he got clearance for his show in a modest 27 markets. Early on, he made a decision to self-syndicate the show, buying his own air time and then signing on big corporate sponsors to fund the venture. It's not a common model, and for Sasseville, who had no financial cushion, it was risky. His big break came when he convinced Overstock.com to sign on as his first major advertiser. While Overstock had been targeting women over the age of 25, the company had plans to pursue the GenY market; Sasseville convinced them that he was the perfect guy to help. He spent two hours talking to Overstock's senior vice president for marketing and customer care, Stormy Simon, convincing her that "I wasn't just a crazy kid who wanted a talk show just to do a talk show." She found him convincing enough to arrange a meeting for him with Overstock's CEO in Los Angeles.

"My thoughts were, 'Here's this kid, and he's funny and convincing, and he wants it,'" recalls Simon. "As he spoke, you started believing him." A month later, he had his first six-figure advertising deal, which he used to get clearance in more markets and to attract other advertisers such as Ford and AirTran.

The show aired in February 2008 on 39 ABC affiliates as a kind of reality show cum talk show—the chronicles of a 22-year-old kid from Maine negotiating to get his own talk show and, at the same time, doing his own talk show. Viewers watched him struggle to make payroll, mull over content with his tiny staff, set up a makeshift studio at a Dunkin' Donuts, and cajole a group of a cappella subway singers to appear on the show.

Celebrity guests were spare but included appearances from Katrina Bowden of *30 Rock*, Rainn Wilson from *The Office*, and recording artist Wyclef Jean. All the while, Sasseville integrated his sponsors into the show

> **"I wasn't just a crazy kid who wanted a talk show just to do a talk show."**
> —Jake Sasseville, "The Edge with Jake Sasseville"

by, say, driving a Ford, doing impromptu makeovers with Bed Head products at a local gym, or secretly tossing a Hillary Clinton nutcracker from Overstock.com into a clothes dryer at a Harlem laundromat. It was all very rough around the edges, but that was the point.

Sasseville is hoping to become known as the late-night voice of Generation Y. His show ran out of money last year after the fourth episode, but as of March 2009, Sasseville had lined up enough new sponsors, including Denny's and FUZE to relaunch on various affiliate channels for a 15-week season in 36 markets starting at the beginning of May. Of course, it's distinctly possible that his show will be just a distant memory in a year or two. The ultimate outcome, however, doesn't diminish what he managed to achieve at age 22: a late-night talk show on major network affiliates with big-company sponsors and ratings that, says Sasseville, topped Conan O'Brien in a handful of markets. And he did it with limited financial resources. "It's all about bucking tradition," Sasseville says. He's a maverick, and he has lots of company.

New Eyes on an Old Industry

Sometimes inefficiencies or outmoded ways of doing business become so ingrained in an organization or an industry that people become numb to the pain. It takes a fresh set of eyes to point out that the emperor has no clothes or at least that he ought to consider updating his wardrobe.

Jared Isaacman, now age 26, was 16 years old when he left high school in Far Hills, NJ, and went to work in the information technology (IT) department of a credit-card processing company. It was there that he stumbled on the inspiration for his company, United Bank Card. "I saw that the banking industry was so interested in putting credit cards in people's wallets that the actual moving of the money from the vendor to the bank was really neglected. The processors in our industry had no technology in place, no efficiencies, and prices for merchants were high and service was poor," he recalls. That was back in 1999, and Isaacman, a mediocre student with a strong entrepreneurial bent who later got his GED, decided that he could do better. So he cashed in a $10,000 stock certificate from his grandfather, an attorney who helped him incorporate, set up shop in his parent's basement, and christened his company United Bank Card. His mom did the bookkeeping, and his dad, who had sales and marketing experience in the alarm industry, wined and dined potential clients because Isaacman could neither drive nor drink alcohol.

At first, Isaacman had an "If I build it, they will come" philosophy. Small merchants, such as florists and pizza parlors, who wanted to take credit cards were being poorly served, making life difficult for the independent salespeople who work as intermediaries between merchants and the processing companies. So Isaacman, a technology wiz, built an online system where salespeople could manage and track their deals, and he promised that merchants would get same-day approval. "All our systems, our marketing, and our public relations were geared toward being the perfect company for salespeople to do business with," he says. "It was like everyone else was a fast-food place that took an hour to deliver a cheeseburger, and we did ours in a minute."

It worked like a charm, and United Bank Card racked up 12,000 new accounts in the company's first few years. But there's just one problem with being a successful maverick: If you identify a void or inefficiency in an industry and then profit by filling it, other surely will follow your lead.

> "It was like everyone else was a fast-food place that took an hour to deliver a cheeseburger, and we did ours in a minute."
>
> —Jared Isaacman,
> United Bank Card

That's what happened to Isaacman; by 2004, revenues were $12.6 million, but the young CEO realized that his business had reached a plateau. "We needed to shake up the market again," he recalls. So he made what was then a very radical decision. He told his sales reps to start giving away the $250 credit-card processing terminals that his competitors were still selling or leasing to merchants. The tactic resulted in the company tripling its new accounts from 12,000 in 2004 to 36,000 in 2005. That spring, Isaacman sold 15,000 of his accounts to a competitor for $44 million in cash, which allowed him to continue financing the free-terminal program; it also helped to propel him to number 6 on the 2006 Inc. 500 list. Continued growth would keep him on the list for the next two years as well.

At this writing, Isaacman is shaking things up again, and his latest innovation actually assumes the obsolescence of the product that helped him grow his business: the credit-card processing terminal. Eighteen months ago, he hired a team to develop an affordable point-of-sale (POS) system for small businesses that could never afford the $30,000 to $40,000 terminals used by large companies. "Credit-card terminals are a thing of the past," says Isaacman. "A POS system does everything a credit-card terminal does, plus it runs the entire business, so it has a better return on investment." The result of the company's research and development (R&D) efforts was a $5,000 system called Harbortouch that hit the market in the summer of 2008 and was already selling well as of this writing. According to Isaacman, Harbortouch is one-quarter the price of its closest competitor and is serviced by a stable of 300 contractors that United Bank Card has trained to install, service, and repair the machines. "There's nothing else like it on the market," he boasts. That probably won't last for long, but by the time his competitors catch up to him, Isaacman most likely will have disrupted the status quo once again.

Challenging the Old Guard

Jordan Goldman, age 26, is a disrupter in his own right. His company, Unigo, was just a startup at this writing, but Goldman already had scored a feature story in a the *New York Times Magazine* and was featured in Walt Mossberg's personal technology column in the *Wall Street Journal*. Unigo, a website with free student-generated information on over 300 colleges and universities, is Goldman's response to what he believes is the traditional publishing industry's failure to serve prospective college students adequately. Books such as the *Fiske Guide to Colleges* offer a few pages on each college, typically written from the admissions department perspective and with little student input. It might have been a good enough resource for previous generations, but Goldman felt strongly that people who were forking over $200,000 for a four-year education in a highly competitive admissions environment deserved something better.

A Staten Island native and Wesleyan University graduate, Goldman had dipped his toe into the world of publishing when he was a freshman, coediting a book called *The Students' Guide to College*. He used unpaid college interns on 100 campuses to provide content; the book, published by Penguin, sold relatively well. But Goldman wanted to take his idea of student-generated content a step further. He had an idea for a Web-based business—a platform really—that would allow current college students to post information (including videos and pictures) about their schools. "I figured that there are about 15 million high school students looking at colleges, 45 million parents and relatives who self-identify as being involved in the process, and another 15 million college students who don't have a place where they can accurately represent what their college is like," says Goldman. Unigo would bring them all together in a dynamic community where information is constantly updated and users can talk directly to one another.

It was not an easy plan to execute. Goldman needed help—capital, advice, and a staff to work the phones and reach out to college students. Like the partners at Higher One (see Chapter 1), he tapped his college's alumni network with the hope of igniting a spark of interest from some well-heeled grads. "I started doing this when I was 23 and just sent out e-mails to people who are respected, and they responded," says Goldman. "You'd be shocked by the level of people who responded." He says that Strauss Zelnick, CEO of Zelnick Media and the former CEO of BMG Entertainment, agreed to meet with him and "stress-tested my business model." Frank Sica, formerly of Soros Private Funds Management, took the bait as well and ultimately signed on as an angel investor, providing Goldman with enough startup capital to hire a staff of 25 recent college grads. "We researched the schools, found the tour guides, the RAs, the people who wrote for the student newspapers," recalls Goldman. "And we built it up one by one. It was a youth movement in its purest form."

There were very few ground rules. Students could upload just about anything, although the Unigo staff reserved the right to remove content that was patently false or offensive. "We're not interested in whitewashing the college experience," says Goldman. "If part of going to a particular college is going to keggers every week, it's better that you know that ahead of time." By the time the company formally launched in September 2008, 15,000 students had contributed content. In Unigo's first week, the site had 1.5 million page views and a long list of advertisers who were eager to buy space on the site.

> "I looked at the old way of doing things and I said 'the world has moved on, but the publishing industry hasn't.' So we're trying to disrupt what has been a stable industry."
>
> —Jordan Goldman, Unigo

Goldman is still in the heady startup days. He's not sleeping much, and he's spending as much time learning about how to run his business as he is refining the website. But he feels pretty certain that he's onto something. Before launching the site, he made a "dream list" of youth-friendly advertisers he'd like to see on the site; within a few days of the launch, they had all contacted him. Current advertisers include Apple, Dell, Barnes & Noble, Textbooks.com, and Victoria's Secret. "I looked at the old way of doing things, and I said, 'The world has moved on, but the publishing industry hasn't.' So we're trying to disrupt what has been a stable industry."

Where Giants Won't Tread

How do you compete against Federal Express, UPS, and DHL? If you are the CEO of a startup international air courier business in New York City, it's a question that's bound to keep you awake at night. But Justin Brown, the 29-year-old CEO of First Global Xpress (FGX), sleeps just fine. That's because FGX doesn't actually compete with the 800-pound gorillas in its industry; it differentiates itself by employing an entirely different business model—one that has helped grow the company from revenues of $1 million in 2002 to $10 million in 2008.

The big guys, says Brown, are "tonnage-driven, hub-and-spoke, infra-structure-owning" companies that make money by filling up their own air-craft with cargo and then typically flying to a centrally situated U.S. hub before delivering overseas packages to their final destination. FGX, which currently works only out of New York, partners with 100 commercial airlines to put its customers' packages on direct flights. That not only saves time and money, says Brown, but it allows FGX to position itself as a "green" alter-native because fewer shipping miles means a reduction in carbon emissions.

The idea for the company came from DHL veteran James Dowd, age 43, who had hired Brown to help him with sales at FGX in 2001, made him a partner, and then ceded the CEO role to him in late 2007. "As Justin gained business experience, it became clear to me that he was becoming a leader and would make a great CEO," says Dowd. "With Justin focusing on exe-cuting the vision, I could devote more time to creating operation efficien-cies." From the beginning, they focused on building volume of shipments into specific areas so that they could better negotiate shipping rates with air-lines. The pitch to prospective clients: "We can get it there faster and cheaper." Their first clients were in two large and very different demo-graphics: international law firms with documents to ship; and distributors of vinyl records. "There are a lot of record distribution companies in Brooklyn and Queens," says Brown. "And there was also a huge explosion of DJs spinning vinyl in western Europe and the Far East. So we plugged into those companies, and within three months, we were shipping thousands of pounds a day." The records were dense, so they didn't take up a lot of room in cargo holds, but their weight was substantial and allowed FGX to negotiate favorable rates with airlines.

Building relationships with airlines was a challenge, but earning customer trust was even tougher. "If FedEx makes a mistake, it's FedEx's fault," says Brown. "But if we make a mistake, it's the fault of whoever decided to use us. We had to do something to help people overcome the fear of using a smaller company." The solution: a "new client challenge" that encourages customers to use FGX's shipping services for a week with the promise that they won't be charged unless they're fully satisfied. An innovative tracking system and the additional promise of cutting 24 hours off transit time lured enough customers to give the company a track record.

Now, it's the troubled airline industry, hungry to fill cargo holds even as passenger seats remain empty, that's courting FGX. But the company has strict standards that not every airline can meet. One international carrier, for example, was looking to lure some FGX business away from Virgin, which flies packages into Heathrow for FGX four to five times a day. The company wined and dined Brown and Dowd, but in the end, says Brown, "Their retrieval time didn't meet our standards." It took three hours for a package to get from the plane to its final destination as opposed to Virgin's one hour. Virgin kept the business.

> "We didn't want to compete against UPS and FedEx, so we're going after niche businesses."
>
> —Justin Brown, FGX

While the company currently ships only from New York, Brown is in the process of raising capital to expand into 10 or so East Coast cities within five years. He and Dowd are undaunted by the recession. In fact, says Brown, "I never thought a recession could be so much fun." As a low-cost shipping alternative with margins more than twice as high as their mammoth competitors and very little debt, FGX actually can use the economic downturn to position itself for growth. "One of our competitors has just slashed the

> "I never thought a recession could be so much fun."
>
> —Justin Brown, FGX

majority of its sales force in New York," he says. "I have my staffing agency screening all of them and forwarding me the top 10, of which I will hire five. Couple that with investing in new technologies to be able to bring a better system for international shipping to our e-commerce prospects, and we have a fairly kicking outlook for 2009." That's probably not something you'll hear from his larger, more traditional competitors.

Supply-Chain Mavericks

For Brown and Dowd, the secret to success lies in the innovative way they're able to serve customers by offering them a cheaper, faster, and greener alternative to traditional shipping. Robert Selleck, the 29-year-old CEO of $25 million Pacific Columns, is making his mark as a maverick through supply-chain innovation. Selleck's stock in trade is high-end architectural columns, but his business role model is Michael Dell, who defied the conventional wisdom that consumers would never buy computers over the telephone. Much to competitors' astonishment, Dell's then-radical direct-to-consumer model and his commitment to mass customization made him one of the richest and youngest CEOs on the Fortune 500 list. Selleck hopes to have a similar, albeit more modest, impact on his own industry. He's made a good start. His Brea, CA, company was number 372 on the Inc. 500 list in 2007 and number 1,081 on the Inc. 5000 list in 2008. More than half that revenue comes from the Internet, but that's only part of his innovative supply-chain strategy.

Selleck worked in his father's specialty woodworking company in high school, gained an understanding of the industry's distribution channels, and detected its weaknesses. "In our industry, everything goes through a two-step distribution system," he explains. "You have manufacturers who only sell to wholesalers, wholesalers who will only sell to distributors, contractors who only buy directly from lumbar yards, and consumers who buy from the contractors." But Pacific Columns challenged the good old boy system and decided to sell to everyone. "No one crosses the different boundaries like we do," says Selleck.

Of course, whenever a company tries something new, particularly in an established industry, there's fear and pushback. And it probably doesn't help when the person who's pushing a new idea is young and relatively inexperienced. But Selleck counters the resistance by offering everyone in the supply chain an incentive. He now works with 45 manufacturers and creates customized websites for them. He also gives them the opportunity to buy co-op advertising at a discount, provides them with return-on-investment (ROI) data, and works with them to create new products. "They're all older, and they're afraid of the Internet, but they know they need it," says Selleck. "So they give us free reign—we're like a marketing partner." He also sells directly to contractors, who like the company because Pacific Columns allows them to design their own custom products right on the website and guarantees delivery in 72 hours. And for the do-it-yourself crowd, the company created a special website called architecturaldepot.com, where consumers can buy columns, shutters, railings, and just about every other kind of architectural trim.

Selleck's system, driven by his extensive use of technology, has enabled him to be highly competitive in terms of pricing, and that has helped the company weather tough times in the construction industry. Revenue and profits have remained steady, although Selleck concedes that his average order size has shrunk. "That means we have to process more orders and grow our customer base," he says. "Market share–wise, we're doing very well. With the industry slowing down, it's forcing the old relationships to be challenged. Now all the margins count, and it's opened up an opportunity for new companies to break into the good old boy chain."

> "With the industry slowing down, it's forcing the old relationships to be challenged. Now all the margins count, and it's opened up an opportunity for new companies to break into the good old boy chain."
>
> —Robert Selleck,
> Pacific Columns

It's worth noting that Selleck's primary goal was not to position himself as a low-cost seller, but to alter the supply chain so that it resulted in greater all-around efficiencies for everyone. So, although he wasn't anticipating a downturn in the market, his supply-chain innovations ultimately gave him a huge competitive advantage when things tuned ugly in the construction industry.

Rocking the Service Supply Chain

Talia Mashiach achieved similar results with her company, Eved Services, which partners with hotels to provide corporate clients with transportation, entertainment, videography, and restaurant reservations—services that hotels typically would need to outsource to a variety of vendors. The idea for the company came to her when she was managing event bookings for her husband's band and noticed that most hotels lack the systems required to coordinate all the outside vendors that are hired for corporate events. Mashiach's biggest not-so-secret weapon: She's a bona fide geek who used her technology skills to assemble and manage a killer list of local vendors that she connects with hotels and corporate meeting planners; the entire system is managed online. "With my technology background, we can build a platform that automates the process that links hotels with vendors," she says. "And there's a big service piece that goes along with that because you have to make sure your vendors show up."

Originally, Mashiach assumed that her hotel partners would use the technology to order directly from the vendors she recommended and managed. But that changed as soon as hotel managers realized that it was far more efficient for Eved's team to handle the entire process. It made perfect sense. Mashiach took potential nightmares—like airport pickups for 4,000 pharmaceutical executives going to four different hotels and 55 different restaurants for dinner—and executed them flawlessly.

Eved, now a $9.2 million company, was number 188 on the 2008 Inc. 500 list, with over 1,200 percent three-year sales growth. Mashiach attributes much of that success to the company's relationships with its vendors. She chooses those companies carefully and puts them through a rigorous certification process that ensures that their services are up to her standards. All vendors are rated by clients after each event and must keep their ratings high enough to remain on Eved's list. Mashiach also raises the service bar for her vendors. All her airport greeters, for instance, wear bright yellow shirts so that they stand out amidst airport chaos, and they carry professionally laminated signs. But it's her technology that brings all her vendor partners together. Every vendor is linked to a Web portal where they're able to upload pictures of their products, along with video and audio content. Eved's sales team then uses that virtual inventory to create proposals for potential clients. If the proposal is approved, it goes back into Mashiach's system, which then sends out purchase orders to the approved vendors. The system works so well that Mashiach plans to expand the company further by licensing her technology to companies outside her markets. "No one else has this model with hotels," says Mashiach. "And they also don't have the technology."

> "No one else has this model with hotels. And they also don't have the technology."
>
> —Talia Mashiach, Eved Services

Both Selleck and Mashiach detected opportunities to revolutionize the way their products or services were sold through the supply chain. And for both, the result was a dramatic shift in the very nature of their customer relationships. These supply-chain mavericks didn't change the products they were offering; they simply made the marketing and selling process easier, more reliable, more predictable, and often less expensive for their customers. In each of their industries, customers had come to take the standard inefficiencies for granted, in the same way that we all assume we'll be kept on perpetual hold by the helpdesk. But the game changes entirely when someone puts into action a business model that makes traditional ways of doing business seem inefficient and obsolete.

Professionalizing a Fragmented Business

The world is filled with fragmented industries that are crying out for a little sophistication. Take a business that's not particularly sexy—think auto repair, trucking, barber shops—pump it up with technology and branding, raise the service bar, and standardize the systems and procedures, and you just may be on the road to market leadership. This is where Omar Soliman and Nick Friedman are. They're both 27—childhood buddies and college grads who clearly never dreamed that they'd one day be partners in, of all things, a junk-removal company. But their company, College Hunks Hauling

Junk, racked up $3.5 million in sales in 2008, and the partners are now franchising their operation from a home base in Tampa, FL. Many of those franchisees, says Soliman, are also young entrepreneurs. The appeal of the franchise—and the success of the business in general—has less to do with what the company actually does than with how it distinguishes itself from the mom and pop operations that account for most of the industry. College Hunks is about as different from your neighborhood junk-removal operation as Craigslist is from the classifieds ads in your morning newspaper.

The summer before their senior year in college (Soliman attended the University of Miami and Friedman was at Pomona College), the two friends, who are from the Washington, DC, area, were looking for a way to make some extra money. Soliman's mother, who owned a furniture store in DC, had a beat-up cargo van and suggested that her son use it to hire himself out for odd jobs. "Nick and I thought that maybe we could clean out people's garages. We thought we could come with a funny name, make a couple of hundred bucks, and go out and party," says Soliman. They chuckled over "College Hunks Hauling Junk," but printed out flyers the next day, and then plastered their neighborhood with them.

"Suddenly, we were doing two jobs a day, and two months into it, I had $15,000 in cash," says Soliman. "The light bulb went off. I was in class a month later, and I'd still get calls on my cell phone." Buoyed by his early and relatively unexpected success, Soliman decided to write a business plan for College Hunks and enter it in the University of Miami's Leigh Rothschild Entrepreneurship Competition. His summer experience gave him a clear advantage over the 130 other entrants: He already had a handle on his market and the key numbers that made the business tick. He walked away with the first place prize and $10,000.

Nonetheless, both Soliman and Freidman came back to the DC area after graduation in 2004 and dutifully settled into traditional corporate jobs. The former landed at the Health Care Advisory Board and the latter at National Economic Research Associates. Within six months, though, they each asked themselves the question that's so common to GenY: "Why am I breaking my back on something that's not exciting to me?" So they took Soliman's $10,000 in prize money and invested in a new Isuzu dump truck. They were turned down for loans left and right, but their families pitched in, and eventually, Bank of America came through with a $50,000 line of credit that paid for a logo, website development, and marketing materials. For a junk-removal company? You bet.

Soliman and Friedman knew that in order to distinguish their company in the fragmented junk-removal industry, they needed to give customers an uncommon experience. That includes clean-cut, polite, collegiate employees dressed in polo shirts and khakis. They drive spanking clean, bright orange trucks emblazoned with the College Hunks muscle man logo and bold green lettering. The company also pledges to recycle 60 to 70 percent of what it collects rather than just hauling all junk to the dump. The green spin appeals to environmentally conscious customers, but also saves the company money since the dump charges by the pound.

In 2007, the company's second full year of business, College Hunks posted $1.2 million in revenue and had a fleet of eight trucks in the Washington, DC area. It was time, the cofounders decided, to start franchising their operation. As a model, they looked to 1-800-Junk, a Vancouver, Canada, company founded by Brian Scudamore when he was just 18. The company, says Soliman, "is the Coke of junk removal—they were the first ones to brand a company with uniformed drivers and commitment to customer service. But we're on pace to be the Pepsi."

Using cash flow from the company's Washington, DC, operation to fund expansion, Soliman spent a total of $150,000 to $200,000 to set up the franchise business. That included $40,000 on customized software and manuals for franchisees that scripted and systemized even the most mundane aspects of the business. The partners also hired a franchise industry veteran of 25 years, George Palmer, as the company's director of franchise development, and they moved the company from DC to Tampa, where call-center employees are plentiful and less costly. A year into the franchise venture, the company has 15 franchisees operating 36 separate business units; four of the franchisees are under age 30, and 90 percent of them are reaching their revenue goals. The hardest thing for Soliman and Friedman? "We thought everyone would be like us," says Soliman. "We thought they'd all have $500,000 the first year, but that's unheard of; we've had to change our thinking." Nonetheless, the company posted 2008 systemwide revenues of $3.5 million.

Like so many GenY entrepreneurs, Soliman and Friedman need to manage the transition from startup to growth company, and that's not always easy. They've got Palmer to guide them through the potential landmines of franchising; their DC operation will serve as an incubator for the new things they may want to introduce to franchisees, such as recycling centers, and they'll aggressively position themselves in the market as a green company. "A production company has approached us about doing a show where we go into garages and show people how they can recycle things," says Soliman. It's all a far cry from the typical mom-and-pop junk-removal business, but that was the point all along. "Within three to five years, we hope to be a household name," says Soliman. In the meantime, there's another business idea in the works: College Foxes Hauling Boxes!

 ## Reinventing the Family Business

According to the 2007 American Family Business Survey, approximately 40 percent of family business owners are expected to retire within the next 10 years. Only a third of those companies will survive the transition to the second generation, and far fewer—12 percent—will make it to generation three. Family businesses are as complex as the families that run them, and they fail for all kinds of complex reasons. But the ones that survive have at least one thing in common: The older generation manages to effectively transfer years of accumulated knowledge to successors while at the same time encouraging their progeny to put their own unique stamp on the business. Those in GenY who are poised to take over family companies would not have it any other way.

> "I think I have a huge respect for the responsibility being passed on to me."
>
> —Emily Powell, Powell's Books

Such is the case for Emily Powell, age 29, who is now ensconced as the heir apparent to what is the largest and quite possibly the most venerable independent retail bookstore chain in the country. Powell's Books started by Emily's grandfather, Walter, and now run by her father, Michael, is a rarity among family-owned companies and within its industry as well, where independent bookstores are under siege from the likes of Barnes & Noble and Amazon. With over $60 million in revenue, Powell's, says Emily "is doing well, which is a little scary because the world is shaking around us."

Michael Powell plans to step down as CEO when he turns 70 in 2010, leaving his daughter in what she calls a "CEO-like role." She's been preparing for that role full time since 2004 but has worked at the store intermittently her whole life, starting as a tot who stood on boxes to reach the cash register. "I lived and breathed this store growing up," she says. "I think I have a huge respect for the responsibility being passed on to me."

That responsibility essentially involves making a good thing better, and that comes with its own set of challenges. "My dad has said that the only thing I could do that would disappoint him would be to enshrine the company in gold and not change anything," says Emily. The company, which has six stores, already has a strong reputation for innovation; Michael Powell put his inventory online back in 1994, pre-Amazon, and now 30 percent of the company's sales comes from the Internet. An e-newsletter goes out to half a million people, and Powell's even has begun making short films with authors and distributing them to other independent bookstores.

But Emily is making her own mark as well. In the used-books division, which represents about 50 percent of the company's sales and yields its highest margins, she called on Powell's store managers to help her come up with ideas to consolidate and standardized the operation. Previously, each manager was responsible for his or her own used-book inventory, and there was little communication among them. "I got them together and said, 'Who knows what works best, what's measurable, and how can we get better information?'" recalls Emily. The result: a used-book retail distribution center that now serves all stores and

> "My dad has said that the only thing I could do that would disappoint him would be to enshrine the company in gold and not change anything."
>
> — Emily Powell, Powell's Books

that buys books in large quantities, creating economies of scale. Powell's also hired a director of used books to manage the operation. The process has been fully operational for a year, and since then, used books has seen double-digit sale increases and significant margin improvements.

"My contribution has more to do with people," says Emily. "My dad was a book person, and I grew up in a book company, but I'm not my dad. I see my job as sitting in a room full of people and coaxing things out of them." In other words, she's creating the kind of classic Upstarts-style work environment that you'll read more about in Chapter 7. If she can consistently leverage the collective intelligence of her 550 employees to come up with creative and innovative ways to the make the business more profitable and sustainable, it will be a mighty legacy for Powell's and for Emily.

Calling the Shots

Kathy Vegh is hell-bent on creating a legacy of her own. Her father's company, Danny Vegh's Billiards and Home, was a household name in Cleveland for more than 45 years when Kathy, age 32, stepped in to make her mark on the family business. "I took over the day I walked in at age 24," she says. Danny Vegh might beg to differ. Vegh fled his native Hungary in 1956 during the uprising against the Communists and landed in Cleveland via Austria, with very little money and no knowledge of English. What he did have was an intense love of Ping-Pong and the skills to match his passion; in the late fifties, he was a state, national, and international champion. He become a local Cleveland celebrity and opened a succession of businesses, including a table tennis club, a pool room, and a company that sold and serviced pool and Ping-Pong tables.

It was that last business that ultimately became Danny Vegh's Billiards and Home, a company that bears very little resemblance to the store where Kathy Vegh started working seven years ago. Back then, 70 percent of the company's customers were commercial pool halls, and, she says, its showroom was messy and congested, with tables stacked one on top of the other. "For two years, I did nothing but clean up," Vegh says. Despite an MBA and a year of law school, her dad gave her the title "Director of Public Relations." "He totally underestimated me," she says, "but I knew I was going to take the industry to a whole new place."

Vegh paid her dues for two years, and then announced that she had run out of business cards and would like new ones printed. One small change: The new cards, she insisted, would read "Vice President of Operations." Her dad acquiesced, won over by his ambitious daughter's dramatic transformation of the business. By 2003, residential sales were outpacing pool halls and game rooms as nesting Baby Boomers sought to outfit their newly finished basements with big new toys for the family. Vegh had redesigned the retail floor to make it more consumer-friendly, retrained the salespeople, and added more products. That year, she convinced her father to open a second store just south of Cleveland; it was her baby, and she had it running in the black in 60 days. And two years after that, a third store followed just to the east of Cleveland; today, Vegh is CEO of the company and 49 percent owner.

A petite powerhouse, Vegh is known as the industry sweetheart. But make no mistake—she takes a no-nonsense approach to running the family operation. She took a very solid but basic business and put a decidedly Upstarts spin on it—one that pays homage to her father's rich history but that speaks to changing demographics and a vastly more competitive retail environment. And like the Upstarts in Chapter 1, who understand the importance of collaboration, Vegh has sought out businesses partnerships that give her customers greater value and allow her to outservice her larger competitors.

> "I took over the day I walked in at age 24."
>
> — **Kathy Vegh, Danny Vegh's Billiards and Home**

The newest store, with its two-story glass front, neon sign, and columns that mimic pool cues, has a showroom that's shaped like a pool table and lighting reminiscent of billiard balls. Around the perimeter of the store are eight themed game rooms decorated in styles that range from retro 50s to rustic to contemporary so that customers can envision an entire room. Vegh partners with architects, lighting companies, and builders so that she can offer customers not only game tables but complete home-entertainment packages that also include the kind of personal service that big companies don't offer. "If we have a customer who really doesn't know what to do with their designated space, we will go to their house and design their game room for them," says Vegh. "We interview them, we take time to understand their style, and we work within the budget they set for us. We don't charge for this service, nor do we impose an obligation to buy."

In typical Upstarts style, Vegh is also forging some high-profile strategic partnerships. Three years ago she signed a contract with the Cleveland Cavaliers to do halftime entertainment on Danny Vegh's game tables and to sponsor an in-store event that hosts the entire team and coaches. And she has the exclusive right to promote the store as "the preferred game room vendor of the Cleveland Cavaliers." That distinction has brought her several lucrative private game room jobs from players. "The traction I'm getting with this right now is truly remarkable," Vegh says. "Plus it's a lot of fun."

It's this kind of relationship building that has helped Vegh to triple sales over the past several years (while she won't reveal exact numbers, she says that the company has annual revenues between $5 and $10 million). "Most of the small family businesses that we've competed with over the past seven years are either gone or on their last leg," she says. "And the big companies don't have the flexibility to do things out of the norm for their client base like we do." While Vegh concedes that the economy has slowed down revenue growth in 2009, she also views the recession as a growth opportunity. "Many other specialty retailers are going out of business nationwide," she says, "so I have pushed hard to refocus efforts on our website to capture some of that business."

Combining High Touch with High Tech

Family businesses in traditional industries are getting slammed by the recession and also by a growing number of competitors, many of which are large and well resourced. The only way to survive and grow is to change the game by differentiating yourself. Kathy Vegh did it by turning an old-school retailer into a one-stop destination for home entertainment. And Rob Van Etten, the 29-year-old CEO of Brighton Cromwell, used new technology systems and the Internet to better serve existing clients and to diversify into new markets. The Randolph, NJ defense contractor, which had revenues of $16 million in 2008, specializes in supply-chain integration,

Van Etten started the company with his uncle, John, and his father, Bill, an industry veteran, in January of 2004 when he was just 23 years old. Van Etten assumed that he'd have years to learn about the business, tapping the expertise of his dad, whom he describes as "my role model and my best friend." Bill Van Etten was a serial entrepreneur who owned a defense consulting and procurement firm, and then acquired a troubled manufacturing company in the late 1980s. Unfortunately, the company bled him dry and he was forced to sell the majority of it to Fischer Scientific in the early 1990s. Still saddled with a mountain of debt, the elder Van Etten was faced with a tough decision. "I remember sitting down with him when I was a young kid," says his son. "And he told us that he could file for bankruptcy and a lot of people would suffer, or our own family could suffer. So we sold our big house in Nutley, NJ, and moved to the Poconos for two years. We struggled, but he paid back every penny."

It was lesson that Rob Van Etten took to heart and one that got him through what he now describes as the worst year of his life. Ten months after the launch of Brighton Cromwell, his Uncle John died of stomach cancer; two months later, in January of 2005, his father died of pulmonary hypertension. "I knew at the funeral that everyone was thinking that I would fail," says Van Etten, "and I wanted to prove every single one of them wrong." He borrowed money from his mother to buy out his widowed aunt and another aunt who was part owner, and he cut his paltry $20,000 salary to $10,000. He brought in his brother, Glenn, and his best friend, Dan Youker, to help him run the company, which was losing money on $1 million of revenue. And he relied on his father's best friend, Fran Scricco, for advice. Scricco, a top executive at Avaya, also was a veteran of General Electric and Boston Consulting and a former CEO of Arrow Electronics. With help from Scricco, Van Etten "went mean and lean" and turned a profit by the end of 2005.

But it wasn't merely fiscal oversight that helped him to grow the company, which posted $8.8 million in revenues for 2007 and had clients such as Sikorsky, Boeing, and Honeywell knocking at the door. As a supply-chain integrator, it's Brighton Cromwell's job to make procurement easier and more efficient for its clients, which include defense contractors as well as the U.S. Department of Defense (DOD). The company started out by assembling aftermarket parts kits for the DOD, which means that it took on the job of procuring and assembling into a single box up to 50 different parts that a mechanic might need for maintenance and repair of a military vehicle. "When we began doing that, everyone thought we were crazy," says Van Etten. The concept was common enough in the aerospace industry but had not been sold to the DOD for land vehicles, "and by then, we were fighting a land war," says Van Etten, referring to Iraq.

The company earned its chops on those contracts and developed a reputation as a reliable and innovative government contractor. That's partly due to the investment Van Etten made in proprietary software that automates the sourcing of thousands of items to the most economical suppliers. Say, for example, that a customer needs 400 items and wants to consolidate its vendor base as much as possible. Brighton Cromwell's system, which taps into a database of approved companies, completely automates that process. "My father was always ahead of the curve with technology," says Van Etten. "A lot of the people in the defense industry came in during the cold war, and we want to blow them away with technology. Our competitors are huge, but they're shrinking and I'm growing."

In the summer of 2008, Van Etten, then 28 years old, was approached by two large companies that wanted to buy Brighton Cromwell for more than $5 million. He was wined and dined and even a little tempted—until he called Fran Scricco for advice. "Are you crazy?" Scricco asked him. "Your father never liked not being in control, and you won't like it either. Here's what you need to do to get to the next level." And so Van Etten poached an executive from his father's former company and also hired a director of business development. The goal: Grow the company to $25 million by going after contracts from original equipment manufacturers (OEMs) and by diversifying the company away from the defense industry. To that end, Van Etten just recently launched a new Web-based company called BCL Hardware, a business-to-business site that sells bulk commercial hardware to, for example, home builders and equipment manufacturers. He's also working on a green product that will help companies to reduce water consumption.

> "Our competitors are huge, but they're shrinking and I'm growing."
>
> —Rob Van Etten,
> Brighton Cromwell

As for the skeptics who might have written him off as too young and inexperienced to run his father's company, Van Etten has proved them wrong repeatedly. With 32 employees, a 14,000-square-foot office, and contracts in the works that could boost business by $10 million, Van Etten has very little to prove anymore.

UPSTARTS PLAYLIST

Track 3: Change the Game

1. **Look for opportunities to be disruptive.** When United Bankcard's Jared Isaacman was working for a credit-card processing company, he was struck by the industry's lack of efficiency and its minimal use of technology. So he started his own company and raised the bar not only by building an online system to track business, but by giving away credit-card processing terminals to merchants. When those practices became industry standards, Isaacman redirected his resources to another disruptive new product—an affordable point of sale system for small businesses. The lesson: You've got to keep changing and disrupting the game to stay ahead of the competition

2. **Be aware of changing customer needs.** Jordan Goldman, the founder of Unigo, felt strongly that a burgeoning population of prospective college students was not being given adequate information to make good choices in a highly competitive admissions environment. Moreover, the tried and true resources (big, expensive guide books) didn't speak to students in the environment where they spent an increasing amount of time—online. Unigo, a free online source of college information, taps into college communities to offer high schoolers information, reviews, and videos that come directly from students. It's a strategy that most traditional publishers would never pursue for fear of cannibalizing their core business.

3. **Look for supply-chain inefficiencies.** Sometimes the most effective innovations have nothing to do with actual products or services but the way in which they're delivered. Talia Mashiach knew that hotels were compelled to hire a variety of outside vendors when serving big corporate clients that were organizing events. Her business, Eved Services, aggregates those vendors—musicians, florists, transportation companies, etc.—into a single highly selective data base that she draws upon to provide services for hotel clients. Her service, driven by a sophisticated technology platform, frees hotels of

the administrative burden of choosing and managing vendors, and of the scheduling headaches that come with servicing large groups. And so Eved also changes the game for its hotel customers.

4. **Professionalize an old-economy business.** There are plenty of industries where consumers have come to expect substandard service. Surprise and delight them by raising the service standard and you'll stand out from the pack. The founders of College Hunks Hauling Junk systematized and branded a very basic business by hiring clean-cut college students, putting a green spin on their company, and consistently branding everything from trucks to uniforms. The result: a $3.5 million franchise operation in the junk-removal industry, where businesses are typically run by mom and pop operators. The company has even attracted attention from Oprah, who is working with them on her "Clean Up Your Messy House" tour.

5. **Ferret out underserved niches.** Justin Brown, the CEO of First Global Xpress (FGX), marketed his fledgling international air courier service to vinyl record distributors to get initial credibility in the industry. It was a small, lucrative niche that the 800-pound gorillas in the industry couldn't be bothered to pursue. But the reputation FGX built within that niche gave the company the track record it needed to compete for more mainstream business with the big players like DHL and Federal Express. The company's other game changing strategy: It uses direct flights on commercial carriers to ship overnight packages. So the company can typically serve clients faster than competitors, and do it without the crippling cost of maintaining its own fleet of aircraft.

6. **Step out of the box.** Before Kathy Vegh joined her dad's business, Danny Vegh's Billiards and Home, the store sold pool and Ping-Pong tables. Now it sells complete home entertainment solutions. Vegh redesigned the main store, opened up two new ones, forged strategic partnerships with architects and lighting companies, and even cut a sweet promotional deal with the Cleveland Cavaliers. While the economy hasn't been kind to retailers, Vegh is doing so well that she's beefing up the company's online presence to capture market share from failing companies outside of her hometown, Cleveland.

Market
Insiders

Marketing Fast and Furiously
to Their Own Generation

Imagine that you had special insight into a very large and affluent demographic—nearly 80 million people with $200 billion in annual income whose ideas about money, music, fashion, education, food, and just about everything else are, well, a little quirky—so quirky, in fact, that major corporations, such as McDonald's and Pepsi, have hired experts to advise them on how to reach the GenY demographic. So if you knew intuitively what buttons to push, you'd have a killer competitive advantage, wouldn't you? And that's exactly what Upstarts have—an instinctive ability to create products and services that speak directly to their generation.

For instance, they're reaching out in innovative ways to the college market to provide goods and services to this burgeoning segment of GenY. The founders of College Boxes and DormAid understand that GenY doesn't really care what companies say about their products; they want to know what their friends are saying. So they hire students to do their marketing. And like some of the entrepreneurs in Chapter 2 (such as Loopt and Aviary), the Upstarts you'll meet here are tweaking existing products and services to make them more user-friendly to their own generation. Mint.com is an easy-to-use online finance tool geared toward GenY, Ignighter.com puts a GenY group spin on online dating, and Indochino.com appeals to this generation's love of customization by selling reasonably priced custom-made suits to young execs. Bobby Kim and Ben Shenassafar, cofounders of The Hundreds, speak to GenY's attraction to indie brands with their line of T-shirts that reflect an "amalgamation of subcultures." Perhaps most fascinating of all, there seems to be an ever-increasing number of Upstarts who make a living by teaching others—big companies, mostly—how to get a clue about GenY. Buzz Marketing and Undercurrent are two leaders in what seems to be a new and rapidly growing marketing/communications specialty.

> ## "They respond negatively when companies market back to them a perceived version of who they are."
>
> —Tina Wells, Buzz Marketing

Not only do Upstarts know what their peers want, but they also know how to use alternative forms of advertising and marketing to reach them. Why is this important? Research has shown consistently that GenY doesn't respond well to traditional marketing messages. "Young people understand marketing and advertising, so you can't fool them," says Tina Wells, the 28-year-old CEO of Buzz Marketing Group, a youth marketing company. "And they respond negatively when companies market back to them a perceived version of who they are." They also don't like being told what they should buy, they hate the hard sell, and they won't tolerate anything that they perceive as inauthentic.

They're tough to please, but their entrepreneurial peers are doing exactly that in virtually every sector of the economy. They know that GenY has some needs that are fundamentally different from those of previous generations (case in point: most people over the age of 30 probably don't care if they're able to locate their friends via a GPS application on their cell phone). And they also understand that even basic needs that don't change from generation to generation are often best met a little more creatively for GenY.

 ## The Student Market

The U.S. college student market totals 13.6 million people and boasts spending power of more than $237 billion annually, says the "Alloy College

Explorer," a 2008 study done by Alloy Media + Marketing with Harris Interactive. It's a lucrative market, and one that's not as easy to serve as you might think. "They get how valuable they are and how they can be used as a resource," says Allison Marsh, vice president of consumer insights at AMP, which is a subsidiary of Alloy. "But they want to know what you can do for them. You have to be relevant, provide access to something of value, and have an open dialogue with them." Bottom line: It's not just the product or service itself that's important; Upstarts know that the way in which they market to and serve their peers is every bit as important as what they're trying to sell.

For Boston-based College Boxes, this involves a two-pronged approach: The company employs college students to market its moving and storage service to peers, and it has constructed a robust technology platform that drives online service and communication. "In general, the moving business is in the stone ages, and one of the reasons we're successful is that we're bringing new technology to an old business," says Josh Kowitt, who cofounded College Boxes with Scott Neuberger (see Chapter 1). Students create online accounts, order packing kits, print out shipping labels, and schedule door-to-door pickup and delivery. They also can arrange summer storage of their belongings to avoid schlepping everything home at the end of the year. The process is simplified through technology that Kowitt says "was built to fit into our customers' comfort zone; we've designed it to be very simple."

The company got its start at Washington University in St. Louis, where Kowitt merged his minifridge rental company with fraternity brother Scott Neuberger's moving and storage business. Like College Hunks Hauling Junk (see Chapter 3), College Boxes

> "In general, the moving business is in the stone ages, and one of the reasons we're successful is that we're bringing new technology to an old business."
>
> —Josh Kowitt, formerly with College Boxes

has professionalized a largely fragmented industry; it aggregates demand for storage facilities and then works with local companies to negotiate the best rates for its customers. Vendors are also screened for quality, freeing students and their parents from the time-consuming task of hunting down a reliable company. "The storage business has been around for 30 years, and typically, a guy would show up with a truck, people would throw their stuff in the back, and they'd get it back in three months," says Kowitt. With College Boxes, students can access their belongings if they need to, inventory everything online, and arrange delivery for the beginning of the fall semester. On the moving end of the business, the company works with UPS and aggregates shipping to specific colleges.

"The colleges like it because we reduce congestion on campus since we'll have one truck moving 40 people," says Kowitt. Another boon to colleges: They get a commission in exchange for endorsing College Boxes, and their students are employed by the company to do local, on-campus marketing. In addition, using students to help spread the word about College Boxes is as smart as it is economical.

The "Alloy College Explorer Study" surveyed more than 1,500 college students, and 64 percent of them said that word of mouth is a key factor when it comes to making purchasing decisions. We all value personal recommendations, of course, but GenY's highly social nature, and its use of online social networks to talk about products and services, makes this demographic more responsive to peer buzz than older generations. So if you want to sell to them, says AMP's Allison Marsh, "You have to talk to them using their own language." And the best way to do that is to deploy a young sales force.

The strategy has worked well for College Boxes, which, at $3 to $5 million in revenue, was the largest company of its kind in the industry when it was acquired by Door to Store, a former vendor, in January 2008. It now does business with 44 colleges and universities. While Kowitt has since left the company, Neuberger remains its president.

Cleaning Up

The college market has also paid off for DormAid founder Michael Kopko, age 24, but not without a good bit of controversy along the way. He founded the company as a dorm room cleaning service at Harvard University in the fall of 2003, when he was a freshman and looking for a way to keep his room clean without actually having to clean his room. It struck him that other students might be faced with similar challenges, so he started a modest business by scheduling a cadre of local cleaning professionals to clean half the rooms in his freshman dorm. He made just enough money to finance his own room cleaning.

The following year, he decided to ramp things up by actively marketing the service to freshman and sophomores; his brother Matthew, a freshman at Princeton, founded a similar business, and the two launched a website for the company, which was then called DorMaid (note the emphasis on *Maid*). That put the company on Harvard's radar screen, and the administration, claiming that DorMaid was an unauthorized business, tried to shut Kopko down. After several months of paperwork and persistence, he finally received official permission to carry on with his business, on the condition that he agree to change the name to DormAid (*Maid* was deemed derogatory).

But not everyone on campus was impressed with Kopko's entrepreneurial fervor. The *Harvard Crimson*, the school's prestigious student newspaper, accused the company of being elitist. "By creating yet another differential between the haves and have-nots on campus, DorMaid threatens our student unity," wrote the *Crimson* staff in March 2005. They also called for a company boycott. The article caught the attention of the mainstream media, and suddenly Kopko was learning the main tenet of public relations: There's no such thing as bad publicity. The campus controversy triggered coverage on the Associated Press and Reuters wire services, and the *Wall Street Journal* and the *New York Times* ran stories on the company as well. Even Rush Limbaugh got into the act, calling the *Crimson* staff "a bunch of leftist journalists," and suggesting that Kopko should be a professor because clearly he had already learned what's taught in most business schools. On the other side of the political spectrum, *The Daily Show* skewered Kopko and colleague Dave Eisenberg with a five-minute-long "interview" with Rob Corddry, who had a field day with his young guests. The result: increased demand for DormAid's services at Harvard and a plan to expand the company to other campuses.

That summer, Kopko retreated to his parents' house in Fort Lauderdale, FL, along with his partners, Rob Cecot, Jorge Aviles, Chris Acton-Maher, and his brother, Matthew. It would become an annual event—a summer strategy session to plan growth for the coming year. On tap for fall 2005: They'd begin offering laundry service to students by partnering with local laundromats, and they'd expand operations not only at

Harvard but also at Boston University, Babson College, Princeton University, and Dickinson College. Each new school would have a local "president"—a student who was paid a part-time salary to manage the business, maintain relationships with local vendors, and drum up new business on campus. It was essentially the same strategy used by College Boxes—using students to market to their peers. "We hire students who feel like the company is their baby," says Kopko.

Kopko's goal is to make DormAid a nationally scalable business. With 65 colleges in the system, he's on his way. He's shifted the business model somewhat, though. Instead of hiring individual cleaning professionals, the company now hires local companies to clean dorm rooms, a change that makes the service more expensive to students but that poses fewer administrative hassles for the company. The company also has expanded its range of services to include water delivery, appliance rental, bedding supplies, online computer backup, and career prep services and tutoring. "We're especially strong in math and science," says Kopko. "We have Ph.D.s in India who work through it with you on virtual whiteboards on the Web." For each service, DormAid partners with a preferred vendor—an efficient use of strategic partnerships that puts Kopco among the "Extreme Collaborators" in Chapter 1.

DormAid's revenues for the 2007–2008 school year were approximately $600,000, but Kopko believes that the business's real value is in what it has taught him about how to run a company. He has at least two more business ideas cooking. The GradeFund is a Web-based education application that allows students to raise money for school by getting paid for good grades by their family members. "Students utilize the concept of a marathon model to encourage family and friends to pledge money toward their drive for good grades," reads the description. "The GradeFund collects those grades, bills sponsors, and sends the money for school." The company will take a 5 percent fee on every transaction. Paying for grades? It sounds like a company that might well generate as much controversy as DormAid. "We hope so," says Kopko. As of January 2008, the site already had 16,000 users.

> **"We hire students who feel like the company is their baby."**
>
> —Michael Kopko, DormAid

Personal Finance Is Fun and Easy—No, Really

Even without cash for grades, GenY's total annual income is pretty substantial—approximately $200 billion. They've got a lot of money, they spend a good percentage of it (about $172 billion), and they are bound to come into quite a lot more through inheritance from grandparents and, eventually, their parents. But do they know how to manage their funds? Does anyone really know how to teach them? Aaron Patzer, age 28, didn't think so. His solution: Mint.com, an online personal finance site that now has over 1 million registered users, half of them under age 30.

"The guys at Fidelity and Citibank are very surprised that we're getting anyone in their twenties interested in finance," says Patzer. On Mint.com, users organize all their financial information—bank accounts, credit cards, brokerage accounts, etc.—and the site breaks down their spending into categories and suggests ways they might save money by, say, switching to a lower-interest-rate credit card or by putting cash into an interest-bearing account. Mint.com does that by linking to 7,500 different banks and brokerage firms, and the company is paid a commission when its users sign up for a new account. "The only ads you see on Mint.com are the ones that will save you at least $50," says Patzer. "It's completely free to the user, and we only make money if we help you save money." That feature has been critical to the company's success; Patzer says that Mint.com's registration rate tripled last autumn when it became painfully clear that the country was in the midst of a recession. In fact, PCMag.com cited Mint.com last October in a list of 10 online tools for weathering a recession.

So how does a 28-year-old get a million people to enter all their bank user names and passwords into the database of a brand-new startup with no track record? This was exactly what venture capitalists asked Patzer back in 2006 when he was seeking funding for the company. "Most venture capitalists told me this would fail because people wouldn't trust a startup with their financial information," he says. Most, but not all. In the last two years, Patzer has landed $17 million in venture capital from some very heavy hitters in Silicon Valley, including former executives from Intuit, Google, and Yahoo!, plus prominent venture capital firms such as Benchmark Capital,

Shasta Ventures, and First Round Capital. But getting cash and support from such an established group of high-tech players wasn't easy.

The idea for Mint.com, in Mountain View, CA, came from Patzer's frustration with existing personal finance tools such as Microsoft Money and Quicken. Patzer always had been tech-savvy; as a kid growing up in Evansville, IN, he taught himself to program batch files in DOS when he was eight years old. By the time he was 16, he had his own Web design company and made enough money to put himself through Duke University, where he earned three undergraduate degrees in computer science, computer engineering, and electrical engineering. He went on to earn a master's degree in electrical engineering at Princeton and then went to work for IBM where, he groused, "You can't do anything interesting until you're 40."

> "The guys at Fidelity and Citibank are very surprised that we're getting anyone in their twenties interested in finance."
>
> —Aaron Patzer, Mint.com

Startups, he reasoned, cared less about how old you were than if you had good ideas and were willing to work hard. So he went to work for a small high-tech company in Austin called Nascentric and distinguished himself there so rapidly that within a few months he was asked to open a San Jose office. By the autumn of 2005, Patzer had been in San Jose for five months, working 80-hour weeks, and, he says, neglecting his personal finances. He had been using Quicken and Microsoft Money for years, but when he finally sat down with the programs after a long hiatus, he was struck with how "tedious and boring" he found them. He also was displeased with how the programs categorized his transactions; all he wanted was a simple pie chart to show him how he was spending his money. "Quicken failed my basic needs," he says bluntly. It was his aha moment—the one in which so many entrepreneurs have the same thought: There must be a better way.

Patzer quit his job, lived off his savings for seven months, and worked 14-hour days seven days a week developing the technology for Mint.com. "I thought, if I go 100 percent on this and I fail, I can live with that. But if I go halfway because I'm trying to keep a full-time job, I can't live with that," he recalls. Nonetheless, it was an emotionally trying time, and Patzer vacillated between extreme self-confidence and punishing self-doubt. "Some days I'd think, 'I'm a 25-year-old guy, so how can I take on Microsoft and Intuit? If this was a good idea, someone would have thought of it already.'"

But his persistence paid off. By the autumn of 2006, he had a beta version of Mint.com completed and had begun giving his elevator pitch at various Silicon Valley networking events. At one, he caught the attention of Josh Kopelman, the founder of Half.com and a partner at First Round Capital. Patzer took Kopelman aside, pulled a battery-powered server out the trunk of his car, and did a live demo for the venture capitalist. Kopelman asked for a business plan, and a week later Patzer had a $750,000 seed-capital commitment from First Round and a handful of angel investors who included Ron Conway, one of Google's first investors; Paul Buchheit, who developed g-mail for Google; Sy Fahimi and Mark Goines, former top executives at Intuit; and others. That money, combined with another $4.7 million in a series A funding round led by Shasta Ventures six months later, allowed Patzer to assemble a highly experienced team of executives and to launch a public beta version of Mint.com in September 2007. "Aaron has one of those brains that we all wish we were born with," says angel investor Mark Goines, a former Intuit executive who managed the company's Turbo Tax and Quicken product lines. "And he scratched an itch I knew existed in the marketplace."

Patzer's investors gave Mint.com visibility and credibility not only with users but also with the financial institutions whose cooperation and trust the company could not do without. As soon as the site launched, though, Mint.com began to sell itself. Users— 50,000 of them at first—got the word out virally via a Facebook fan page, Twitter, and blog posts. But Patzer's best friend was the mainstream media. "We did no advertising," he says, "but we were on *Good Morning America*, in the *New York Times*, *Forbes*, *Fortune*, the *Wall Street Journal*, and *Inc.*" Mint.com was named the top presenter at TechCrunch40 in September

> "Some days I'd think, 'I'm a 25-year-old guy, so how can I take on Microsoft and Intuit? If this was a good idea, someone would have thought of it already.'"
>
> —Aaron Patzer, Mint.com

2007 and got glowing reviews on GigaOm, NetBanker, and Lifehacker and in *PCWorld*, *Time*, and *BusinessWeek*. To date, says, Patzer, the company also has been mentioned in approximately 6,000 blog posts.

Mint.com is by no means perfect, but it suits the needs of the GenY demographic brilliantly. It's fast (you can set up an account in about six minutes), free, educational (you can learn how to roll over your 401(k) or buy a new car), and the site design is clean and attractive. Mint.com also e-mails you when your checking account balance is low, reminds you when your credit-card bill is due, and will warn you that you're over budget in a particular spending area.

Patzer won't reveal revenues, but he does say that they've doubled every quarter for the past year and that he expects the site to break even by the end of 2009. In January 2009, he says, "We signed up 175,000 users and made fully half as much money as we did in all of 2008." With another $12.1 invested in the company by Benchmark Capital in the spring of 2008, there's a lot riding on Mint.com's success. Patzer doesn't appear concerned. Intuit launched an online Quicken program in December 2007, but Mint.com, he says, is still five times larger and growing faster. Goines, who is now on Mint.com's board, says that the company has some strategic advantages over its larger competitors. "Mint.com offers the product for free and gives customers very specific savings suggestions," he says. "Intuit doesn't do that and never will because it would threaten their legacy software business." Also, he notes, Intuit and Microsoft would have a tough time encouraging consumers to change their financial relationships because many of their large customers are the same institutions that a model like Mint.com's might recommend against. "Mint.com had none of those shackles," says Goines.

For his part, Patzer is focusing on doubling Mint.com's membership to 2 million by the end of 2009. When we last spoke, the company had just launched a new Mint.com iPhone application that helps users to make buying decisions by evaluating their budget on the go. The application became the number one finance application for iPhone within 24 hours. "You ask it if you should buy something, and it'll say yes, no, or probably not," says Patzer. It's parental, but without the nagging. Applications like this should help him continue to attract the under-30 demographic that's so important to the growth of his company.

Indie Brand Appeal

Patzer's dream is for Mint.com to gain mass acceptance among GenY consumers. For Bobby Kim and Ben Shenassafar, both age 29, that would be a complete nightmare. The two are passionate about remaining true to the roots of their popular streetwear apparel brand, The Hundreds. This is not as easy as you might think. When a brand gains significant traction, there's a huge temptation to take it to the masses because that's where the fast, easy money is. But Kim and Shenassafar have so far resisted that allure. Their logo—a little atom bomb with a slightly alarmed expression—says it all. "The bomb never explodes," says Shenassafar. "And that's like our brand. It's not going to explode; it will never become this mainstream thing."

The two met at Loyola Law School and, at the end of their first year, were struck with same liberating realization: "We hated the law profession, and we didn't want to be attorneys," says Kim. While studying for finals and facing a summer of mind-numbing internships at law firms, the two came up with what they thought was a far better alternative: They'd start a T-shirt company. "We had friends telling us, 'Why are you doing this? There are a million T-shirt companies.' But we didn't care because we were just doing it for fun," says Kim, who wore the design hat, whereas Shenassafar played the role of sales guy.

"This was never really just about T-shirts or apparel specifically," says Kim. "We refer to it as a lifestyle project." And the lifestyle was Los Angeles street culture, which, for the partners, meant skateboarding, hiphop, and the music, designers, and artists who helped to define that movement. "When we started, street brands were a New York and Tokyo phenomenon—it was a tiny little niche of the men's apparel industry," says Shenassafar. The Hundreds would put its own LA spin on that niche, and from the beginning, the partners took a contrarian approach. "At trade shows, people would ask if we were a hiphop brand or a skate brand, and we'd say both," recalls Kim. "It was stupid of us from a business perspective because we knew we wouldn't sell as well if we didn't position ourselves in a particular direction. But we were staying true to our brand, which is an amalgamation of subcultures."

The best reflection of that brand identity was not just the T-shirts but also The Hundreds website and blog, which the partners designed as an online magazine that featured interviews with designers and artists who were identified with LA street culture. Their goal: Enlighten the rest of the world about what was going in LA, and establish brand credibility by focusing not on products but rather on the iconic figures who inspired them. Today, the site gets over a million readers a month.

Shenassafar and Kim never wanted their brand to have mass appeal. "When we first started out, we had a white board, and on it we wrote the names of the 50 stores in the entire world that we would feel comfortable in," says Kim. One of those stores was Fred Segal Street, a trendy Santa Monica boutique. The folks at Fred Segal, however, had very little interest in The Hundreds. "We were told no by buyers many times," says Shenassafar. "Then we kind of snuck up on Tony Johnson, the owner, as he was coming out of the store. We had a box of shirts with us, and to be honest, they were really bad shirts because they were Bobby's first designs." But Johnson was impressed enough to give them an order, which gave the brand enormous street credibility in LA.

> "This was never really just about T-shirts or apparel specifically. We refer to it as a lifestyle project."
>
> —Bobby Kim, The Hundreds

With no formal marketing or advertising plan, the brand took off, gaining traction via word of mouth and The Hundreds website, which contained essays by Kim, along with YouTube videos, and interviews with artists and designers. Fans also could download branded icons, flyers, and wallpaper to put up on their MySpace pages. And the company happily sent out thousands of stickers to kids who would plaster them, well, everywhere. The fans built the brand, and in 2007, the partners opened up their own retail store in LA. Suddenly that tiny list of 50 acceptable retail outlets grew substantially. Their merchandise—T-shirts, but also hats and hoodies—was selling in 100 stores nationwide and in 10 foreign countries.

Today, The Hundreds has a second store in San Francisco and sells in 400 other stores worldwide. But Kim and Shenassafar have made a conscious choice not to be lured into mass distribution, which they felt would tarnish their brand. "We say no to stores all the time," says Kim. "Streetwear has become so popular that a lot of people are jumping on the bandwagon because there's money in it at the moment. But they have no sense of the history behind Streetwear, and in a few years, they'll move on to something else." For The Hundreds to be positioned next to one of those newbie brands in a store that's clueless of the distinction is unacceptable. Less selective distribution also would send a message to brand loyalists that The Hundreds may be going mainstream, and that, according to the partners, might be the road to fabulous revenue growth, but ultimately it would lead to the commoditization of their brand.

It may come as a surprise, then, that Kim and Shenassafar have agreed to partner with the most mainstream of companies, Disney. Kim had always been a fan of the Lost Boys, Peter Pan's Neverland tribe of unruly orphans. "I would liken our brand and the way it was created to the Lost Boys, never having to grow up and always creating mischief," he says. He had actually created Lost Boys–inspired T-shirts, but "only used their silhouettes because I didn't want to be sued by Disney," he says. Nonetheless, Disney is highly protective of its brands and had been keeping a close eye on The Hundreds. When it became clear that the brand was a rising star, an executive from Disney approached the partners with an irresistible deal: Disney's own illustrators would reconceive the Lost Boys, dress them in urban gear, and portray them as skaters, heavy-metal musicians, and graffiti artists, and give The Hundreds permission to put each new character on T-shirts and baseball caps. The two companies would share the revenue on sales of all the cobranded products, which would have limited distribution in The Hundreds' own retail stores and in select other U.S. specialty retailers. What about Disney stores? No way, say the partners. The new, edgy Lost Boys characters just wouldn't look right next to Mickey, Pluto, and Goofy. Besides, Kim and Shenassafar understand that their GenY brand loyalists are watching this emerging partnership very carefully.

Customizing for the GenY Market

The Hundreds and Threadless (see Chapter 1) specialize in the unofficial uniform of youth: the T-shirt. But the influx of GenY's significant ranks into the world of work means that once in a while, everyone needs to look like a grown-up. For those rare occasions, it's nice to have a suit in your closet. Except that good ones are awfully expensive, and cheap ones look cheap and frequently don't fit very well. This was Heikal Gani's dilemma and the catalyst for his company, Indochino.com.

"The stuff he wanted was way too expensive, and the stuff that fit him didn't speak to him," says his friend and co-founder, 24-year-old Kyle Vucko. The two were classmates at the University of Victoria, British Columbia, and had talked frequently about starting a business together. So they noodled around for a solution to Gani's dilemma on the assumption that other young men shared his frustration with finding affordable, well-fitting suits. They came up with what they thought was an innovative solution and wrote a business plan: They'd start an online tailoring company, where customers would measure themselves or be measured by their own local tailor, choose from a variety of styles and fabrics online, place their order, and receive their new suit within two weeks. The suits would be made in China. Average price: $200 to $400, including shipping and alterations. The final product was good, cheap, fast, and customized—the perfect GenY brand.

If you're wondering who on earth would buy a custom-made suit online, consider the original skepticism surrounding BlueNile.com's business model. Now the largest online retailer of certified diamonds, the company won the trust of its customers through its focus on education about the diamond-buying process and its reputation for customer service. For Indochino's founders, BlueNile.com was proof that it was possible to make customers feel comfortable with purchasing high-end items online. And the partners knew from experience that there was a market opportunity among young men who craved custom-made suits but couldn't afford a traditional Hong Kong tailor. The target market: budding executives, aged 28 to 35; young men buying suits for high school or college graduation; and wedding parties.

So Gani and Vucko entered their business plan in a competition at the University of British Columbia, but they failed to generate enough interest among the competition's judges. "We made it to the individual finals but fell short of the money round," recalls Vucko. But that didn't dampen their enthusiasm.

Gani headed to Shanghai, where he lived with his sister and got the lay of the land; Vucko stayed behind in Vancouver to raise money. His university had put him in touch with a variety of mentors, one of whom was Hannes Blum, the CEO of AbeBooks.com. Blum liked the concept enough to bring on three other angel investors, and together they seeded the company with $40,000. "It was proof-of-concept money," says Vucko. The company started doing business offline, with Vucko remaining in Victoria; he threw himself into sales, measured customers, and generated public relations for his young company. He also traveled to Shanghai frequently, where he and Gani sought out relationships with individual tailors who were willing to make one suit at a time. "We went to over 100 tailors before we had one guy who was willing to buy into our model," says Vucko. "But it's an interconnected community, so now we have over 50 tailors." Two of those tailors, he says, have grown the bulk of their businesses based on the work they get from Indochino. That's an element of the company that Vucko's especially proud of and one that he believes resonates with GenY consumers and their interest in sustainable business practices.

The Indochino.com website went live in September 2007, and by January 2008, it had landed a second round of financing for $250,000 from Burda Digital Ventures, a Munich, Germany–based venture capital firm that Blum brought to the table. Vucko and Gani had budgeted for a 10 percent return rate from customers who were dissatisfied with their purchases but were pleasantly surprised when the number held steady at just 3 percent. Plus, they kept raw material and inventory costs low by buying fabric only as they needed it at end-of-roll shops, where the cost per meter was comparatively low.

> "We looked at BlueNile.com as a model for how to make someone comfortable with a high-end purchase online."
>
> —Kyle Vucko, Indochino.com

"We have zero inventory, and this is a big advantage because it's something traditional fashion retailers can't match," says Vucko.

At the end of 2008, Vucko moved to Shanghai, where he and Gani (who no longer has trouble finding suits that fit) launched a wholly owned Chinese subsidiary. At that time, the company, which has eight full-time employees in addition to its network of 50 tailors, was in the black. Since then, sales have been increasing steadily, as has Indochino.com's average order. "Turns out the economy has been a good thing for us," says Vucko. "The value message is really hitting home and people who were only interested in higher priced suits before are now in a place to try us out and are being surprised by the results."

In March of 2009, Vucko and Gani landed a small investment—$55,000—from Jeffrey Mallet, the former president and chief operating officer of Yahoo!. Mallet, who now owns a small percentage of the company and has a board seat, will "continue to help us find top level talent and keep me in the right frame of mind as we grow," says Vucko. He expects revenues of $1.5 million in 2009.

Dating 2.0

Online dating hasn't been around for as long as the custom-made suit, but it's still old news as far as GenY is concerned. Companies such as Match.com and eHarmony.com were started over 10 years ago, and they're now widely trafficked by people looking for love and companionship. According to Quantcast, a company that tracks the demographics of website visitors, approximately 65 percent of Match.com and eHarmony visitors are over the age of 35. Adam Sachs, age 26, Daniel Osit, age 27, and Kevin Owocki, age 25, think they know why. "The Match.com model was created 15 years ago and wasn't made for this generation," says Sachs, a cofounder of Ignighter.com, an online dating site with a GenY flavor. "They haven't changed their model to meet our needs." GenY's most basic social needs revolve around groups, and the idea of a blind date, says Sachs, "seems awkward, unnatural, and potentially dangerous."

So Sachs and Osit, who met at Northwestern University, came up with an idea in June 2007 for an online dating site where users would register in groups and then arrange to meet other appealing groups of people at a physical location, such as a bar or a park. Meeting new people, they reasoned, wouldn't be so awkward if you did it with your friends. So they tested their idea as an application on Facebook in January 2008 but soon realized that a stand-alone website was a better alternative. They signed on Owocki as their lead developer, and that summer the team was accepted into the Boulder-based incubator and funding program TechStars. By the end of the summer, Sachs and Osit had a functional website and had landed $1.2 million in funding from a private equity fund and a group of angel investors.

At this writing, Ignighter had registered 15,000 groups worldwide, with an average of 3.5 people per group. The site allows groups to post their pictures and their profiles and to contact other groups that look compatible.

There's a also a section of the site with ideas for group dates; the local watering hole works, of course, but users also might consider laser tag, a volunteer project, or Frisbee in the park. Sachs says that Ignighter will do a city-by-city marketing campaign to rustle up registrants. In August 2008, for example, the company sponsored a New York City group date (aka "party") for Obama and Clinton supporters. The guest of honor: "Obama Girl" (Amber Lee Ettinger) from *Crush on Obama* video fame. The event landed them in the *Wall Street Journal* the next day.

> "The Match.com model was created 15 years ago and was not made for this generation. They haven't changed their model to meet our needs."
>
> —Adam Sachs, Ignighter

The biggest challenge for Ignighter now: making money. There's always advertising, if you can get it, and Sachs says that while the site is now free, he won't rule out charging a subscription fee in the future. He's confident that if he builds up his user base, he'll have a number of ways to create revenue. He also believes that the economy just may be his best friend. "When you look at crappy economies, one thing that does really well is diversions—things that help people have fun and enjoy their lives," he says. "In a cheap way."

Reading the GenY Mind

If online dating sites such as Match.com and eHarmony were interested in reaching the GenY demographic, they might have added a "group" option to their existing sites or perhaps started spin off websites targeting younger users. Of course, that's never as easy as it sounds. Companies that want to market to GenY frequently struggle with both their messages and the media through which those messages are delivered. They often fail miserably, particularly when it comes to using social networking to reach young people. "Companies are intrigued and terrified," says Charlene Li, coauthor of *Groundswell: Winning in a World Transformed by Social Technologies* (Harvard Business Press, 2008) and CEO of Altimeter Group, a consulting firm. "Most have no clue what to do, and they make a huge number of mistakes."

There's probably no better example of that than Wal-Mart, which has made several attempts at using social networking to reach young consumers. In July 2006, the company launched a social network called The Hub, a highly controlled, sanitized alternative to MySpace that bloggers immediately labeled "uncool," citing a suspiciously high number of posts that sounded like corporate messaging. The site was shut down in just 10 weeks. Then, in September 2006, a blog called "Wal-Marting Across America" made its now infamous debut. It was ostensibly written by a married couple named Jim and Laura who drove their RV across America, parked for free in Wal-Mart parking lots, shopped at the stores, and made pals with employees, none of whom complained about low wages or lack of health insurance. But the blog turned out to be a "flog" (fake blog); Jim and Laura (who weren't even married) were being paid by Working Families for Wal-Mart, an organization started by Wal-Mart's public relations firm, Edelman. The blogosphere went crazy, and the campaign became a textbook case for what happens when companies aren't completely transparent on the Web: They get caught; they get trashed.

But Wal-Mart did not give up on social networking. In August 2007, it spent $100,000 to start a Facebook group called "Roommate Style Match" that encouraged future roomies to take a quiz that revealed their decorating style. The idea was for Wal-Mart to capture some of the $1,113 that the National Retail Federations says the average college freshman spends on room decor. But something unexpected happened: Students used the group to post highly negative comments about Wal-Mart, referencing what they perceived as the company's antiunion reputation and its detrimental impact on local communities. To its credit, Wal-Mart now seems to be on the right track with a blog called "Check Out" that is written by a group of relatively young Wal-Mart buyers who talk about "the latest in gadgets, green, gaming, and more," apparently without corporate vetting. Is the fourth time the charm? Maybe.

Calling in Reinforcements

Wal-Mart is not the only company that seems befuddled about how to connect to GenY. If that were the case, it's doubtful that we'd be noticing such a conspicuous increase in the number of marketing and consulting firms whose primary purpose is helping companies market to young consumers. And many of these firms are started by—no surprise here—Upstarts.

Among them is Tina Wells—an early mover in this nascent consulting niche whom you met earlier in this chapter. Wells, age 28, is the CEO of Buzz Marketing Group, a $3 million youth marketing firm in Voorhees, NJ, that has helped clients such as American Eagle, Esprit, Hard Candy, and Nike tap into the teen market. She got her start in June 1996 when she was just 16 years old, writing product reviews for a magazine called *New Girl Times*. Companies liked her style and the comments she made about their products and soon began contacting her. "By the fall, I realized I had a business," recalls Wells. So she started a company called The Buzz that organized events, conducted surveys, and did research for companies targeting teens.

Wells refined her business at Hood College with help from Anita Jose, director of the MBA program. "We met every Friday for three hours," says Wells. "We wrote a business plan and worked on a marketing plan. I started the company right around the Internet boom, but Dr. Jose told me that the online piece was great but that I had to have a bricks-and-mortar company." Wells took heed. She did consulting projects throughout college, organizing youth focus groups for such clients as Verizon Wireless and DaimlerChrysler. Along the way, she aggregated a group of 250 young people she called "buzz spotters," whose advice and opinions she could solicit on behalf of her clients. Buzz spotters typically received free products and a bit of cash for every market research project in which they participated.

> "My clients didn't know I was 16. They though I was a cool girl that understood teens, not that I was a teen."
>
> —Tina Wells, Buzz Marketing

"In 2000, *Cosmo Girl* wrote about the buzz spotters, and all of a sudden everyone wanted to be one," says Wells. "We had 15,000 applications." Her 25 original buzz spotters vetted those applications, and Wells now has 9,000 young men and women aged 16 to 24 in her buzz-spotting tribe; she uses them for market research, idea generation, trend spotting, online marketing, and focus groups. "We have them in every state and in 20 countries, and in every campaign, they're a central part of what we're doing," she says. For instance, a cosmetics company recently hired Buzz Marketing to help launch a new line of makeup with each item priced at $1. "We tapped 100 buzz spotters and told them to go on the client's site and pick out five products for themselves and five for their friends," recalls Wells. Clients like this not only garner the collective intelligence of a large and opinionated community, says Wells, but they also get a better shot at brand loyalty from that community. "Including them in the process makes them feel like they have ownership," she says "And this generation likes ownership."

Let Me Entertain You

This generation also likes to be surprised, delighted, and entertained. Who doesn't? But the bar is higher for GenY, and these days, a company has to do a heck of a lot more than throw a party or give away free stuff or produce a cool television commercial to get into the wallets of young consumers. "We were born digital," says 25-year-old Josh Spear, a blogger turned digital marketing savant. "And so we have certain expectations as consumers in the way a brand moves in that space." Spear is a founding partner of Manhattan-based Undercurrent, and big firms such as Pepsi, Virgin, and McDonald's have paid him handsomely to advise them on how to market to GenY. Undercurrent's revenues were $2 million in 2008 and Spear expects a jump to $5 million in 2009,

He was 18 when he first developed an interest in youth marketing and trends, but he didn't know he could turn that passion into a business until he had a conversation with his father's friend, Elissa Moses, author of *The 100 Billion Dollar Allowance: How to Get Your Share of the Global Teen Market* (Wiley, 2000). "She said I was a trend spotter and a strategist and told me that if I wanted people to take me seriously, I needed to start cataloging my own finds and insights," he recalls. A year later, he was sitting in the back of the room in a Journalism 101 class at the University of Colorado when boredom drove him to start writing a blog on products that he liked and the youth trends he saw emerging. Within six months, Audi was advertising on the site, and large companies were offering to pay Spear for his advice.

Spear's enormously popular blog is now written by a staff of writers around the world because he has bigger fish to fry with Undercurrent, which he founded with "co-conspirators" Aaron Dignan and Rob Schuham. He's now known as one of the youngest marketing strategists in the world, has spoken at Google Zeitgeist, was nominated to the Global Agenda Council at the World Economic Forum, and named a "Young Global Leader" by the Forum. In his 18-minute speech at Zeitgeist in 2007, he told the audience how to go about marketing to a composite GenY girl named Ally by taking her through a typical day. "When it comes to reaching or selling anything to Ally or to digital youth, it's not about finding her," he concluded. "And it's certainly not about interrupting her. We know that; we learned that a long time ago. It's about creating content and functionality that she's going to seek out, use, or interact with on a day-to-day basis." The core of

> "We were born digital. And so we have certain expectations as consumers in the way a brand moves in that space."
>
> —Josh Spear, Undercurrent

what he does involves teaching companies how to reach youth in the digital space without using traditional advertising. And to do that, sometimes you need to get creative.

Last year, for instance, Undercurrent was involved in a digital marketing campaign for BMW that had traditional marketers scratching their heads. BMW and its advertising agency, GSD&M, produced a "mockumentary" entitled *The Ramp*—a 35-minute film that lives only online and chronicles the story of "Rampenfest," an event (that never happened) conceived and orchestrated by marketing genius Franz Brendl (not a real guy), who builds a gigantic wooden ramp (digitally concocted) from which to launch the BMW 1 Series (an actual car) from the Bavarian town of Oberpfaffelbachen (doesn't exist) across the Atlantic to the United States.

It was a spoof cooked up by two young men named Scott Brewer and Ryan Carroll at Austin-based GSD&M, to get the relatively economically priced 1 Series on GenY's radar screen. Once the film was in the can, the two realized that they needed help making it come to life online. Enter Spear and his team at Undercurrent. To build buzz before BMW's March 2008 launch, Undercurrent created a blog for *The Ramp*'s "filmmaker," Jeff Schultz, an actor. More teasers followed, including trailers on YouTube and a Rampenfest fan page on Facebook. Closer to the March launch, GSD&M built micro-websites for the characters and businesses in the film, including a site for the mythical town of Oberpfaffelbachen, a Facebook page for Franz

Brendl, and a store selling Rampenfest souvenirs on Café Press. The result: Within the first two weeks of the launch, 1.2 million people had been exposed to some element of the campaign. It's worth noting that BMW isn't even mentioned until six to seven minutes into the film.

The campaign is less about the actual product than it is about delivering a specific message to the GenY target market: We understand what gets your attention, so we're going to plant our brand where you live and give you fun stuff to look at and play around with online, and we're going to facilitate an ongoing conversation that will engage you far longer and more intimately than a 30-second television commercial (and at a fraction of the cost, by the way). So did it sell cars? Jack Pitney, vice president of marketing at BMW North America, told CNN last June that the video, which racked up 10 million views, was a hit; two-thirds of the BMW 1 Series were presold.

UPSTARTS PLAYLIST

Track 4: Get Clued in to the GenY Market

1. **Go back to school.** Annually, 13.6 million college students spend $237 billion, but they're selective consumers who often view traditional advertising/marketing messages as irritating interruptions. Their social nature makes them highly receptive to word-of-mouth marketing; recommendations from friends trump just about every other form of selling. Enlist students to market and sell your product or service, such as College Boxes and DormAid, and you'll have a better shot at tapping into this demographic.

2. **Scrutinize existing products.** Look for points of pain that might be particularly irksome to GenY. Aaron Patzer's Mint.com was born out of his frustration with personal finance programs such as Quicken and Microsoft Money. He thought they were too cumbersome to set up and that they weren't accurate enough when it came to categorizing his expenses. Budget-conscious young people hate spending more time than they have to on personal finance, so Patzer developed a service that makes the process fast, easy, and fun. Ignighter.com is a GenY spin on Match.com; it uses a group date model that's more in sync with how GenY socializes.

3. **Think customization, not mass production.** GenY is highly individualistic and responds negatively to anything mass produced. Conversely, products and services that allow them to either customize or express their individuality are typically a hit. Witness the success of Loopt (see Chapter 2), one of the many iPhone applications that allow users to call the shots on how they use their mobile devices, and Threadless, whose community-designed T-shirts will never be mass produced. Likewise, the founders of The Hundreds know that the appeal of their indie brand of T-shirts relies on the company's connection to youth subculture, so they've wisely rejected offers from big retailers to carry their merchandise. They've still managed to grow their brand through strategic partnerships and highly selective distribution.

4. **Sell your [fill in the blank] online.** GenY lives online, so everyone who wants to sell to them needs to be there too. When Kyle Vucko and Heikal Gani founded their custom-made suit company, they eschewed the traditional model and opted instead for a Web-based business that shows customers how to measure themselves. Low overhead, relationships with independent Shanghai tailors, and smart purchasing of raw materials helps them keep costs down so that they can offer reasonable prices to their target demographic: their own GenY peers.

5. **Draw in your customers.** Buzz Marketing's clients pay the company for access to a select group of young "buzz spotters" for product testing and market research. Companies get feedback directly from consumers in their target market and also engender brand loyalty from people who feel connected to a product because they helped develop it. The Hundreds gathers its community of customers, called the "bombsquad," on its website, which doubles as an online magazine. Customers can download branded MySpace wallpaper, icons, and flyers to spread The Hundreds' message. And a section called "photo booth" posts pictures of customers, fed to the site via a Web cam in The Hundreds' two retail stores.

6. **Offer content that's entertaining.** GenY hates the hard sell but will listen to your message if it's fun and engaging. BMW paid a fraction of the cost of a 30-second television commercial to produce a "mocumentary" for the launch of its 1 Series car to the United States. The campaign attracted 10 million online viewers who were engaged not just by the film but also by websites, Facebook pages, and a Café Press store that brought the film's quirky characters and fictional town to life. The result: far more buzz than a traditional ad campaign.

Brand
Builders

A Brand Is a Dialogue,
Not a Monologue

U pstarts have created some of the most important and innovative brands in recent times: Facebook, YouTube, Flickr, Digg, Yelp, Threadless, and Etsy, to name just a few. The concepts behind these brands are as original as their names, and if you think that their most significant common element is that they live on the Internet, then you're missing the point. For these companies—and other Upstarts that are not Web-based—the Internet is a tool that facilitates the creation of community and the sharing of information and entertainment. It's a vehicle for companies to communicate consistent and meaningful brand identities—an essential high-speed train that delivers the goods, but that's not nearly as important as the precious human cargo it transports. As Seth Godin says in *Tribes: We Need You to Lead Us* (Portfolio, 2008), "the real power of tribes has nothing to do with the Internet and everything to do with people."

Nonetheless, the Internet, along with constantly evolving mobile technology, fundamentally changes the way companies go about the process of branding. It's worth repeating what you heard from Ed Moran at Deloitte in Chapter 2: "Branding is not in your control anymore," he cautions. "People will assemble around a product or service, and they've got a much stronger affinity for your product than they do for your company. They create a tremendous amount of buzz." And the Internet is the buzz train.

This is all very familiar terrain for Upstarts. They know how to collaborate and foster community, they're fearless with new technology, and they're drawing on the standards they use when judging other brands to brand their own companies. "This group of younger people really understands that brands have cultural power and that you can express ideas through brands," says Rob Walker, author of *Buying In: The Secret Dialogue Between What We Buy and Who We Are* (Random House, 2008). "The popular notion is that the younger generation rejects mainstream brands, and that's sort of true, but it misses the real point—that they reject mainstream brands in favor of creating their own brands."

> "Branding is not in your control anymore. People will assemble around a product or service, and they've got a much stronger affinity for your product than they do for your company."
>
> —Ed Moran, Deloitte

So what are the characteristics of Upstart brands? First and foremost, Upstarts understand that a brand isn't set in stone; it's an ongoing conversation between a company and its customers, a dialogue rather than a monologue. This conversation often takes place online, but savvy Upstarts, such as Sittercity.com, and Etsy (which you'll meet in this chapter), as well as Ignighter.com (from Chapter 4), know that brands need face time. And brands that are all about face time, such as Meathead Movers and JW Tumbles, also use community building to distinguish themselves from their competitors. Upstarts in the consumer goods business, such as Happy Baby Food and Feed Granola, play up the organic elements of the brands but know that's not enough to survive in their cutthroat industry. So they use their youth, their brand stories, and street marketing to drive brand loyalty. And in a flagging economy, Upstarts sometimes have to get really creative when it comes to brand expansion. Kenny Lao at Rickshaw Dumpling Bar is an expert at this. Lastly, Upstart branding is very often infused with higher meaning, and while you'll hear more about this in Chapter 6, here you'll meet Rob Kalin of Etsy, who views his online craft marketplace as a catalyst for the creation of sustainable small businesses.

The Community Is the Brand

Genevieve Thiers, age 31, didn't set out to build a national multimillion-dollar brand that would one day become an Inc. 500 company; she just wanted to create an easy way for desperate parents to find trustworthy babysitters. The result was Sittercity.com, a company that uses its own online databases of sitters and families to facilitate connections between members of the two groups. Sittercity's revenues were $2.6 million in 2007, landing it the number 287 spot on the Inc. 500 list. And while Thiers won't reveal numbers for 2008, she says that the company is growing steadily at 300 percent a year. If you're wondering who would use the Internet to find a babysitter, you've probably never had the teen down the street cancel at the last minute on a Saturday night. But creating this highly successful and expertly branded community was not child's play.

The oldest of six children, Thiers babysat her way through Boston College (BC) and was the go-to girl for 30 local families. So she was keenly aware of the trials of busy parents. One day back in 2001, she saw a pregnant mom struggling up the 193 steps that link BC's upper and lower campuses carrying a stack of flyers that she was posting in search of a babysitter. Thiers was horrified and offered to post the flyers for the grateful mom. While she was doing the good deed, her entrepreneurial wheels began turning; there had to be a better way for a desperate parent to find a babysitter. Sure, you could always go through an agency, reasoned Thiers, but a sitter from an agency could cost $50 an hour, and that was beyond the means of most parents (witness the stair-climbing pregnant woman). And so Thiers decided to start a business that would connect sitters directly with families. In that respect, you might also put her in the "Game Changer" category of Upstarts.

> "This group of younger people really understands that brands have cultural power and that you can express ideas through brands."
>
> —Rob Walker, author of "Buying In"

Thiers sought out investors but was turned down consistently by guys in suits, who scoffed, "We don't invest in babysitting clubs." So she called her father and asked to borrow $120 to register the domain name. Dad's reaction: "Here's my credit-card number; don't tell your mom." By that time, Thiers had graduated from BC and was working for IBM, so she was able scrape together a bit of money to hire two college friends to build a website for her. Then she printed 20,000 fliers and posted them in 400 dorms around Boston. The idea was to replicate the online dating service model, like Match.com, by creating a meeting place where sitters would register and parents could review their credentials and then contact them directly. By September 2001, Sittercity.com had 600 Boston babysitters signed up on its website; the 30 families that Thiers had worked for agreed to register as well, paying a $39.99 registration fee and then $9.99 a month thereafter. Sitters could register for free. People were so pleased with the service that "we had cake and cookies arriving in the mail the first two weeks," recalls Thiers. The company was profitable right out of the gate.

The obvious question (and one that Thiers' mom fretted about when her daughter started Sittercity) was: "What about liability?" Because Sittercity doesn't hire the sitters the way brick-and-mortar agencies do, liability is low, says Thiers. "We give you the tools to screen each other, but we don't actually do any of that," she says. "And everyone on the site has to sign a terms-of-use agreement." The site also allows parents to publicly rate sitters on a one- to five-star basis, and it encourages sitters to run background checks on themselves (offered through the Sittercity site), which then are displayed on their profiles. The company runs all sitter information through an algorithm so that when a parent searches for a sitter, the most highly ranked ones appear at the top of the list. If a sitter neglects to run a background check on himself or herself, "they plummet in the list," says Thiers. Sitters are encouraged to post comments on the families they work for so that other sitters will know, for instance, if parents are chronically late or if their kids are perpetually bratty. The system, which fosters transparency and accountability, is a crucial element of the Sittercity brand.

It didn't take long for the word to spread about the company. With little or no marketing effort, parents and sitters in other cities began signing up on the Sittercity site, and Thiers sometimes received e-mails from parents alerting her that the sitter count in a particular city was low. That was her cue to get on a plane so that she could distribute flyers in local dorms to find sitters, just as she had done in Boston. By 2002, San Francisco, Cleveland, New York,

Chicago, and Dallas were thriving Sittercity markets. That year, Thiers moved the company to Chicago so that she'd be better positioned for bicoastal travel; she also decided to pursue her other passion—opera—and enrolled in a graduate program at Northwestern University's School of Music.

Thiers' market and customer base grew organically, but she left nothing to chance. She promoted her brand like a pro, at first positioning herself as a babysitting expert to local mothers' groups and then attracting the attention of national media outlets. In 2004, Thiers became the iVillage.com babysitting expert, which soon landed her in multiple spots on *The Today Show* when NBC bought iVillage.com. Interviews on the *Ellen DeGeneres Show*, *The View*, *The Early Show*, and *Good Morning America*, as well as hundreds of other media outlets, soon followed. The company also landed over 12 major business awards, including the Small Business Administration "Champion of the Year" award in 2006, received in the White House. While Thiers did plenty of online marketing, using paid search and e-mail campaigns, her most effective branding efforts came from good old-fashioned public relations, events, and television appearances. Frequently, she burst into song, positioning herself as an operatic Mary Poppins. "It's memorable," she says. "You have to build mojo around a brand." That brand-building mojo also includes a book (*Love at First Sit*, BookSurge Publishing, 2008) and a CD of children's songs ("Sittercity Sings").

Thiers was the reassuring face of the Sittercity brand and a bona fide expert on caregiving. This was critically important because not all parents were comfortable choosing their babysitters on a website. To give her Internet company even more "face time" with potential customers, she spun off a new division that sponsored "speed-sitting" events. "It's like speed dating," says Thiers. "We run an event, and we have 50 parents and 50 sitters, and they talk to each other for a few minutes. We do it for press, but also to give people a sense of who we are and to build a brand." It's a bit like Ignighter's (see Chapter 4) group dating parties, held in targeted cities in order to beef up the number of registrants for the online dating site. The events also build local brand buzz.

> "You have to build mojo around a brand."
>
> —**Genevieve Thiers, Sittercity**

Now that Sittercity has gained traction as a recognizable and trusted brand, Thiers is marketing its services to human resources departments at companies such as Pitney Bowes, Avon, and MasterCard, which pay the company a bulk rate to offer the sitter-finding service to their employees. And partnerships with several companies, including PetCo, iVillage, Discovery Health, and Humana, are in place to promote the company's expansion into the pet-sitting and elder-care markets.

Thiers concedes that copycat services, encouraged by her success, have begun to spring up. But she's ready for them. "When industries are just getting started, you're just running to let people know that the industry exists," she says. "But when you really begin to capture market share, the leader has to protect her space, and we're already beginning to lay our defensive strategy." At the end of 2008, the company landed $7.5 million in equity financing from Point Judith Capital and Apex Partners. "We realized how powerful our brand was when we were sealing our capital in the end of 2008," says Thiers. "In the middle of a huge economic crisis, we were getting more attention than ever before, not less." She adds that "the best time to grow is in a recession. A lot of things get cheaper, and there's an influx of talent on the market."

> "When you really begin to capture market share, the leader has to protect her space, and we're already beginning to lay down our defensive strategy."
>
> —Genevieve Thiers,
> Sittercity

Thiers won't elaborate on her long-term plans except to say that "there's a huge international and domestic market for Sittercity." She's confident that her brand mojo—and her new venture partners—will help the company maintain its impressive growth trajectory.

Differentiating Your Brand

Genevieve Thiers built the Sittercity brand by connecting two communities of people who desperately needed each other but had no direct, efficient, and economical way to meet. Because the concept of a Web-based parent and babysitter matching service was new, Thiers faced a very particular set of branding challenges: She needed to educate users, establish trust, and give her Internet company a public face and a physical presence in the communities it served. Companies in established industries have a different set of issues when it comes to branding: How do you differentiate yourself from your competitors, wow your customers, and avoid being viewed as a commodity?

The Steed brothers think they've done a pretty good job of that. "We wanted to defy the stereotype of the dumb jock moving furniture and show that we could establish a high-quality, client-oriented business," says Evan Steed, age 26, who started San Luis Obispo, CA–based Meathead Movers with his brother, Aaron, age 28, in 1997. The two were high school athletes (Aaron was a wrestler; Evan, a football player) who started a moving business to make some extra money; the work was also great exercise. When they couldn't handle demand on their own, they enlisted other athletes to help, and soon their tiny operation earned a reputation as a company that employed hardworking, clean-cut, polite, and honest young men. Before long, the company became a full-time pursuit for the Steeds, who realized that they had a valuable branding opportunity on their hands; they'd use their employees to define their brand identity.

Like College Hunks Hauling Junk, they took a look at the industry standard and figured that they could distinguish themselves by doing a whole lot better. The labor pool that they originally tapped simply out of convenience—student athletes—became their biggest differentiating factor. On the Meathead Movers website, 90 employee pictures and short bios are posted on the "Starting Lineup" page, and customers can actually choose their movers. The company, which does $3 million to $5 million in sales, has 30 to 40 full-time employees and another 120 or so part-timers.

The Steeds are demanding employers and make no apologies for their strict standards; they're not just looking for brute strength. "When we hire, we gauge character," says Aaron Steed. "They're told ahead of time to show up to the interview in a collared shirt, and if they don't, then they don't get hired. And if they're not on time, they don't get hired."

> "We wanted to defy the stereotype of the dumb jock moving furniture and show that we could establish a high-quality, client-oriented business."
>
> —Evan Steed,
> Meathead Movers

But it's not all tough love. Meathead has an on-site gym and provides employees with free massages and chiropractic appointments. According to Steed, employees also "feel comfortable telling us if they don't feel well. We'll pay them to clean the warehouse or wash the trucks." The Steeds know that a mover who isn't feeling up to snuff is more likely to get injured, but might slog through a job anyway to avoid loss of pay. For every four consecutive months without injury, the company throws a big party, racking up an annual party tab of $50,000. "If we can create a culture and a job that is the best job for young, strong student athletes, we will have the best moving company," says Aaron Steed, who you might also call a "Workplace Renegade" (see Chapter 7).

Meathead also distinguishes itself by being a "Game Changer." Unlike other moving companies that typically consolidate shipments, Meathead has a one-move, one-truck policy so that the company can focus on one customer at a time. Customers are also assigned a Meathead "Quarterback"—essentially the equivalent of a concierge—who suggests landscapers, babysitters, attorneys, housecleaners, or any other service provider that a newcomer might require. The service is free, and Steed says that no commissions are involved. While Steed concedes that the company's hourly rates are typically higher than those of competitors, he says that Meathead's movers usually complete jobs in less time than a competitor might because they move a good bit faster than the average moving professional. A trademark company policy: Meatheads must jog when they're not carrying something, a practice that not only saves time but also provides customers with a little theater. "Everything we do is meant to impress the customer," says Steed. "We want to wow them and shock them." Before the truck is unloaded, customers give the movers a tour of their home and then are asked to sit in the VIP Meathead chair—a folding chair with a cup holder—and simply to tell the movers where everything goes as furniture and boxes are unloaded. "When we run past them, we run extra hard," says Steed. "At the end, we give them a present—a plant

> "If we can create a culture and a job that is the best job for young, strong student athletes, we will have the best moving company."
>
> —Aaron Steed,
> Meathead Movers

and a deck of cards—and the price is almost always less than the estimate. It makes them love us."

In fact, Meathead Movers' website "Trophy Room" bears out that claim. In 2008, the company was named "best moving company" in San Luis Obispo, Santa Barbara, and Ventura counties, and it's the largest moving company between Los Angeles and San Francisco. But *best* is far more important to the Steeds than *biggest*. While they easily might have pursued franchising or expansion to other areas, the brothers have resisted that temptation. "We've always been concerned with quality, and we've been very conservative," says Aaron Steed "Once quality goes down, we can't demand the same rates, and the whole business model is screwed." Not to mention Meathead Movers' brand identity. More than one company's brand franchise has been eroded by fast and imprudent expansion tactics, typically employed in pursuit of short-term gains rather than long-term sustainability. The Steeds have decided that their brand is too important to risk the commoditization that so often comes with fast growth.

Repositioning a Brand in a Tough Economy

When Ashley Robinson, age 28, bought San Diego–based JW Tumbles in June 2007, the company was suffering from exactly the kinds of growing pains that the Steed brothers have sought to avoid. Still, she knew that there was a solid and growing market for the company, a franchisor of gyms for children. The U.S. Census Bureau estimates that there are approximately 40 million children under the age of 10, and an alarming number of them are in danger of developing obesity-related illnesses such as type II diabetes. According to the Centers for Disease Control and Prevention, in the past three decades, obesity rates have more than doubled in children aged two to five and tripled in those aged six to 11. A company focused on health and fitness for young children seemed like a worthwhile investment.

Robinson first started working for the previous owners of JW Tumbles, Jeff and Melissa Woods, as a part-time accountant in 2003, when the company was still just a regional chain with six gyms. She took on more responsibility, helping Tumbles launch 17 new franchise locations. When the couple decided to sell the company, Robinson, who had grown up with an entrepreneurial father, decided she was game for the challenge of running a company. She believed in the brand, even though the company was bleeding cash and was suffering from severe growing pains. She found investors, including one of the company's franchisees, put in a chunk of her own money, and bought JW Tumbles in June 2007.

"The franchise was in bad shape," she recalls. "So it was a turnaround situation." Early on in her new role as CEO, she saw more problems on the horizon. Home values in southern California were already beginning to drop—a harbinger of the tough times to come. "I knew we had to make sure that we weren't just branding ourselves as touchy feely and fun, but something that's a necessity in the minds of parents," she says. "We needed to become more of a lifestyle resource." She subtly changed the company's logo tagline from "A Children's Gym" to "A Learning Playground," which, she says, "gives us a bigger umbrella for our brand." She also contracted with a local company to develop toddler art classes for her franchisees. Her goal: to create an essential community resource and gathering place for her customers.

The most important part of Robinson's rebranding strategy involved aligning the company with other complementary brands that would help her to expand JW Tumbles' offerings to kids and parents and thus increase its value proposition. So, yes, she's also an "Extreme Collaborator." She invited public health specialists from the San Diego State Nutrition Program to come to the gym for Q&A sessions with parents, and she joined forces with the Juvenile Diabetes Research Foundation (JDRF), agreeing to host the organization's annual 5K walk/run and also to sponsor family fun days for kids with diabetes and their families. The JDRF partnership and other local charity events cost the company $25,000 to $50,000 a year just for San Diego activities, but Robinson thinks it's money well spent because it helps to establish the company as a community business. A strategic partnership with Baby Boot Camp, which offers a stroller fitness program, is also under way. The companies will coordinate their fitness classes at JW Tumbles' facilities so that moms can do a stroller workout with their babies while older children take their own classes.

Robinson's rebranding has been successful, but not without casualties. Between November 2007 and December 2008, she closed down eight franchisees that were not performing well. The good news: She opened another 13, and among them were five current owners who were expanding to second, third, or fourth locations. Ironically, the lousy economy gets part of the credit: Commercial lease rates were a bargain, allowing for expansion without a punishing drain on cash flow. The company now has 36 franchisees in 12 states, plus four in Singapore, two in Hong Kong, and two in Mexico. A 50-unit franchise in China is in the works. Systemwide, the company racked up $12 to $13 million in 2008, with JW Tumbles corporate on track for $1.9 million in revenue, up from $1.2 million in 2007.

JW Tumbles' brand expansion has had some unexpected consequences for Robinson. Last September, she was searching for a strategic partner to offer music classes to franchisees and found Manhattan-based Kidville. A month into discussions with CEO Andrew Stenzler, also the founder of Cosi, it became clear to both parties that a merger was an attractive option. Kidville, a public company that posted revenues of $8.3 million for the first nine months of 2008, acquired JW Tumbles for $500,000 in cash and 2.5 million shares. "It's a great deal for both companies," says Robinson, who is now head of Kidville's franchise division. "And it's validation of how we were able to turn the company around. Tumbles has a lot of brand equity."

> "I knew we had to make sure that we weren't just branding ourselves as touchy feely and fun, but something that's a necessity in the minds of parents."
>
> —Ashley Robinson, JW Tumbles

Guerrilla Branding

Ashley Robinson built up her brand equity by using strategic partnerships to create more value for her customers. She knows that customers can be fickle, particularly in a flagging economy, when every product or service that isn't viewed as essential is in danger of being cut from the family budget. And so she came up with some creative ways to build brand loyalty.

Shazi Visram, age 32, and Jessica Rolph, age 34, the founder and founding partner of Brooklyn-based Happy Baby Food, did the same thing with their frozen organic baby food company. This meant not only creating a new product that was fundamentally different from competitors but also using customer evangelists to spread the word about it. In the burgeoning but highly competitive $20 billion organic food and beverage industry, fast and effective branding is crucial for two reasons: Copycats will highjack your idea in a heartbeat, and stores often will test new products readily and then private-label their own similar products if the sell-through is good. If you haven't established brand loyalty, consumers may drift toward cheaper private-label alternatives.

Happy Baby Food, now a $2.1 million company, manufactures organic frozen baby food that's now distributed in 4,500 stores nationwide after just three years in business. A serial entrepreneur, Visram founded the company after a friend complained that she desperately wanted to make her own baby food but was too pressed for time. Visram had been raised on her mother's homemade baby food and felt strongly that there should be an alternative to jarred baby foods that typically have a supermarket shelf life of three years. With her business partner, Jessica Rolph, a former account manager at SPINS, an information provider on the natural products industry, Visram developed a line of fresh-frozen organic foods that maintain the color and flavor of "real" foods: Yes Peas and Thank You Carrots are flavored with mint, and Indian-inspired Baby Dahl is made with organic red lentils, potatoes, coriander, and cinnamon—a nod to Visram's own childhood menu.

The two raised money in the six-figures range from a variety of angels who invested anywhere from $2,500 to $450,000; they included Honest Tea founder Seth Goldman and Bear Naked Granola cofounder Kelly Flatley, who both sit on the Happy Baby Food board of directors. Visram and Rolph launched their product on Mother's Day 2006, with local distribution through Fresh Direct, a New York City–based grocery delivery service, Gourmet Garage, and a select few Whole Foods stores. They expected to take things slowly, but the products were so well received that within a year the company went from making the food in 40-pound kettles to producing 4,000-pound batches using a contract manufacturer in the Midwest. Soon, the company's products were in 1,400 stores nationwide. When the company came out with a dry cereal in 2007, the number spiked to 3,500 stores.

As it turned out, they were riding the wave of two huge trends. According to The Nielsen Company, a global information and media company, organic baby food sales increased 16.9 percent to $109.4 million in 2006, compared with a 2.1 percent increase for all baby food that year. The trend continued over the next two years, with organic baby food sales hitting $172.7 million in

2008. Between 2005 and 2008, says Nielsen, sales for organic baby food increased by 84.7 percent, compared with just 6.9 percent growth for all baby food during that period. This was due in part to increased awareness of and interest in organics, of course, but there was something else going on as well: There were simply more babies to feed. The National Center for Health Statistics reports that in 2006 U.S. fertility rates hit their highest level—2,101 births per 1,000 women—since 1971.

> **"We actually give out our recipes. It's part of our brand authenticity."**
>
> **—Shazi Visram, Happy Baby Food**

While there certainly were a number of baby food choices available to those new moms, there wasn't anything quite like Happy Baby Food. And for retailers, the product was a welcome change from jarred baby food, which yields such low margins that it's typically a loss leader on the shelves. So Happy Baby Food not only gave them an innovative, new product to offer consumers, but it also gave them much more attractive margins. "We really pioneered the category of organic frozen baby food," says Visram. That turned out to be a challenge as well because moms were not accustomed to shopping for baby food in the freezer aisle. But Visram and Rolph had a secret weapon—one that worked particularly well with the GenY demographic.

To educate consumers about their product, Visram and Rolph hired a handful of "community marketing specialists" to do in-store demonstrations. They were all new moms who were looking for alternatives to reentering the workforce full time, and they became an important part of the company's viral marketing strategy—GenY moms talking to their peers about a product they truly believed in. They also went to pediatricians' offices and to Mommy and Me classes and handed out coupons for Happy Baby Food: they gave talks about the health benefits of organics; and they even taught other moms how to make their own baby food. "We actually give out our recipes," says Visram. "It's part of our brand authenticity. Plus we want people to spend time making their own food so that they can appreciate the process."

When I last spoke to Visram, the company had 45 community marketing specialists nationwide who were helping the company roll out another new product—an organic snack puff for toddlers that has been a "runaway hit," according to Visram, who predicts 2009 revenues of $5.5 million. "The marketing specialists bring their kids to the stores, and they really get behind the brand," she says. That peer-to-peer marketing is especially effective with GenY because while health concerns may bring them to organics initially, it's the story of the brand and the trust that's created through personal connections that will earn their loyalty as customers.

Using Your Story to Generate Brand Buzz

No one knows the power of a brand story better than "The Granola Guys," aka Jason Wright, age 30, and Jason Osborn, age 31. They started the Manhattan-based Feed Granola Company back in 2003, when they were both modeling for Wilhelmina Models. Osborn, who liked to cook, starting making his own granola to satisfy his craving for a natural snack, tweaking a recipe he found online to make it healthier and tastier—*and* organic. Friends declared it good enough to sell, and soon the roommates, who were then living in Manhattan's West Village, were selling the granola to local restaurants. It was a classic case of a kitchen experiment turned commercial venture.

But the story behind the product was anything but classic. Here were two strikingly handsome young men who lived double lives: glamorous international fashion models who also donned hair nets and plastic gloves to bake and bag trays of granola in their sixth-floor walkup apartment. Soon enough, they were "The Granola Guys," an Upstart company unintimidated by their high-profile progenitor, Bear Naked Granola. Bear Naked, acquired by Kellogg in 2007, had a good story and great distribution, but it wasn't organic. Besides, it wasn't run by two men who seemed willing to give up the high life to stay home and bake.

As demand for their product grew, Osborn and Wright moved from one commercial kitchen to the next, seeking out bigger and more professional manufacturing partners. A $75,000 loan from the Small Business Administration (SBA) helped, as did advice from the Service Corps of Retired Executives (SCORE), a nonprofit small-business counseling organization that works with the SBA. By October 2006, Osborn and Wright had incorporated their business, had put modeling on the back burner, and were ready for a bigger playing field.

So they headed to the Natural Expo East Trade Show in Baltimore, where they introduced Feed Granola to the growing but highly competitive natural-products industry. Osborn admits that they were babes in the woods. "We were just there to learn," he says. "We didn't know about brokers and distributors, but we had this incredible response." The product, combined with the cofounders' story, made a huge splash, and the company received a best packaging nomination and was featured in the show's "New Product Showcase"—an enviable accomplishment for a newbie. A broker they met at the show was intrigued enough to arrange a meeting with Whole Foods, and says Osborn, "We were cleared for the Northeast region right there on the spot." After a highly successful launch in a new Whole Foods store in the East Village, Feed Granola was in every Whole Foods store in the Northeast. That meant ramping up production from 1,500 pounds to 24,000 pounds a month—a potential nightmare that they managed to pull off.

The combination of a high-quality organic product and an irresistible story made Wright and Osborn media darlings. Donny Deutch featured them on his CNBC show *The Big Idea* in September 2007; he then did a much bigger story on them in October 2008 for a new show called *The Entrepreneurs*. Rachel Ray declared Feed Granola a favorite snack, and *Men's Fitness* magazine named Wright and Osborn among their "25 Fittest Guys in America." Feed Granola even had a cameo appearance in the Tina Fey movie *Baby Mama*.

Small wonder, then, that the company posted revenues of $1.8 million in 2008 and had nailed down nationwide distribution not only in Whole Foods but also in Publix, ShopRite, The Fresh Market, and Vitamin Cottage. "I think Feed has been lucky," says Osborn. "We got into the market a little bit earlier than our competitors, and we've been fortunate with the press. That helps us stand out." But Osborn knows that what's important now is having "our feet on the floor in the store." Like Shazi Visram and

> "It's a really important factor of the brand. You have to be there to interact with the customers, giving out the product, shaking their hands, and educating them on the benefits of the product."
>
> —Jason Osborn,
> Feed Granola

Jessica Rolph of Happy Baby Food, Osborn and Wright spend a lot of time in grocery stores. Wright is still on the East Coast, in Hoboken, NJ, but Osborn has moved to Santa Monica, CA, and Brent Church, a third partner brought on to manage sales and operations, is in Chicago. Along with up to 10 part-time employees, they manage to visit most of Feed Granola's major national accounts on a regular basis. "It's a really important factor of the brand," says Osborn. "You have to be there to interact with the customers, giving out the product, shaking their hands, and educating them on the benefits of the product." The brand message is pretty clear: We're healthy, we're young, and there's a great story behind our brand.

Expanding the Brand

Once your brand has gained acceptance in the marketplace, it's time to start thinking about spreading your wings. Upstarts such as Ashley Robinson and the cofounders of College Hunks did this through franchising; Happy Baby Food added products to its line; the guys at *Mental Floss*, the trivia magazine and website, added games, books, and T-shirts to their offerings; and Kenny Lao, age 32, just assumed that he'd one day have a small empire of dumpling restaurants.

There are probably as many Asian restaurants in New York City as there are tourists in Times Square, but that didn't bother Lao, who "had these childhood memories of wrapping dumplings all night long and then frying them with my mother." After a short career in finance in Boston, he hightailed it to New York, where he finagled his way into a job with Myriad Restaurant Group, which owns two of Manhattan's trendiest restaurants, Nobu and Tribeca Grill. He bused tables and took reservations at the former and checked coats at the latter until finally working his way into a job that involved opening new restaurants for the company's consulting division.

In 2002, Lao decided to get his MBA at New York University's Stern School of Business but says, "I just had this idea burning in my head. I wanted to do dumplings." He mulled over the idea of starting a restaurant, even tapping the expertise of Stern alumnus Andrew Stenzler, the founder of the popular eatery, Cosi. He made his move in the spring of 2004 when he and classmate David Weber wrote a business plan for Rickshaw Dumpling Bar for a class assignment and then submitted it to Stern's

Maximum Exposure Business Plan Competition. The concept: a fast, casual, sit-down Asian restaurant that would specialize in dumplings and get them to you as quickly as your morning latte. Average tab: $9. Weber had a consulting background, and Lao knew the restaurant business and had rubbed elbows with plenty of high-profile chefs. Among them was Anita Lo, the proprietor of the popular restaurant, Annisa, who had once schooled celebrity chef Mario Batali on *Iron Chef*. She became an investor and a partner; she doesn't cook, but her input on recipes and menu development, along with her keen eye for detail, gave the restaurant the cachet it needed.

It was a perfect Manhattan brand: It was ethnic, it had star power, and it had Lao's youthful, enthusiastic, somewhat in-your-face personality behind it. The judges of the business-plan competition thought so too, and the partners walked away with first prize and a fistful of cash. The restaurant opened in February 2005, and says Lao, "We were cash-positive in four to five months, and we broke even the first year."

Lao and his partners opened up a second restaurant near NYU in Greenwich Village and originally had plans for another one in 2008. A third Manhattan restaurant right in midtown was in their sights, but the flagging economy and exorbitant rents triggered a little reconceiving. At $300 to $400 per square foot annually, it would have cost Rickshaw $300,000 to $400,000 to rent an adequate space. So Lao's partner, David Weber, came up with an ingenious solution. Instead of a third restaurant, they would sell dumplings out of a truck, which they'd park at different Manhattan locations each day of the week. So they bought an old postal truck, painted it red, retrofitted it with a mobile kitchen, decorated it with funky, retro-looking art, and hit the streets in late September 2008. Total cost: $60,000. On a particularly tense day on Wall Street, the truck's chalkboard menu declared, "Don't Jump, Eat Dumplings."

Those high Manhattan rents may turn out to be a blessing in disguise. In a recession, having another expensive lease to finance might have been disastrous for the company. And the truck, originally a money-saving way to expand, is now spreading awareness of the Rickshaw brand all around Manhattan. It's not just a dumpling truck; it's mobile advertising. Hungry Manhattanites can find out where the "Dumpling Truck" is by visiting Rickshaw's website or by following "RickshawTruck" on Twitter. Another unexpected benefit: The truck gives Lao, who typically operates it for at least one shift a week, a chance to experiment with exactly how small he can make the operation in terms of menu offerings and kitchen space. "It's taught me from a resource and equipment perspective how to make things more efficient for the new stores," he says. With Manhattan rents now falling, a new midtown location is on the table again.

 ## Your Brand and the Company It Keeps

Your brand will be judged by the company it keeps. When Happy Baby Food and Feed Granola landed distribution at Whole Foods, that sent a message to consumers that their products had passed a high bar for quality. And Anita Lo's investment in Kenny Lao's Rickshaw Dumpling Bar drew diners who knew and trusted the celebrity chef's impeccable standards.. Likewise, if you own a sports-related media company that targets 12- to 24-year-old men, then LeBron James, Terrell Owens, and Reggie Bush are pretty good friends to have. If those superstar athletes can help you to assemble an eager community of young men, then you'll also find yourself with some new best friends: big companies like Nike, Gatorade, and Under Armour that rely on that ever-growing, brand-conscious demographic for steady sales. Chad Zimmerman, age 27, and Nick Palazzo, age 28, former college athletes at Carnegie Mellon and Harvard, have done exactly that with Stack Media, a $3 to $5 million company that launched a magazine called *Stack* along with a website for student athletes that focuses on athletic training and performance.

The high school friends, who grew up in Cleveland, founded Stack in 2004 after winning two business-plan competitions—one at Harvard and another at Cleveland's Council of Smaller Enterprises (COSE). The latter awarded them $15,000, which allowed them to create a prototype magazine for high school athletes. They reached out to trainers and nutritionists of professional athletes for content and found that these unsung heroes were more than willing to pass on their wisdom to young athletes. The prototype's cover story was on LeBron James and his trainer, and while the bulk of the content came from the latter, James, who had recently been drafted by the Cleveland Cavaliers, also agreed to give the local founders some original quotes for their new magazine. "It's a passion point for athletes to talk about training and fitness," says Zimmerman. "Most media just want to talk about how many points they scored, or they look for scandals."

Nike, Reebok, and Rawlings, all eager to reach a targeted demographic of young men who typically outgrow their gear every few months, were featured advertisers in the prototype issue. And that gave the company additional credibility with the people who would be instrumental in helping it grow a circulation base: high school athletic directors. Just as Bryan Sims at Brass Media tapped financial companies to help him target a large audience of young people hungry for money advice, Palazzo and Zimmerman reasoned that marketing to students through athletic directors would give them a way to reach hundreds of readers at a time. "We bought a database of school athletic directors, and we sent out 6,000 prototypes with a cover letter," says Zimmerman. "And we had such phenomenal success that we had to turn off the marketing efforts." Within three weeks, 3,200 athletic directors had signed up to receive the magazine, which was distributed for free; at an average of 100 copies per school, that gave Stack a controlled circulation of 300,000 by the end of 2004.

Current events gave the company a big boost as well. Steroid use among professional athletes seemed to be in the press on a daily basis as one iconic sports superstar after another was tarnished by reports of drug use. In October 2004, President Bush signed into law the Anabolic Steroid Control Act of 2004, which added 26 compounds to the existing list of steroids that are classified as controlled substances. Shortly thereafter, Jose Canseco's book, *Juiced: Wild Times, Rampant 'Roids, Smash Hits and How Baseball Got Big* (William Morrow, 2005), hit the stands and was all over the news. "We were very antisteroid," says Zimmerman, "and it helped us to get into schools because we were helping to educate athletes on supplements and what not to take."

The magazine was a Brand Builder that helped the company develop a loyal readership base and a solid stable of advertisers, but, says Zimmerman, "it's by no means the crown jewel of what we are." That would be Stack Media's website, which is loaded with training, nutrition, and recruitment content delivered on the "StackTV" platform, which has more than 20 channels with thousands of originally produced videos. They might include, for instance, Phoenix Suns' trainer Erik Phillips coaching point guard Steve Nash on an overhead medicine ball throw, Joe Thomas of the Cleveland Browns demonstrating agility drills, or a sports medicine doctor explaining the symptoms of postconcussion syndrome. "We've never paid a dollar to work with any athlete, and we've got some of the biggest names in sports," says Zimmerman. "They know we're not asking them curve-ball, 'gotcha' questions, so now their public relations firms come to us."

On the strength of its content and its growing audience, Stack Media was able to negotiate distributed media deals in 2008 with a number of online retailers, including Footlocker.com, EastBay.com, iHigh.com, and Varsity.com, as well as a recruiting site called BeRecruited.com. Stack Media distributes its branded content to those sites, sells advertising for the sites, and takes a cut of the revenues. Those partnerships boosted Stack Media's Web traffic to 4.9 million unique visitors in December 2008, which made it the ninth most popular Web-based sports network according to comScore Media Metrix, which measures Web traffic. While the magazine, which now has a circulation of 800,000, in 9,000 high schools, still reaches its original high school athlete demographic, Stack Media's digital property broadens that reach out to active young males aged 12 to 24 who seek out authentic and authoritative advice from top athletes and trainers.

> "We've never paid a dollar to work with any athlete, and we've got some of the biggest names in sports."
>
> —Chad Zimmerman, Stack Media

Palazzo and Zimmerman have been highly strategic about building Stack Media. They started with the magazine and then expanded their digital property only after they knew they had enough credibility in the marketplace to attract advertisers. As they expanded their demographic reach to slightly older males, they also were able to attract another important strategic partner: the military, which is always on the lookout for creative ways to attract recruits. The U.S. Army is a Stack Media advertiser, but Stack also shot a series of 69 videos at the Army's Fort Benning, GA, training facility. They appear on a custom Army Strong channel on StackTV and include physical training footage as well as information about Army careers. It's essentially a recruiting vehicle for the Army.

Stack Media now has 20 employees, half of whom are in Manhattan with Palazzo, working primarily on ad sales, whereas the others hunker down in Cleveland with Zimmerman and work on content. And there are new projects in the works, such as nationally syndicated reality show featuring top National Football League athletes and a book deal. "We're not just creating a media company," says Zimmerman, "we're creating a brand."

Brand with a Mission

Cause branding is nothing new; companies have been affiliating themselves with nonprofit organizations or worthy community projects for years. It's good for employee morale, casts a socially responsible glow over the company, and with luck, tips the scales when it comes to consumer spending. But there's something fundamentally different about the way in which Upstart CEOs approach this practice. And while I'll talk more about this in Chapter 6, suffice to say here that they are frequently driven to infuse their companies with a greater sense of purpose right out of the gate—before they're profitable or have achieved any notable scale. And some of them build their entire organizations, and hence their brands, around a single passionate cause. Such is the case with Rob Kalin, age 28, the founder of Etsy, an online marketplace where a community of 375,000 independent crafters sell their creations.

On the Etsy website, you can buy anything from homemade laundry soap for extrasensitive skin to a hand-wrought diamond ring and everything in between (including a taxidermy squirrel-foot necklace and earrings to match). Crafters pay the company a 20 cent per item listing fee and 3.5 percent commission on every completed transaction. For Rob Kalin, though, the business is not so much about the stuff sold as the impact of the sale. "This is a way for hundreds of thousands of small businesses to thrive without having to funnel into larger businesses," says Kalin. Each seller has his or her own Etsy store within the site, and all members pledge that they'll post only goods that are handmade, altered by hand in some significant way, or vintage. Reselling is not allowed.

Approximately 15,000 of Etsy's sellers have sold over 100 items on the site, and more than 550 people have made over $30,000, says Kalin. The Etsy brand is about the Etsy community, and to illustrate what this means, Kalin often refers to the classic children's book *Swimmy*, by Leo Lionni. Swimmy is a small fish who rallies his tiny pals to swim together in the shape of a large fish, and their collective might allows them to survive without fear in an ocean filled with large and threatening predators. Swimmy is the eye, and, said Kalin in a blog post last year, "We want Etsy to be the eye. We do not want Etsy itself to be the big tuna. Those tuna are the big companies that all of us small businesses are teaming up against. Those big companies are holdovers from the days before the Web existed."

The "teaming up" involves more than just providing an online space for craftspeople to sell their goods. On the Etsy website, there are forums where members can talk to one another about their crafts or how to charge out of state sales tax. They also can form Etsy "street teams," organizing themselves according to geographic location or craft medium to extend their virtual relationships to the real world so that they can network, support, and help to market one another's products. Those teams provide Etsy with some viral buzz, important to Kalin because he does no traditional advertising. There are also virtual labs—online training classes that teach viewers how to, say, make their own natural dyes or fuse together plastic bags for craft projects. The company also partners with its Brooklyn neighbor, 3rd Ward, to offer craft education programs, hosts "Craft Night" every Monday from 4 to 8 p.m., and allows the Church of the Craft, a national organization that supports and encourages information sharing among crafters, to hold its "service" on the first Sunday of every month at Etsy. All this builds community in a way that other online marketplaces, such as eBay and Craigslist, for example, do not. And it keeps the company intimately connected to the human hands that have made Etsy so successful and so popular.

> **"I see the company itself as a handmade project."**
>
> **— Rob Kalin, Etsy**

So is this a brand or a cult? It's a little of each, actually, and Kalin is its outspoken and slightly quirky public face/evangelist. Over the past several years, there's a been a resurgence of interest in handmade goods, driven largely by younger people who are more likely to create, say, Steampunk jewelry and Möbius scarves than quilted oven mitts and macramé plant hangers. Kalin counts himself among them. He's an amateur carpenter, and, he says, "I'm making my own wardrobe, so I'm learning how to sew. And I made my own stereo. I have to make something physical at least once a month or I go crazy. But most of all, I'm making Etsy." You can read more about how Kalin is doing that in Chapter 8.

Upstarts Playlist

Track 5: Make Branding a Group Project

1. **Give your high-tech brand a high-touch element.** Because trust is so important in the child-care industry, Genevieve Thiers knew that a faceless online service would not fly. So she established herself as a highly visible and entertaining expert—a GenY Mary Poppins—to give the company a personal vibe. She also holds "speed sitting" events to give the company a physical presence in new markets. Likewise, Etsy's Rob Kalin offers up space in the company's Brooklyn location for independent craftspeople to meet one another, learn new skills, and connect personally with the company that helps them to sell and market their goods online.

2. **Use your customers to spread brand awareness.** Happy Baby Food employs 45 part-time community marketing specialists nationwide to help spread the word about the company's frozen organic baby food. All are moms who buy and feel passionate about the product. They visit pediatricians' offices, give out discount coupons at Mommy and Me classes, and do in-store demos. They even share Happy Baby Food's recipes with customers and show them how to make the food, which CEO Shazi Visram says gives moms an appreciation for how much time and effort goes into creating a great product.

3. **Brand your culture.** Your employees can be your biggest brand asset. Meathead Movers employs clean-cut college athletes, posts a "lineup" of movers on its website, and allows customers to assemble their own moving team. When they're not carrying heavy loads, they jog between house and truck while customers sit in a "VIP chair" and enjoy the show. The company also created a calendar that featured its beefy young movers; all the proceeds went to charity.

4. **Expand your brand creatively.** When times are tough, you can either hunker down and wait for a better time to expand your brand or you can get creative. Kenny Lao and his partners at Rickshaw Dumpling Bar opted for the latter by investing in a roving dumpling

truck rather than a third restaurant. They're not only saving money on rent but they're also literally driving brand awareness in preparation for better times. At JW Tumbles, Ashley Robinson selectively sought out strategic partnerships to help her expand her brand and establish the company as a necessity in the lives of children and parents, and not just an entertaining indulgence.

5. **Make friends selectively.** Your brand will be judged by the company it keeps. Stack Media, which publishes a magazine and has a website for young athletes, built instant credibility by partnering with top athletes and their trainers—people eager for ways to build their own brand franchises on the Web. And when he was first starting Rickshaw Dumpling Bar, Kenny Lao pestered celebrity chef Anita Lo to look at his business plan and convinced her to sign on as a partner. Her high profile and contribution to menu development and recipes were critical to the restaurant's success.

6. **Brand your mission.** Everyone is in business to make money, but if you also have a positive impact on your little corner of the world, so much the better. In fact, having a higher purpose can help to drive growth and profits, as it did for Etsy. Founder Rob Kalin didn't just build an online marketplace for independent crafters to sell their handmade creations; he helps them to build sustainable small businesses by providing workshops and online training. Etsy also helps its members make personal connections with each other for support and advice.

Social
Capitalists

Capitalism and Social Mission
Make a Lovely Couple

elieving that you can and should change the world is a perennial characteristic of youth, but some generations just seem more determined
than others to shake things up. Granted, GenY's social activism bears
little resemblance to the counterculture zeitgeist of their Baby-Boomer parents, but they are still by all accounts a generation that takes social responsibility very seriously and acts on those convictions. In the two years I spent
interviewing young entrepreneurs, I was consistently surprised and
impressed with the way in which so many had woven social missions into the
very fabric of their companies. For instance, Etsy's Rob Kalin (see Chapter
5) wants to help independent crafters create sustainable small businesses,
Tom Szaky of TerraCycle is in business to change the way we all think about
recycling, and Pinnacle Services' Nick Thomley is enabling the mentally
disabled to lead more independent lives. Jake Kloberdanz and his partners
at OneHope donate a hefty 50 percent of profits on wine sales to various
charities. But even when social mission isn't front and center in their business plans, Upstarts frequently find creative ways to integrate good works
into their day-to-day operations.

Ami Kasser, chief innovation officer at the credit-card company Advanta, has made a similar observation about young entrepreneurs. At the end of 2007, Kasser spearheaded the launch of an Advanta website called IdeaBlob that runs a monthly competition in which entrepreneurs can pitch new business ideas to a community of 100,000 people. Each month, the community votes for the most promising ventures, and a lucky winner receives $10,000 in startup funding. It was a way for Advanta, a company with a very traditional small-business customer base (think contractors and small retailers), to reach out to a different demographic. "We used to joke that we weren't Web 2.0, we were Web 2.Joe," says Kasser. While he says that the company had no preconceptions about the types of visitors the website might attract, the IdeaBlob name, the site's design, and its community-based nature seemed custom-made for younger, tech-savvy entrepreneurs. And indeed, that's exactly who showed up. But there were some surprises as well.

One year and 4,000 ideas into the program, Kasser found that fully 35 percent of all ideas could be categorized as social entrepreneurship ventures. Perhaps even more intriguing, 80 percent of all finalists and winners had social entrepreneurship characteristics, indicating that IdeaBlob's larger community had a clear preference for these types of companies. Kasser says that Advanta is currently noodling around ideas to tweak IdeaBlob so that it will address the large number of young, socially minded entrepreneurs on the site.

So what exactly is *social entrepreneurship*? In the strictness sense, a social entrepreneur defines value in terms of the positive impact his or her business has on society or on a particular marginalized or disadvantaged group. Think Muhammad Yunus, the founder of Grameen Bank, who won the 2006 Nobel Peace Prize for his microlending work in the world's poorest countries. The late Paul Newman, who donated all of Newman's Own profits to the camps he founded for chronically and terminally ill children, is another social entrepreneur. By contrast, a business entrepreneur defines value in terms of revenue, profit, new markets, and other standard capitalistic measures of success. It sounds pretty clear-cut, but it's really not. At least not for GenY.

Yes, there are plenty of traditional social entrepreneurs in the larger community of Upstarts; among them are the four mentioned earlier. But more often than not, this segment of the Upstart community is a fascinating hybrid of profit-driven capitalist and values-driven philanthropist. And they don't view those two roles as mutually exclusive. Like the founders at Happy Baby Food, they commit a percentage of sales to a nonprofit that somehow relates to their business; they start their own foundation, the way Billy Downing at ESM did; or they give back to their communities, donating time and company resources to good causes, like Night Agency and DNS. None of this would be unusual for established entrepreneurs, but it's never been all that common among startups, where founders usually are singularly focused on getting their businesses off the ground and turning a profit. The "giving back" typically comes later.

But this is an impatient generation, and its members are eager to make an impact sooner rather than later. According to a 2008 Cone report on the history of cause marketing, 88 percent of Millennials, another name for GenY, would switch from one brand to another if the second brand were associated with a good cause and price and quality were similar. The percentage for all adults was 79 percent. And 51 percent of Millennials had bought a cause-related product in the past year compared with 38 percent of all surveyed adults. Another survey, conducted by Deloitte, revealed that 62 percent of GenY respondents prefer to "work for a company that provides opportunities for me to apply my skills to nonprofit organizations." So is it any wonder that when they start their own companies they bring along that sensibility?

 ## Social Entrepreneur

You might say that social entrepreneurship is in Nick Thomley's DNA. His grandmother, mother, and aunt were all psychologists, and his grandfather worked at the Minnesota Department of Rehabilitation Services and routinely invited needy clients home for dinner. "It was part of our family culture," says 29-year-old Thomley, CEO of Pinnacle Services in Minneapolis. Pinnacle, a $9 million company, provides employment, housing, and in-home services to seniors and people with disabilities in Minnesota. "Having a social mission at the core of the company impacts everything we do," says Thomley.

The seeds for Pinnacle were planted back when Thomley was 16 years old and working part time at a residential facility for people with disabilities.

As a sophomore at Concordia University, St. Paul, he decided that he wanted to open his own group home for the disabled. "I thought it would be manageable, but it's a fairly heavily regulated industry, and at 20 years old, I wasn't aware of the complexities," he recalls. It took all of 2000 for Thomley to navigate the licensing requirements and then to win a county contract for his company. He put the group-home idea on hold and started out by providing in-home services to disabled individuals; he also helped them find jobs and housing. Payment for those services came primarily from Medicaid, so Thomley began to learn how that system worked.

> "Having a social mission at the core of the company impacts everything we do."
>
> — Nick Thomley,
> Pinnacle Services

That served him well, and in late 2000, he responded to a request for proposal (RFP) from Hennepin County for a financial management contract that would set up Pinnacle as an intermediary between Medicaid and individuals, meaning that his company would manage Medicaid dollars on behalf of recipients and make payments for services rendered. "We won the proposal, and we beat out companies that had been around for 30 years," he says. "A lot of older companies are sluggish. The government is looking for more cost-effective ways of serving people, and I can typically figure that out." While other companies were proposing fees that were based on the amount of service provided to consumers, Thomley proposed a flat monthly rate that remained stable regardless of how much or little a consumer used Pinnacle's services. "It wasn't exactly a revolutionary concept, but it differentiated us in a cost-effective way from just about everyone else," he says. Being young and indifferent to the status quo was clearly an advantage, so Thomley is also a "Game Changer."

Thomley continued to differentiate not only through the services that Pinnacle offered but also with the way in which he marketed the company. One of the programs that distinguished Pinnacle was its employment program for the developmentally disabled. Traditional employment opportunities for the disabled often consisted of day programs that gave workers assembly-line-style piecework that paid less than minimum wage. Over time, that evolved into a system of work enclaves, where groups of disabled people might work for a specific business for a few hours with the support of job coaches. But Thomley felt there was a better way.

"When we decided to start our employment program, we rejected the notion that people with disabilities needed to work in a sheltered warehouse or needed to work in groups of other people with disabilities," he says. "We wanted to work with community businesses to create jobs that were competitive. We believe that everyone deserves a right to at least earn the minimum wage and work with coworkers who are not disabled." Pinnacle now helps to provide this type of employment for 30 individuals. The company's big success story is a man with autism who was hired at a grocery store, was promoted, and is now supervising nondisabled coworkers. "This service is better for the person we serve, better for the community, and in most cases cheaper for the government," says Thomley.

At the core of Thomley's mission is the belief that people with disabilities should be supported in a way that gives them as much independence as possible. While Pinnacle now operates five group homes, the company also started an innovative program called "customized living" two years ago in response to the limited number of housing options for people with mental illness. Thomley went out on a limb and purchased an 11-unit apartment building in northeast Minneapolis with the intention of filling it with "people coming out of institutionalized settings and other places, including some who were homeless," he says. "We had no guarantee that we would have consumers move in or that we could make it work. It was really a risk for us." But a year later, the building was filled, and Pinnacle had staffed it with employees who help with laundry, cleaning, meal preparation, medication administration, and a variety of other services. "The government likes it," says Thomley, "because it costs less than a nursing home or residential treatment center." More important for Thomley, it fills a community need for more independent living options for the disabled.

Providing innovative services is one thing, but getting the word out is quite another. Privacy laws prevent Pinnacle from marketing directly to disabled consumers, so instead the company relies on county social workers and nurses to recommend the company to clients. "I like to think no one in our industry outmarkets us," says Thomley. At Minnesota's statewide human services conference, Pinnacle buys a booth and staffs it with employees who don full-body animal costumes and toss out stuffed animals with the company logo on them. "It's like being at a sporting event with a team mascot," says Thomley. "People go crazy for the stuffed animals." At the booth, Pinnacle draws in attendees with "Guitar Hero" competitions; Thomley was considering hiring break dancers this year. "This all probably seems a bit over the top and strange, but it keeps us in the minds of people who make referrals, and it's fun, which makes it memorable."

Pinnacle has been profitable every year and has accumulated an impressive number of accolades. It made the Inc. 5000 list in 2007 and 2008, and Thomley also was named by the *Minneapolis/Saint Paul Business Journal* as "one of the top 40 businesspeople under 40" in 2006; that same year, he also made *Inc.* magazine's "30 Under 30 Coolest Entrepreneurs" list and was on *Winning Workplaces'* "Top Bosses" list. "Starting a business was the best decision I've made in my life," says Thomley. "We make a reasonable profit, and we have a positive impact in the lives of others while doing it."

 ## Cause Branding 2.0

Companies have been affiliating themselves with good cause for years. From the Ronald McDonald House charities, to Susan G. Komen's Race for the Cure, to Product Red, we've become accustomed to companies tugging on our heartstrings in order to make us feel good about doing business with them. According to the Cone study that I mentioned earlier, 85 percent of adults surveyed in 1993 and 2008 said that they had a more positive image of a company that supports a cause they care about. But today, more consumers are letting those perceptions drive their purchasing choices: 38 percent have bought a product associated with a cause in the past 12 months compared with 20 percent in 1993, and 79 percent would switch to a cause-branded product provided quality and price were similar, compared with 66 percent in 1993. Are consumers really more socially conscious today, or do they simply see a pink ribbon as an easy way to cut through all the marketing noise generated by an increasing number of products? Either way, cause branding generates increased revenue.

That's what Jake Kloberdanz, CEO of OneHope Wine (formerly Hope Wine), noticed back in 2005 when he was spending eight hours a day stocking grocery shelves with Gallo wine. "There was a huge increase in cause-related marketing," says Kloberdanz, age 25. "I'd notice that products associated with a cause would get the best displays—end caps or the lobby—and that those products would get huge sell-through," meaning the number of stocked products that were actually sold. Companies usually would run cause-related campaigns for a finite period of time, even though sales spiked significantly when a product was associated with a good cause. "After seeing those results, it just made sense to me to create a brand that donated to charity and helped raise awareness all year round," he says. He continued to mull over the idea, but the final push came in April 2006 when a good friend was diagnosed with Hodgkin's lymphoma at age 23. "The day after she began her treatments, I incorporated Hope Wine," he says. Eventually, he brought on seven young friends who also worked at Gallo as managers and sales executives to help him get the company off the ground.

"We're the perfect balance between hardcore capitalism and democratic socialism," says Kloberdanz about OneHope. Based in Newport Beach, CA, the company sells five varietals of wine and gives away 50 percent of its profits to charity. Each wine is labeled with a circle ribbon and branded with a specific cause, such as breast cancer, autism, AIDS, families of fallen U.S. military personnel, and environmental initiatives. Last year, the company's first full year in business, revenues were $1 million, and OneHope had given away $150,000 in cash and in-kind donations, plus "a ridiculous number of volunteer hours," says Kloberdanz. If you don't think that sounds much like capitalism, think again.

After he incorporated, Kloberdanz continued to work for Gallo as a district manager in Los Angeles while he set up his business. He also nailed down a startup round of capital of just under $2 million from friends, family, and angel investors. He contracted with a wine negotiant—a broker who buys grapes on the open market—and with Sonoma Wine Company's veteran winemaker David Elliott to blend the wine. Kloberdanz knew the wine had to stand on its own to create a loyal following. "People will just cut a check to their favorite charity rather than buy a crappy bottle of wine," he says. The goal: Deliver good wine at a comfortable price point (under $20) that customers might try because of the

> "We're the perfect balance between hardcore capitalism and democratic socialism."
>
> —Jake Kloberdanz,
> OneHope Wine

associated cause but come back to for the quality. The first bottles came out in February of 2007, and by June, Kloberdanz was confident enough to bring on his seven friends from Gallo—four women and three men, all under age 30. While Kloberdanz remains the largest shareholder, all seven have equity in the company.

At the start, distribution was not terribly sophisticated. "It was the eight of us selling out of the trunks of our cars," recalls Kloberdanz. "We'd cold-call grocery stores, wine shops, and anyone who would listen to us." The company also worked with charities, providing wine at events and generating exposure and publicity for the OneHope brand, which was unique in the wine world and just happened to be run by eight young, attractive men and women. They quickly became media darlings. The best part: OneHope's marketing and publicity budget is miniscule; the brand itself generates buzz virally, as do the charities that the company works with.

Kloberdanz and his team choose their not-for-profit partners carefully. The company has a board of advisors who have either started or worked as marketing executives at not-for-profit organizations. Last year, OneHope donated to 20 organizations, including Susan G. Komen for the Cure, AIDS/Lifecycle, Act Today (an autism-related not-for-profit), and Snowball Express, which serves families of fallen soldiers. The company also has served its wine at 200 events, where Kloberdanz estimates he and his partners put in 3,400 volunteer hours; last year, five of them participated in the 550-mile AIDS/Lifecycle ride between Los Angeles and San Francisco, raising $20,000 for the organization. While the company is still in the red and is essentially giving away its profit margin, Kloberdanz predicts that OneHope will be in black in 2009, with $3 to $5 million in revenue. The wine is now sold to over 500 accounts in 10 states and online at the OneHope website, which sold its product to customers in 27 states in the 2008 holiday season. Kloberdanz just hired two top executives from a major spirit company and has signed a distribution deal with Young's Market Company, which he says is "one of the best distributors on the West Coast."

> "When people see OneHope and the circle ribbon, they'll think 'socially conscious and cool.'"
>
> —Jake Kloberdanz, OneHope Wine

Perhaps most significant is the rebranding of Hope Wine into OneHope early in 2009. It's a strategy designed to make the name more distinctive (President Obama had made the word *hope* a bit too ubiquitous!) and to position the company to branch out into other products. "We're trying to become the first cause brand," says Kloberdanz. "When you see Nike, you think 'athletic and cool.' And when people see OneHope and the circle ribbon, they'll think 'socially conscious and cool.'"

Market-Based Mission

Even if their core business is not in the social entrepreneurship space, Upstarts are frequently driven to infuse their companies with a greater sense of purpose right at the start-up stage—before they're profitable or have achieved any notable scale. While the desire to do good may be sincere, there's also an awareness that philanthropy should enhance or at least be consistent with a company's primary business and its brand.

When Shazi Visram and Jessica Rolph launched Happy Baby Food, which makes frozen organic baby food (see Chapter 5), they knew that they wanted to align their company with a nonprofit whose mission was complementary with their product's brand identity. Since they were in the business of feeding babies, they searched online for an organization that was fighting childhood hunger globally. They found Project Peanut Butter (PPB), which is run by Dr. Mark Mahary, a St. Louis pediatrician who developed Plumpy Nut, a peanut-based paste fortified with vitamins and minerals that boasts a 90 percent success rate in treating severely malnourished children. The organization works primarily in Malawi, where 70 percent of all children are malnourished. "There was a particular resonance with PPB because my family is from Tanzania, which borders Malawi," says Visram. "So the idea of giving back to a population so close to home was also very appealing."

The partners decided that for every unit of Happy Baby Food sold, they would donate to PPB the cost of feeding one child in Malawi for one day. "We build the donation to PPB into our model based on unit sales," says Visram. In 2008, the company's first full year in business, Happy Baby Food contributed to feeding roughly 600,000 children for a day—a notable achievement for a company that isn't even profitable yet. But Visram and Rolph wouldn't have it any other way. "Of course, the concept behind the business is to create a strong profitable model," says Visram, "but also to create abundance and give back."

Adelaide Fives, age 29, and her partner, Amy Abrams, age 35, felt that way too when they started In Good Company (IGC), a Manhattan-based shared worked space created specifically for women entrepreneurs. Fives and Abrams were consultants working with women who were making career transitions. They noticed that a common complaint among entrepreneurial women was the isolation that frequently came with starting a business or running an ongoing operation as a soloist. So they decided to address that need in September 2007 by starting In Good Company Workplaces, which offers loft-style office, meeting, and conference space designed specifically for women entrepreneurs. Clients pay a flat annual membership fee of $400 and then rent space on an as-needed basis.

IGC's offices are sleek and fashionable, with exposed-brick walls, gleaming wood floors, a lounge with cushy sofas, fresh flowers, and a rotating gallery of art by female artists. "It's a feminine approach to business," says Fives. "There are other companies that offer shared office space, but what sets us apart is the community aspect." IGC also runs networking programs, seminars, classes, and events where its members brainstorm and collaborate with one another; Fives and Abrams offer consulting for an additional fee. The company's 200+ members include financial advisors, fashion and graphic designers, online retailers, coaches, and consultants.

> "Of course, the concept behind the business is to create a strong, profitable model, but also to create abundance and give back."
>
> —Shazi Visram, Happy Baby Food

Fives and Abrams give back to their community by donating office space to not-for-profit organizations that support the professional development of women and girls. For instance, the company has hosted groups such as GEM Girls, which serves young women who are victims of sexual exploitation and domestic trafficking, and the VIBE Theatre Experience, a performing arts education organization. IGC also has a relationship with Step Up Women's Network, which runs teen empowerment programs for underserved girls and offers women's health education, advocacy, and professional mentorship. Fives is a mentor for the organization, and last January, IGC conducted a class for teen girls on entrepreneurship. The company also has raised funds for Nest, a microcredit organization that serves female artisans in developing countries, and last year, IGC rallied its members to raise more than $500 for the popular microlending organization Kiva. The company's latest initiative, says Fives, is a scholarship fund that would enable low-income female entrepreneurs to join IGC to grow their companies. "It's really important for us to have In Good Company be a vehicle for good," says Fives. "It's our hope that our business helps elevate the status of women entrepreneurs, so we partner with nonprofits that have the same mission."

Volunteering Is a Win-Win Proposition

Having a social or philanthropic mission is more than just an effective way to project your company's value to consumers. It also happens to be great for employee morale and retention. This wasn't what partners Darren Paul, age 31, Evan Vogel, age 30, and Scott Cohn, age 32, had in mind when they started their Manhattan-based interactive advertising agency in 2003, but that's how it turned out.

Giving away their valuable time and expertise wasn't in their original business plan for Night Agency. But that changed when Vogel met activist Leigh Blake, who had just cofounded a nonprofit called Keep a Child Alive (KCA) that supplies antiretroviral drugs and medical support to children and their families with AIDS in Africa. Blake, who also founded Artists Against AIDS Worldwide, had teamed up with performing artist Alicia Keyes in 2003 to start KCA and was just beginning to raise funds and awareness for the organization. "It was just the three of us," recalls Paul, "and we didn't really have a whole lot we could give, but we liked Leigh and wanted to be part of getting her message out to the masses." After many discussions about how much sense it made for a revenue-hungry startup to give away creative services, the partners decided that working with Blake was "the right thing to do." It also was the smart thing to do.

Blake was no ordinary bleeding-heart philanthropist. "KCA is a rock and roll nonprofit," says Paul. "They push the limits." One of the organization's first fund-raising campaign slogans was "Who Wants to Be a Drug Dealer?" which, of course, referred to the antiretroviral drugs that would save lives. Night Agency worked with KCA and the advertising agency Fallon to build a website for the controversial campaign, helped to publicize it, and generated a fair amount of buzz, says Paul. Over the years, he says, the relationship has evolved as the agency has grown. Night Agency is now a $7 million company with 37 full-time employees and paying clients such as Champion, Hanes, Dial Corp., and MTV. Cumulatively, those employees spend approximately 20 hours a week on KCA projects that have included everything from designing invitations for events, building Web pages, and helping to make a fund-raising video for a song by Alicia Keyes and Bono. For the agency, the work is a tremendous morale-builder. "I can't tell you how psyched up our staff gets when they get to sit around with Leigh, and she tells them how she couldn't do this without them," says Paul. "We've got a young staff that feels they can make a difference, and they become really impassioned. People who I've never seen pull all-nighters will pull an all-nighter for KCA."

Two years ago, the partners at Night Agency and some folks at KCA brainstormed about tapping into that youthful enthusiasm in a more systematic way. Blake, after all, certainly had no trouble reaching out to big celebrity donors, but a grass-roots campaign designed for the youth market was altogether different. The result of the brainstorming was KCACollege.com, a Web-based social network with a platform that allows college and high school students to create their own school-based fund-raising chapters. Night Agency built it, recently updated it, and also put up a Facebook fan page for it. There are now over 200 chapters, says Paul, and KCA has begun including the student chapter presidents in its annual "Black Ball" fund-raising event—a pricey, star-studded fund-raiser that Keyes hosts. Last year, Night Agency even got an onstage mention from Keyes.

> "We've got a young staff that feels they can make a difference. . . . People who I've never seen pull all-nighters will pull an all-nighter for KCA."
>
> —Darren Paul,
> Night Agency

Thanks are nice, but so are paying clients, and the agency did get one of those from its relationship with KCA. STA Travel, the largest student travel company in the world, has been a Night Agency client for almost three years, thanks to an introduction by Blake. Paul and his partners don't seem to be keeping score, however. The relationship helps to brand the company to other paying clients, gives employees a morale boost and occasional exposure to celebrities, and validates its founders' original decision to give back before they had much of anything to give.

Get What You Give

Every year, half a dozen employees at Dynamic Network Services (DNS) in Manchester, NH, spend as much as 20 hours a week for 10 weeks with students at nearby Manchester West High School. This may seem excessive, but building robots is time-consuming, and that is exactly what the DNS crew is helping students do. The finished projects are entered into a worldwide robotics competition run by the not-for-profit FIRST, which is also located in Manchester. The high school's team, called the "PowerKnights," is mentored by DNS employees, who are given paid time off from work to participate in the program; the company also started making a $10,000 annual sponsorship grant to the team in September 2007.

It's not all altruistic, though. According to DNS CEO Jeremy Hitchcock, the program benefits the company in two important ways: It's a recruiting venue for interns and future employees, and it gives employees the opportunity to develop additional skills.

"We started out as a minor sponsor of the program in 2005, but this will be our third year of working one on one with students," says Hitchcock. DNS is a provider of domain, zone, and e-mail services with more than $5 million in revenue, and it relies on top-notch engineers to keep its technology ahead of the curve and to expertly serve its 2.5 million clients. There's just one problem. "There's a huge decline in engineering and math enrollment in our schools," says Hitchcock. "We're selfish," he concedes. "We want those kids to go into engineering and come back and work for us. It becomes a natural pipeline." Indeed, the company routinely cherry-picks promising students for internships and/or summer employment, and Hitchcock hopes that some will turn into full-time employees.

But there are other benefits to the company as well. FIRST gives DNS's employee volunteers the opportunity to flex their mental muscles in a scientific discipline that's outside their area of expertise, and that's ultimately good for morale and productivity. But more important, says Hitchcock, the program gives employees in nonmanagerial positions the experience of teaching and mentoring, which helps them to develop the "soft skills" they rarely practice when they're writing code. It also gets employees out into the community and makes the company more visible. That's particularly important for DNS because it's an Internet company that isn't linked in an obvious way to the local economy. "We really wanted to have a connection to the community," says Hitchcock.

For-Profit Meets Not-for-Profit

Billy Downing has two companies: ESM Group runs a youth sports and educational services firm in northern California, and The Edge College and Career Network, cofounded with his former high school guidance counselor, Rick Singer, provides tutoring and college coaching to high school students in 60 U.S. cities as well as Tokyo, London, Hong Kong, and Athens. The businesses, with over $2 million in revenue, are growing, fueled by increased demand for coaching and tutoring services from high school students who are faced with a highly competitive college admissions environment. In 2009, 3.2 million high school seniors graduated—the largest class in our nation's history. Students whose parents can afford pricey tutoring and coaching have an undisputed advantage, and that's how Downing's companies make money. But he wasn't entirely comfortable with that, so to mitigate the inequity, Downing started his own not-for-profit called Education Now to help disadvantaged students afford college. "Anyone can work with rich kids to help them get into college," he says. "But what about the kid in East Palo Alto who's got nothing?"

For the past four years, Downing has put the equivalent of 1 percent of ESM's revenues into Education Now. Those contributions, plus additional money from private individuals and fund-raising events, have allowed the organization to make approximately $100,000 in grants to 12 students every year. This year, Downing decided to ratchet up his involvement with underprivileged high school students by starting a spin-off not-for-profit called the Game Plan Academy (GPA). Its mission is to provide high school athletes in impoverished communities with a combination of free coaching and tutoring—the kinds of services that ESM and The Edge provide to paying clients.

Two NFL veterans, Alex Van Dyke, formerly of the New York Jets and the Philadelphia Eagles, and Gio Carmazzi, who played for the San Francisco 49ers, agreed to coach for GPA, and Downing drew from his network of tutors to find five who were willing to donate their time to the program. Hiram W. Johnson High School in Sacramento donated space for GPA, which gathers 40 students for coaching and tutoring every Sunday for nine weeks. The students are nominated by teachers and guidance counselors.

> "Anyone can work with rich kids . . . , but what about the kid in East Palo Alto who's got nothing?"
>
> —Billy Downing, ESM

Downing estimates that each nine-week session will cost $65,000, and he's confident that he'll be able to support the program through donations. Sacramento Mayor Kevin Johnson's chief fund-raiser has signed on to help Downing fill GPA's coffers. He already has funding commitments from Wells Fargo Bank, Positive Coaching Alliance, and Avanti Solutions. And as of this writing, Mayor Johnson has agreed to speak at GPA's graduation.

 ## Doing Good and Doing Well

Rajiv Kumar, cofounder of Shape Up The Nation (see Chapter 2) cut his entrepreneurial teeth at the not-for-profit he started in 2006 when he was a first-year medical student at Brown University. He used the model for that program, Shape Up Rhode Island, a team-based statewide wellness competition, to launch a for-profit company with partner Brad Weinberg, a fellow Brown medical student. Shape Up The Nation, the for-profit, now manages employee wellness programs for huge clients such as Medtronic and the Cleveland Clinic, but Kumar is still intimately involved in Shape Up Rhode Island.

Kumar and Weinberg developed sophisticated software to manage their corporate wellness programs—software that they now license to Shape Up Rhode Island for free. They also help with organizational efficiency. "We're learning on a national scale," says Kumar, "and we pass that on to the not-for-profit." This means sharing marketing materials that have been highly effective, giving advice on outsourcing administrative functions, and training the staff of Shape Up Rhode Island to use SupportTrio, an e-mail management software, and Salesforce.com to manage sales leads. From a customer perspective, there was a danger that Shape Up The Nation would attract local Rhode Island clients who might otherwise generate revenue for the not-for-profit. So the company donates all income from Rhode Island clients to Shape Up Rhode Island. Last year, this amounted to $20,000; in 2009, it could be as much as $40,000, says Kumar.

> "Our not-for-profit is our way of thinking globally and acting locally. It's fulfilling our desire to bring about change in the world."
>
> — Rajiv Kumar, Shape Up The Nation

The relationship benefits Shape Up The Nation as well. In 2007, the partners coauthored a paper with Dr. Rena Wing, director of the Weight Control and Diabetes Research Center at Brown Medical Center, that analyzed data from Shape Up Rhode Island. The study, which was scheduled to be published in a medical journal this year, showed that the program helped lower body mass index (BMI) for a significant number of participants. "That will help us by documenting the effectiveness of our program," says Kumar. Plus, he says, "Our not-for-profit is our way of thinking globally and acting locally. It's fulfilling our desire to bring about change in the world."

The "Green" (Entrepreneurial) Revolution

Is the green revolution GenY's civil rights movement? Icons of the environmental movement such as Al Gore and Tom Friedman exhort them to don the mantle of "greenest generation"; it's GenY, after all, that will bear the bulk of the burden for cleaning up the mess they inherited from their elders. There's plenty of evidence that they take this responsibility seriously, but their approach to activism is fundamentally different from that of their parents. "There's the old green and the new green," says Rob Reed, the founder of Max Gladwell, a blog and consulting firm that focuses on the convergence of green living and social technologies. "The new green is entrepreneurial and is centered on the idea that we can create businesses around solving the climate crisis; we can approach it from a profit-driven place. The old green is crunchy and NGO (nongovernmental organization) driven, but that's on the wane." While it will surely take both nonprofit organizations *and* entrepreneurial innovation to solve the massive environmental problems that are on the horizon, Reed is spot on in his assessment that GenY embraces the "new green."

If there is a poster boy for the new green, it's Tom Szaky, the 27-year-old founder of TerraCycle, in Trenton, NJ. He leads an impassioned environmental charge at a company that *Inc.* magazine called "The Coolest Little Start-Up in America" in an October 2006 cover story. For his part, Szaky calls TerraCycle "green in the extreme," a claim that rings true because just about everything the company sells is made out of garbage.

By now, TerraCycle's humble roots are the stuff of entrepreneurial lore. Szaky was an undergraduate at Princeton in 2002 when he became intrigued with a homemade fertilizer that a friend had developed to spur the growth of some indoor plants whose buds would be harvested for recreational purposes. Yes, it was exactly what you think. The fertilizer was made with worm castings (aka poop) produced by a colony of red worms that were fed table scraps. The stuff seemed to make the plants and, hence, their owners very happy. So Szaky became intrigued with the idea of developing the fertilizer as a commercial product for home gardeners. He teamed up with a Princeton friend, Jon Beyer, who knew a thing or two about worms because his dad, an ecotoxicologist, had studied them.

The two partners maxed out their credit cards, cleaned out their savings accounts, and borrowed from friends and family to pay a Florida inventor $20,000 to develop a "worm gin" to automate the process of delivering waste to the worms. Princeton agreed to donate garbage from its dining halls. There were fits and starts, and Szaky and Beyer were tempted to throw in the towel. But unexpected support from a local entrepreneur kept them afloat, as did winning half a dozen business-plan competitions in the autumn of 2002. In the spring of 2003, they hit what looked like pay dirt: The

> "There's the old green and the new green. . . . The new green is entrepreneurial and is profit-driven."
>
> — Rob Reed, Max Gladwell

company won the extraordinarily competitive Carrot Capital Business Plan Challenge. The purse: $1 million. There were just a couple of problems:

Carrot Capital wanted Szaky to tone down his passionate environmental message, and the partners made it clear that the handful of dedicated managers that Szaky had hired were not invited to come along for the ride. Szaky said thanks but no thanks and walked away from the million bucks. At the time, there was $500 in TerraCycle's bank account.

In retrospect, poverty was the company's great good fortune. Short on funds, Szaky recruited a small army of students to root through Princeton's recycling bins for used containers in which to package TerraCycle's liquid fertilizer. The process, which actually was illegal in Princeton, led to a revelation: If the company made a practice of using plastic bottles headed for the recycling plant, TerraCycle not only could break new ground with a product that was made completely from garbage but also could save itself a boatload of money on packaging. It was the moment that set the company on its current path and one that led to $1.2 million in financing by angel investors.

Szaky and his team have moved far beyond filching recyclables under the cover of darkness. The company started a "Bottle Brigade" program that paid schools and nonprofits 5 cents for each used bottle that was collected for the company. TerraCycle provided the collection bins and transported the bottles back to its plant in Trenton, where they were filled with what is graphically described as "liquefied worm poop" and dressed with green and yellow shrink-wrap labels. The spray tops came from companies that were discarding them as extras; the shipping boxes were misprinted rejects.

TerraCycle's product and business model, combined with its founders' ecological evangelism, made for a compelling story—one that big retailers like Home Depot thought would resonate with an increasingly eco-conscious consumer base. Indeed, the fertilizer gave Scotts Miracle-Gro a run for its money both online and in the handful of stores in Canada and New Jersey where Home Deport initially stocked it. And that success put the tiny company on the radar screen of an 800-pound gorilla that was highly protective of its turf.

By the spring of 2007, TerraCycle was still relatively small—just $1.5 million in sales—but it was making big waves. Scotts, then a $2.1 billion company, sued TerraCycle, claiming that TerraCycle had copied its label design and had falsely asserted that its organic products were better than the chemical-based fertilizers made by Scotts. Szaky responded in a very GenY manner: He launched a blog called suedbyscotts.com, where he wrote about the suit, sometimes humorously, and solicited financial support to help pay for TerraCycle's legal defense. It was reminiscent of Ben & Jerry's "What's the doughboy afraid of?" grass-roots public relations campaign, launched in 2004 against Pillsbury, when the company reportedly tried to strong-arm a distributor into favoring its Häagen-Dazs brand over Ben & Jerry's. That campaign spurred an avalanche of public support for the scrappy upstart, and the same thing happened for TerraCycle. The blogosphere went crazy for Szaky's posts, and the mainstream media picked up the David-versus-Goliath story, making much of Scotts' 59 percent market share and its apparent fear of a tiny but formidable competitor. While the publicity was great for TerraCycle—Szaky says that sales increased 120 percent during the lawsuit—the company was nonetheless compelled by its burly rival to change its packaging and to back off on the claim that its organic product was better or as good as Scotts' products. But Szaky has no regrets. "I think the lawsuit was a big blessing," he says. "It was one of the biggest boosts we've had."

Since then, the company has moved on, fueled by Szaky's mission-driven zeal to, well, clean up. At last year's Inc. 500 conference, just outside Washington, DC, the perpetually rumpled and somewhat scruffy CEO gave a rapid-fire, impassioned talk on how TerraCycle has transformed its business over the past year by expanding its line of products made largely from waste. "Ninety-nine percent of everything you consume will be garbage in six months," he explained. "America's biggest export is waste." Szaky is doing his best to keep some of it at home by using his bottle-brigade system to collect other kinds of garbage—Capri Sun and Honest Tea juice pouches, Oreo and Chips Ahoy! packages, Clif Bar wrappers, Bear Naked Granola bags—and turning it all into tote bags, umbrellas, shower curtains, and pencil cases, among other products. He's done this by establishing relationships with some of the biggest consumer goods and retail brands in the country—partnerships that helped to boost revenue to over $7 million in 2008 and that also raised $100,000 for not-for-profit organizations. I'll tell you more about TerraCycle's evolution as an "upcycler" in Chapter 8.

Solar Power Hits Its Stride

Aaron Hall, the 29-year-old CEO of Borrego Power Systems, was just a baby when a family friend founded the company in 1980. But it was Hall who led

Borrego, which founder James Rickard concedes was probably 20 years ahead of its time, to new heights. In 2008, the company racked up $60 million in revenue, up from $30 million in 2007 and $11.7 million in 2006. With alternative-energy-friendly President Obama in the White House, Hall thinks that he's poised for ever more dramatic growth.

James and Grace Rickard, who lived in the desert community of Borrego Springs, CA, were making a decent living installing solar thermosystems and off-grid solar electric systems. But when federal tax incentives for solar installation began to dry up in the early 1990s, the company suffered and finally went dormant a couple of years later. It stayed that way until their young friend, Aaron Hall, was assigned by a Northwestern University economics professor to write a business plan as a final project. "My father and I were talking about what I could write the plan on, and that's when the solar idea came up," recalls Hall. It was 2001, and California was in the midst of its now-famous energy crisis, when deregulation led to sky-high electricity prices, frequent blackouts, and widespread public disdain of the electric companies. The state also had initiated a rebate program that reimbursed ratepayers for half the cost of a solar energy installation. So Hall and his dad contacted Rickard and, with his help, came up with a plan to resurrect Borrego.

Hall got an "A" on the paper, and Rickard got a new partner in Borrego when Hall graduated from Northwestern. Hall's parents loaned him $20,000 to buy 50 percent of the company, and he and Rickard got to work on their first project—installing solar panels on Hall's family home in San Diego. An installation for an uncle was next, and then the uncle's coworker signed on for an $80,000 system. It was a good partnership. "Jim taught me physics and contractor law and solar technology," says Hall. "He was my mentor, and the first year, I called him five times a day. And he'd go with me when I pitched clients because I was so young. He'd make them feel comfortable by talking about the 60s; then I'd do the numbers, and we'd close the deal."

The company grew organically, with Hall living at home and frequently answering early-morning calls from customers, dragging himself out of bed, and trudging upstairs to the home office in his boxers. He put the company in the Yellow Pages, spoke at Rotary Club and Kiwanis meetings, and hired his older brother to help him out. A year and a half into the business, Rickard decided to retire and sold his stock to Hall, who, in turn, granted some to his brother and another employee to give his fledgling staff some "skin in the game."

Borrego rode an increasingly powerful wave of interest in alternative-energy solutions, fueled by worries about global warming, energy security, and terrorism. Al Gore brought the climate message to the masses, and California encouraged its residents to take up the cause by passing the 2006 California Solar Initiative, which provides $3.3 billion in financial incentives for residential and commercial solar installations. The goal: solar panels on a million roofs within 10 years.

Between 2003 and 2007, Borrego's revenues surged from $2.3 million to $30.3 million, and Hall expanded the company into San Jose, Berkeley, and Sonoma County. In mid-2007, he also made a bold move and opened an office in Massachusetts, home of solar-friendly Governor Deval Patrick. That spring, Patrick had announced a $150 million expansion of a local solar panel manufacturer called Evergreen Solar—a project made possible with $44 million in state incentives. Evergreen is now Borrego's supplier in the Northeast region, which accounted for a whopping one-quarter of Borrego's revenue last year.

> "For the first time in eight years, we have a pro-alternative energy president. Now we'll have the political support."
>
> —**Aaron Hall,**
> **Borrego Power**

Hall is confident that Borrego will continue to grow. At the end of 2008 he raised $14 million in capital from a large publicly traded foreign investor, and in February of 2009 he sold the residential division of the business to another solar company. "We'll focus all efforts on the commercial and public sectors," he says. "These markets have a lot of potential and will allow us to more easily realize our mission statement to accelerate the adoption of renewable energy. For the first time in eight years, we have a pro-alternative energy president," he added. "Now we'll have the political support."

UPSTARTS PLAYLIST

Track 6: Grow Your Business with a Social Objective

1. **Support causes that are synergistic with your business.**
   When you're thinking of aligning your company with a cause, limit
   your choices to organizations whose missions resonate with your core
   business. For instance, the founders of Happy Baby Food forged a
   relationship with Project Peanut Butter, which feeds children in
   impoverished Malawi. And Meathead Movers (see Chapter 5) partners with local women's shelters to help relocate women in dangerous
   and abusive relationships. In each case, the partnership sends a message to customers, employees, and the community that the company's
   philanthropic efforts are well thought out and authentic.

2. **Involve your customers in your philanthropic efforts.**
   Adelaide Fives and Amy Abrams, cofounders of In Good Company
   (IGC), give their clients the opportunity to contribute to the organizations they support, primarily not-for-profits that fund the professional
   development of women and girls. The company, a membership
   organization that rents shared workspaces to women entrepreneurs,
   involves its clients in a microcredit loan fund, a holiday gift drive for a
   local nonprofit focused on girls, and in various fund-raising initiatives.
   IGC frequently donates work space to not-for-profit organizations
   and helps them to recruit board members among its membership.
   This inclusive approach to philanthropy establishes IGC as a community builder among its clients rather than just a landlord.

3. **Think about a "cause product."** Jake Kloberdanz, founder of
   OneHope Wine, noticed that cause-branded products were given
   premium shelf space in supermarkets and sold like hotcakes. Despite
   their impact, though, most cause campaigns ran for limited periods
   of time. So Kloberdanz decided to create products that were perma-
   nently linked to a cause and make that an integral part of his brand.
   While this strategy isn't viable for every company, consider choosing
   just one product or service and designating it as cause-related on a
   permanent basis.

4. **Pump up employee morale with pro bono work.** Night
   Agency's 37 employees do plenty of interesting work with paying
   clients like Juicy Couture and Nike, who hire the company to create
   interactive advertising campaigns. But CEO Darren Paul says the
   biggest morale booster for his employees is the 20 hours a week they
   collectively devote to pro bono work the agency does for a not-for-
   profit called Keep A Child Alive, which provides antiretroviral drugs
   to children with AIDS in Africa. "Working to help broaden commercial brands is exciting," says Paul, "but when our staff understands
   that their talent can go toward helping save lives, they really become
   impassioned."

5. **Use community work as a recruiting tool.** Dynamic Network
   Services (DNS), which provides domain, zone, and e-mail services to
   2.5 million clients, is heavily involved with its local Manchester, NH,
   high school's participation in an international robotics competition.
   But it isn't all altruism, says CEO Jeremy Hitchcock. Hitchcock
   hopes that his employees, by mentoring students, are sparking student interest in math and engineering—skills that are in decline in
   our country and ones on which DNS relies heavily. The company
   cherry-picks the best students for internships at the company and
   even keeps in touch with them after they head off to college. "Each
   year, there may be a student or two who we could pick up for full-
   time employment," says Hitchcock.

6. **Make sure your "good" products sell themselves.**
   Associating a product with a philanthropic or green mission may
   land it in a shopping cart once, but consumers won't come back for
   more unless the product can stand on its own. Studies show that
   even the most socially conscious buyers won't sacrifice quality and
   fair prices to buy cause-related products. Jake Kloberdanz of
   OneHope Wine partnered with a respected Sonoma winemaker so
   that his wine would appeal to customers' palates as well as their
   sense of social responsibility. Sacrifice quality, and your buyers will
   simply write a check to their favorite charity rather than buy your
   product.

Workplace
Renegades

**Redefining the
World of Work**

The Upstart workplace is a reaction against traditional corporate culture, which members of GenY often find inflexible, joyless, and mindlessly hierarchical. They may have worked briefly in the corporate world and become disillusioned or impatient, or perhaps they eschewed it altogether. Who can blame them? "At Lehman Brothers, I looked around at guys who were in their 40s, and I said, 'I don't want to be those guys,'" Anderson Schoenrock, CEO of ScanDigital (see Chapter 1), told me more than a year ago. "They've worked here all their lives, and they could lose it in a minute." Sadly, they did lose it. Lehman filed for bankruptcy in September 2008, one of the first victims of a massive corporate meltdown that only reinforced how risky it was to hitch your star to a big company.

Statistics from the Small Business Administration (SBA) reveal an increase in business startups during the last two recessions (1990–1992 and 2001–2003), and I believe that our current recession will follow this trend, perhaps even more dramatically. It's a reasonable expectation that the recession will fuel startup activity among GenYers who are unable to find jobs. And I expect this new crop of business owners to create workplaces and company cultures that will look very different from their entrepreneurial predecessors. For clues about how GenY will lead and manage, you need only to look at what's being said about them as employees.

"Generation Y is changing the face of global business, possibly the most dramatic upheaval in business culture since women entered the workplace during World War II," says Randstad USA's 2008 "World of Work" survey conducted with Harris Interactive. "They don't accept all the tried and true principles and practices." So what does GenY expect from employers? According to Randstad, they want training and achievement-based advancement, direct communication and honest feedback, more frequent performance reviews and incentive programs, and a fluid, open work community that values shared knowledge.

> "At Lehman Brothers, I looked around at guys who were in their 40s, and I said, 'I don't want to be those guys.'"
>
> —Anderson Schoenrock, ScanDigital

Author Don Tapscott, who refers to GenY as the "Internet Generation," or "Net Gen," does not think these are unreasonable demands. In fact, in *Grown Up Digital*, he emphatically proposes that "the old HR [human resources] mode—recruit, train, supervise, and retrain—should be shelved. Instead, companies should adopt a new model—initiate, engage, collaborate, evolve. . . . Our research shows that companies that selectively and effectively embrace Net Gen norms perform better than those that don't. In fact, I'm convinced that the Net Gen Culture is the new culture of work."

The long, slow climb up the corporate ladder holds little appeal for Upstarts, so their entrepreneurial pursuits reflect a desire not only to opt out of the mainstream but also to build companies where employee success is achieved through hard work and good ideas, not adherence to a corporate game plan. You may think that this sounds wildly idealistic—maybe even unrealistic—but the classic command-and-control perspective is typically not in the Upstart DNA. And, as it turns out, this can be very good for business. When you're operating in a highly competitive, fast-moving business environment, your company needs to be firing on all cylinders all the time. What better way to ensure that than by establishing a company culture where employees know that good ideas, creativity, and innovation are encouraged, appreciated, and rewarded?

A small segment of corporate America has begun to realize that its employment playbook must be amended to attract and retain GenY. Best Buy, for instance, redesigned its corporate culture to appeal to its predominantly young workforce. In 2006, the company started a program called "Results Oriented Work Environment (ROWE)" at its Richfield, MN, corporate offices. ROWE flies in the face of traditional corporate work environments by evaluating employees on their results, not on face time at the office. As long as deadlines are met and work gets done well, employees are encouraged to work wherever and whenever they choose—a policy that initially irritated older workers as much as it appealed to younger ones. But ROWE was so successful—Best Buy increased productivity by at least 35 percent—that the company has spun off a consulting division, called Culture RX, to market ROWE to Fortune 500 companies. Perhaps best of all, Best Buy now has a solid reputation as a GenY friendly employer.

This is an enviable position to be in, and many companies are pulling out all the stops to play in this league. Consider Deloitte, which has deliberately placed its finger on the GenY pulse. When 80 percent of the 18- to 26-year-olds that the company surveyed described themselves as volunteers, and a staggering 97 percent said that companies should offer employees volunteer opportunities, Deloitte decided to put its research to good use. In 2008, the company worked with United Way to host an "Alternative Spring Break" program for college students to do community-service projects in Katrina-ravaged Hancock County, Mississippi. Eighty students from 35 U.S. colleges and universities—potential Deloitte recruits—worked side by side with company employees not only to do good works but also to "learn more about our people and organization than they ever could otherwise, while allowing us to make a one-on-one connection with many of our future employees," says Deloitte managing partner James Jaeger.

> "Generation Y is changing the face of global business, possibly the most dramatic upheaval in business culture since women entered the workplace during World War II."
>
> —Randstad USA, 2008 "World of Work" survey

And why, exactly, should companies care about the specific needs of this high-maintenance generation? The Bureau of Labor Statistics (BLS) estimates that GenY currently accounts for approximately 25 percent of the workforce. With 10,000 Baby Boomers turning 60 every day, however, GenY will make up a rapidly rising segment of the workforce over the next several years. And the ranks of GenX, with just 45 million people born between 1965 and 1976, some 15 percent of the population, won't be sufficient to fill in for retiring Boomers. Whether or not you believe that these numbers set the stage for a labor shortage, the fact remains that GenY will be an increasingly dominant presence in the workforce. The burden will fall on members of GenY to step into management jobs at younger and more inexperienced ages than their predecessors. Companies will need a new bag of tricks to make sure that the young employees they hire today will be prepared to assume the management and leadership positions of tomorrow.

The cultural and managerial shifts that companies are beginning to make for GenY may look like indulgences but are in fact the underpinnings of a new architecture for the future of work. These workplace transformations are competitive tools that serve companies in good times and bad because they attract, retain, and motivate a growing segment of the workforce. Upstarts know this intuitively. They don't need formal corporate initiatives to attract their peers; they're simply building the kinds of companies they'd want to work for, and they're doing it from the ground up. This allows them to attract the best and the brightest of their generation—people who value monetary compensation but who also place a high premium on training, opportunities for advancement, flexibility, and company cultures that are both fun and meaningful.

> **"I'm convinced that the Net Gen Culture is the new culture of work."**
>
> —Don Tapscott,
> "Grown Up Digital"

 ## Culture Drives Performance

Josh Spear, Aaron Dignan, and Rob Schuham want to know if you "bleed pink." If not, the cofounders of Manhattan-based Undercurrent (see Chapter 4) would really prefer that you look for a job elsewhere. "Pink is our company color," says Dignan, age 29, "and to bleed pink means you're always on, always connected, and you're part of an ecosystem of people who are doing what they were born to be doing." Specifically, that would be creating digital marketing campaigns for major corporations or, as Undercurrent's partners like to call it, "making the Internet a better place."

This starts with making Undercurrent a great place to work. But not for everyone. "We're rewriting the HR rule book," says Dignan. "It's a very unstructured work environment, and everyone makes their own hours. People here have very strong relationships with one another; it's more like a club than a business." And in this respect, it's a lot like many of the other Upstart companies I researched. Undercurrent has a growing staff of 15, and to gain access to this exclusive club, candidates compete with as many as 25 other prospective employees before the partners find one person who "we all would like to spend time with." But make no mistake: With clients like Yahoo!, CNN, Ford, Pepsi, and Mountain Dew, Undercurrent, which has $2 million in revenue and is "highly profitable," is as much of a business as it is a club.

Most of Undercurrent's employees are in their twenties, and Dignan concedes that they do seem to need a lot of encouragement and feedback. So last year the company initiated a quarterly reward system that gives employees three different levels of perks if they land three, six, or nine repeat business deals from existing clients. In the team spirit of the company, individuals don't compete against one another but work together to reach the goals. Three deals earn everyone a Friday afternoon at the movies; if the staff lands six, the reward is free full-body massages for all; and nine earns the team a 15-minute shopping spree at nearby Whole Foods. To keep things interesting, the second- and third-tier awards change every quarter. All of the incentives are "good for the company culture," says Dignan. "People are bonding and having fun." And since the contest rewards repeat business, it also compels every employee to think about boosting revenue by forging deeper relationships with existing clients to discern their needs. It's a goal that makes good bottom line sense as well because repeat business almost always costs a company far less than marketing to new clients.

Also in the vein of frequent feedback, every four months the company runs two-day off-site meetings where everyone discusses business strategy, service, client issues, and lessons learned over the past 120 days. "We might start out in the park under a tree, then go to a coffee house or a partner's house, and then end up at a conference room at a hotel," says Dignan. Staying put in one place would be far too corporate. Besides, "We wouldn't be able to focus," he says. Each day ends with a celebratory dinner. In addition to the meeting, there's also an anonymous survey that asks employees questions about their satisfaction with, say, HR processes, their coworkers, the partners, and so on. "We come away with an incredible amount of insight," says Dignan. For example, one survey revealed that employees were having trouble connecting the dots between their individual job responsibilities and the company's larger objectives. The result was a vision document that spelled it out. "We want to be the company that people think about when they think about reaching consumers with digital marketing," says Dignan. But to get there, everyone will need to "bleed pink."

> **"People here have very strong relationships with one another; it's more like a club than a business."**
>
> —Aaron Dignan,
> Undercurrent

Pure Meritocracy

Upstarts don't put a lot of stock in seniority or longevity. The big question is, "Can you get the job done?" While they may strive to foster corporate cultures that are fun and egalitarian, this doesn't mean that they're pushovers as bosses. This would go double for Tom Szaky, CEO of TerraCycle (see Chapters 6 and 8), which makes organic garden fertilizer and a variety of "upcycled" goods from waste. Perform to his standards, and you'll be running your own show before you know it; disappoint him, and you're likely to be shown the door. If you want a glimpse into TerraCycyle's meritocracy, you just need to have a conversation with Albe Zakes.

Zakes interviewed for a lowly public relations position at the company in September 2006, when he was 21. "I wore a suit and tie and was sweating profusely in TerraCycle's conference room, which had no air conditioning," he recalls. "Tom came in wearing shorts and a T-shirt, and he asked me this question: 'You move into a new market, and you have a negative $10,000 budget. How do you break even?'" It's a question that Szaky asks all potential employees so that he can suss out their critical-thinking ability. Zakes fumbled and left the interview sure that he had blown it, but he later e-mailed Szaky several times with more answers. He was hired.

"Later, Tom told me that he liked the fact that I didn't give up," Zakes says. "I gave half-assed answers, but that was better than no answers at all." There was a precondition to his employment. Since he had never done public relations before, he'd need to work as an unpaid intern for a month so that his performance could be evaluated. Zakes agreed. On his first day, though, Szaky fired the head of public relations, who was in charge of training Zakes, leaving the new intern to sink or swim. He was briefly joined by a young woman who had a year of experience, but, says Zakes, "They let her go after three months for lack of results."

At TerraCycle, public relations is done in-house and it's an immensely important function because Szaky doesn't believe in traditional advertising. He relies exclusively on the press to get the word out about the company's environmental message, its recycling programs, its inner-city employment initiatives, and its increasingly lucrative partnerships with prestigious consumer brands and big-box retailers. But it isn't all about spreading good news. Six months into his tenure, Zakes was charged with handling two major product launches and managing the press when Scotts Miracle-Gro

> "If you stick around this company and work hard, you're going to be promoted very quickly. But we don't want people who just want to punch in and punch out."
>
> —Tom Szaky, TerraCycle

sued TerraCycle for packaging infringement and false advertising. It was a classic David versus Goliath story, and Zakes helped to make sure that the media was all over it. "I got us in the *New York Times*, the *Wall Street Journal*, [and] *BusinessWeek*," he says. "I had to call people that a 22-year-old has no business calling." That summer of 2007, he was named director of public relations; a year later, Szaky rewarded him again by naming him vice president of media relations.

The warm and fuzzies are few and far between, though. "Every day is a challenge, and Tom wants you to be hungry all the time," says Zakes. "I'll walk in and say, 'We got a feature in *Fortune Small Business*,' and he'll say,

'Did we get the cover?'" The payoff for Zakes and his 46 colleagues: stock options for everyone and the promise, says Szaky, that "if you stick around this company and work hard, you're going to be promoted very quickly. But we don't want people who just want to punch in and punch out."

Every Upstart Is an HR Company

But what happens when you're an Upstart with a business that employs people who, for the most part, literally punch in and out? Managing hourly employees has always been tough, and no one knows that better than restaurateurs. "I feel like an HR company that happens to sell dumplings," says Kenny Lao, cofounder of Rickshaw Dumpling Bar (see Chapter 5), which has two fast, casual Asian restaurants in Manhattan. Most of his 60 employees bus tables, serve dumplings, and work the register; Lao knows that these hourly people can make or break him. But he thinks that he knows the secret to retaining them and keeping them engaged.

"We spend a lot of time training," he says. "Everyone is trained on everything from customer service to menu. I want to give every employee the tools they need to feel super-duper comfortable in front of customers so that they can handle anything that comes up." Lao tells his employees that customer trust is vital and that "as soon as a customer sees that you don't know something, they'll distrust everything after that." The knowledge base involves not only being familiar with every ingredient in every dumpling but also being able to answer casually curious questions like "Who designed the restaurant?" (superstar designer Hiromi Tsuruta) or "What are these cool countertops made of?" (a Corian-like solid surface called Avonite). It's the kind of training that sets employees up for success because it helps them to connect more intimately with customers.

After employees are hired, they're briefed on the Rickshaw Dumpling story and the brand identity. They shadow veteran employees, study the menu and ingredients, and take a written six- to eight-page quiz before they're deemed ready to do their jobs. If they can't, for instance, name the spiciest items on the menu, suggest a vegan dish, or describe the Chocolate Shanghai Soup Dumpling adequately, they're shown the door. Those who make the grade are awarded white, gray, or black sweat bands as they become more proficient in their jobs; a raise plus responsibility for training others comes with the color upgrades.

Lao is also paying employees who are native Spanish speakers to participate in an interactive English-language learning program called "Sed de Sebar." Employees listen to tapes on their own time and take a quiz after each of the 10 lessons. Lao pays them $20 for each passed quiz. While it's a

> ## "I feel like an HR company that happens to sell dumplings."
> —**Kenny Lao,**
> **Rickshaw Dumpling Bar**

benefit for employees, Lao is also ensuring that every employee—even the ones who don't yet have direct contact with customers—is able to communicate effectively.

Upstart University

For Talia Mashiach, CEO of Eved Services (see Chapters 1 and 3), the decision to ramp up her company's training program was borne of almost desperate necessity. The rapidly growing company serves Chicago-based hotels by hiring and managing outside vendors for corporate events at the hotels. Mashiach knew that she needed systems in place in order to continue providing her hotels clients with consistently good service. She had labored over training manuals and, over time, realized that it was the best thing she could have done to prepare her company for growth. With multiple new hotels signing on for Eved's services, though, she knew that she needed to do more than just hand employees a book of standardized procedures. So last year she formally launched a new training program called "Eved University," an in-house continuous-learning initiative that Mashiach says helped her grow the company to $9.2 million in revenue in 2008, up 12 percent over 2007. Eved U. also won the company a 2008 "Right Workplace Award" from the Chicagoland Chamber of Commerce.

Corporate universities are nothing new, of course. Disney, Motorola, McDonald's, Pixar, Apple, and a number of other large companies have their own universities, and some of them have been so successful that they market their courses to other companies that are eager to tap into their corporate zeitgeist. But smaller companies are jumping on the bandwagon as well. Take, for example, Zingerman's, the famous Ann Arbor deli that launched an entire community of related businesses, largely by training and empowering its employees. One of its spinoff companies is Zing Train, a training company that teaches other companies how to do business "the Zingerman's way." While Mashiach may follow Zingerman's lead and ultimately market Eved U. externally, for now, she's just happy to be able to educate her own employees in "the Eved way." And this means course requirements not just for new employees, but continuing education for all 30 employees, 75 percent of whom are under age 30.

A new account manager, for example, must earn 25 credits a year and can fulfill that requirement in a variety of ways: He or she might take on-site classes in transportation, decor, and sales in Eved's training room; participate in online classes; visit vendors; go to conferences; or read a business book and write a review. Employees also can earn credit for teaching a course; Mashiach, in fact, teaches a leadership class for employees who are headed for managerial positions in the company. As with a real university, there are always core requirements that must be fulfilled. And after an initial training period, all employees are required to earn 15 credits a year to keep their existing skills sharp and to hone the new ones that Eved's growth requires. Next year, for instance, Mashiach will add a photography course so that her staff can learn how to take pictures of decor for the company's website.

Eved U. is especially appealing to the company's young employees, who crave specific goals and are "used to a lot more interaction and hand holding than older employees," says Mashiach, who at age 32 is the mother of four children under age 11 and thus not unaccustomed to holding hands. The program gets high marks from her employees, who not only appreciate the investment in their training but also recognize that they're developing skills that they can take anywhere.

If it sounds expensive, well, it is. Out-of-pocket costs run $25,000 to $50,000 a year, but add in the cost of taking employees away from revenue-generating jobs, and the tab balloons to around $300,000. Nonetheless, it's worth every penny, and Mashiach can quantify the return on investment (ROI). "We created metrics," she explains. "We measure profit per employee, revenue per employee, customer-service satisfaction, and retention of clients. Customer retention is 99 percent, and the reason for that is consistency, something we know our competition struggles with." Revenue per employee recently went up 67 percent, and profit per employee increased 300 percent, says Mashiach, who attributes those gains to Eved U.

The Virtual Workplace

Upstarts are uniquely suited to working virtually, which gives them a clear advantage when tough economic times dictate that companies cut back on their fixed costs wherever possible. They don't seem to need constant face time with coworkers to get things done. Social networks such as Facebook, MySpace, and Twitter serve as virtual watercoolers; texting and instant messaging are the equivalent of popping your head around the corner.

"Our company is virtual," says DormAid CEO Michael Kopko. "Office space is a tremendous suck of cash." The 24-year-old CEO has just three full-time employees but 34 part-time "presidents" who run their own DormAid student service operations on college campuses. It may sound like an organizational nightmare, but, says Kopko, "We use e-mail, Skype, GChat, Facebook, e-mail photos, conference calls, text messages, wikis, and anything else that tries to simulate being together." Does he worry that employees aren't as productive as they would be under his watchful eye? Sure. But, he notes, "Realistically, it is no different than having people come to an office because if they aren't fundamentally engaged and intellectually involved in their work, they will find other ways to shirk."

While virtual offices often work well for small, cash-strapped startups like DormAid, they also can be a boon for established companies. The cofounders of *Mental Floss* (see Chapter 1), Mangesh Hattikudur and Will Pearson, started their media company eight years ago in Pearson's hometown of Birmingham, AL. After a year and half, though, Hattikudur decided that he wanted to be closer to his friends and family in Manhattan. So was there a parting of the ways? Not at all.

Hattikudur moved six years ago and now manages three employees in Brooklyn, whereas Pearson oversees four in Birmingham. Toby Maloney, who manages marketing, publicity, customer service, and fulfillment, has four employees in Cleveland, and there are two full-time researchers/fact-checkers just outside of Detroit. "If we find talent and they're in another part of the country, they can stay there," says

> "Our company is virtual. Office space is a tremendous suck of cash."
>
> —**Michael Kopko, DormAid**

Pearson. "Our flexibility has been a positive but also a challenge for the company; it's hard to replace face time." While it's rare for the entire staff to get together, Pearson and Hattikudur travel frequently to the various locations, which, Pearson says "function as independent divisions of the company."

Virtual Expansion

The virtual nature of 31-year-old Rachael Krantz Herrscher's company has allowed her to take her Salt Lake City–based venture to a national playing field. Herrscher, a mother of three, came up with the idea for TodaysMama back in 2004, when she and a friend were walking through the mall, each with a double stroller. "We were talking about what to do for fun in the summer with the kids," she says. "There were no books out there in the bookstores, so we decided to write our own." With a $55,000 loan from the SBA, Herrscher and her friend, Stephanie Petersen, produced 20,000 copies of *Utah Mama's Handbook*. The book sold out within the first few months, the partners paid off their loan, and they were pleasantly surprised by requests from moms in other states for similar handbooks.

While there was demand for their product, there also was precious little infrastructure at their company, so the partners decided that the best way to expand was though licensing agreements with people just like them—moms who had ambition and talent but also preferred to work at home. Since then, the company has expanded to 19 markets nationwide and also has forged strategic partnerships with local newspapers and magazines that publish local cobranded *Mama* guides through their targeted publications divisions. So Herrscher is also an "Extreme Collaborator." There's also a TodaysMama website, where users can access general parenting-related content, participate in a Twitter-like micro-blogging forum, and click through to the geography-specific local portals run by licensees. Herrscher, who owns the majority of the company, has eight employees in Salt Lake City, one in Kentucky, another in Montana, and 15 independent contractors in addition to her growing number of licensees. The operation is entirely virtual, with even the Salt Lake City employees working from home. So how does Herrscher make it work?

"We actually have quite a bit of structure since we're virtual," she says. She uses project-management and collaboration software called Basecamp, an "awesome tool" that allows the 42 people involved with her company to communicate with one another, track their progress on projects, and manage editorial content. "When you're in an office, it's easy to poke your head around the door and say, 'What are you doing?' We can't do that, so we go through Basecamp instead," says Herrscher. The program allows her to separate staff communication from interaction with licensees, who also use Basecamp to access templates, art files, and content that they plug into their local websites. And there's also a dedicated Basecamp section for the company's graphic designers and creative staff.

"I encourage a lot of entrepreneurship and ownership in each position, which is part of what makes the tracking and communication so important," Herrscher says. "Ideas and information have to be shared to be implemented, and progress has to be tracked to see the roadmap." To that end, she also asks each of her eight employees to write her own quarterly business plan, typically a two-page document that reviews the previous quarter's projects and sets goals for the coming months. Herrscher then integrates those individual plans into a larger company document and revisits it throughout the year.

To make sure that her licensees are all on the same page, she hosts an annual summit in Salt Lake City, where they meet each other and the TodaysMama staff for both casual face time and formal training. There are classes on public relations, book production, marketing, promotions, and other topics, run by Herrscher's staff as well as some independent contractors who fly in for the meeting.

While TodaysMama is still a relatively small company—revenues for 2008 were just $500,000—Herrscher's systems feel, well, big. There's a reason for that. Like all small companies planning for growth, she needs to have her ducks in a row before she expands. She launched 10 new online markets in the beginning of 2009 and had another 10 scheduled for the year. So it's critically important for her to have her collaboration and communications systems in place, especially since she has no plans for a formal office. "Our long-term goal is to remain a virtual business," she says. "We're moms, and we want to work at home."

Work Hard, Play Hard

Foosball tables, Guitar Hero, and Wii in the break room; dogs wandering around the office; beer and pizza every Friday; refrigerators filled with energy drinks. Well, yes, lots of Upstart companies may look, at first blush, like playgrounds for young, ADD-riddled employees who just can't seem to keep their minds on work for a solid chunk of time. But look again. What's really happening is the convergence of work and life in a 24/7 world where fierce competition and an increasingly global business environment make it difficult to operate within the traditional boundaries of time and space. And that suits GenY just fine.

"For this generation, work and life are no longer two separate things," says Cali Williams Yost, a work/life flexibility expert and CEO of Work+Life Fit. "My experience isn't that they don't want to work hard; it's that they're not linear about work; they see it as much more fluid." Take, for example, Ben Kaufman, CEO of Kluster (see Chapters 1 and 8), whose first company, Mophie, was based in Burlington, VT. Fresh powder on the nearby ski slopes routinely lured more than one employee to take the afternoon off, but that was okay with Kaufman as long as there wasn't deadline-sensitive work to be done. For their part, employees put in plenty of evening and weekend hours to help the company grow. Their mentality was typical of GenY: "If I'm getting the work done well and on time, don't give me a hard time about when I'm doing it."

While older workers may go out of their way to separate work from their personal lives, members of GenY not only don't mind integrating the two, but they also tend to crave the crossover. They want their coworkers—and their bosses—to be their friends. Most Upstart CEOs wouldn't have it any other way. "There's this preconceived notion that when you go from college to work, you have to be a different person," says Joel Erb, the 26-year-old CEO of Richmond, VA–based INM United (see Introduction), a Web design and marketing company. "But then there's an internal struggle." So Erb ties hard to hire employees who will fit into INM's collegial culture by focusing more on personality than on skills when he's interviewing candidates. Skills can be learned, he reasons, but it's important to know that a new employee will be the kind of person who'll go play pool at lunchtime with his or her coworkers at Stool Pigeons, a neighborhood eatery where at least a few of INM's 12 staffers gather every day.

But Erb doesn't rely on impromptu gatherings to keep his staff tight. Every month there's a "family dinner" for everyone; employees take turns hosting. "At my house growing up, we always had people over for dinner; it was a way to break down the stress of what may have happened at work that day," he says. When he's the host, Erb goes all out; he might whip up some fried chicken, macaroni and cheese, and Swedish meatballs because "I want them to see how much I appreciate them, plus it's humbling to cook dinner for the people who work for you." After dinner, people might break up into groups to play Wii or watch a movie.

> "For this generation, work and life are no longer two separate things."
>
> — Cali Williams Yost, Work+Life Fit

So what happens when the company gets too big for such intimate get-togethers? Erb says he'll think of something else—maybe dinner at a restaurant, for instance—but he won't end the tradition. "It's essential that you maintain the aspects of your company that your staff appreciates," he says. "They're your biggest investment, and to eliminate that bonding experience would be like ending family game night because you have too many kids."

Good Vibrations

Of course, the environment in which the work gets done is also important. "Our workspaces have always provided a warm, casual, but fun and modern vibe," says Cyndee Sugra, the 31-year-old CEO of Studio 7 Media, an $8 million Los Angeles–based technology, design, and marketing firm. "This happened naturally because at times we would be required to spend many late nights there. There's a lot of stress, and we have crazy deadlines."

When Sugra first started the company in 2001, she used her industry contacts from former employers such as BMG and DirectTV, plus word-of-mouth buzz, to nail down high-profile clients like Michael Jordan and Hewlett-Packard. She controlled costs by keeping her company virtual, hiring contractors on an as-needed basis and allowing them to work remotely while also maintaining a small office space in the converted warehouse where she lived. "They were designers and programmers, so they already had all the tools and equipment they needed," she says. "They loved this because it provided them freedom with their work schedules." Programmers in particular preferred to work in the wee hours and liked to sleep in. Or designers sometimes would feel stuck and need to revisit their projects in the evening with no distractions. "As long as the work was being done, and done well, it put me at ease to accept and encourage the flexible and creative nature of everyone working from their home," says Sugra. But as the company grew rapidly—to $3.1 million in 2007—Sugra decided that she needed more formal office space. Bigger clients were demanding more face-to-face meetings, plus living and working in the same space was taking a toll on Sugra. "I found myself having to stay in a hotel room on the weekend so that I didn't work the whole time," she says.

So in 2008, she purchased a large commercial warehouse that she converted into office space for her seven full-time employees and the 10 to 15 contractors who come into the office once or twice a week. If you worked at Studio 7, you could ride your bike or skateboard through one of the large garage-door openings right into the huge, open office, gliding on pebbled concrete floors over to your glass desk, lit from underneath for ambiance. Sugra's 160-pound mutt, the office mascot, might lumber over for a pat. You'd work with music streaming in the background, and every few days it would be your turn to choose the tracks. You might take a break to play Foosball or PlayStation 3 or catch part of a movie on the plasma television. If you wanted to hit the beach and then come back to work, you could rinse off under a rain shower and then spend the rest of day working on a large roof deck, where there's also a fire pit.

> "We work hard, and I have always felt the need for a balance of life at work to make us feel that it's not just a job."
>
> —Cyndee Sugra,
> Studio 7 Media

If you're a musician, you'd certainly be tempted to grab one of the 20 or so guitars hanging on the wall and duck into one of the two fully soundproofed studio rooms that are filled with instruments and equipped for recording, mixing, and editing. These particular toys are mostly from Sugra's personal collection. She was a rocker with a record deal at age 16 and is now in a band with her chief technical officer (CTO)/husband, Marlon Mehr. She claims to play a mean Metallica solo.

You might reasonably ask if anyone actually does work at this company. Well, yes, says Sugra. For instance, Studio 7 recently developed proprietary digital copy software and sold it to 20th Century Fox. It allows users to easily copy movies to their PCs or to their portable devices. Fisher Price hired the company to develop Web-based software that enables its customers to customize products, and CNN called on Sugra's team for a quick fix when the company discovered that its video Pipeline service wasn't Vista-compatible. Work like this pushed Studio 7's revenues to $8 million in 2008. In the first quarter of 2009, Sugra started a new division to focus on food-service industry clients. So her employees are likely to be busier than ever. "I've found that all the fun stuff is used during lunch breaks or when we're having a really stressful day and just need a time-out," says Sugra. "I think it just feels good to know that there are outlets in the office, so they're not abused."

Perks Pay Off

When times are good, companies tend to be generous with employee perks, and when cash is tight, everything that's viewed as nonessential is stripped away. Nothing could be worse for morale, which is why it makes sense to make sure that your perks are sustainable in good times and bad. How? Align employee perks with business goals, and view them as investments rather than expenses.

This is Raj Lahoti's thinking. If you do business with his company, OnlineGURU, in San Diego, CA, you may want to schedule a meeting at the company on a Thursday. Chances are that Lahoti, age 27, will treat you to a chair massage from either Manuel or Heidi, the two massage therapists who come to the company every week to work the kinks out of his 20 employees. The company, which grosses just under $10 million in revenue, is a Web publisher that owns the site www.dmv.org, "The Unofficial DMV Guide." It provides information on departments of motor vehicles nationwide to simplify and streamline the often less than pleasant DMV experience. But if dealing with the DMV can be stressful, so can running a company.

"I was getting a full massage every week because I'm on the computer all the time and I have back problems," says Lahoti. "So I figured, maybe all my employees don't have the problems I do yet, but isn't it just a matter of time?" And wouldn't those aching employees ultimately be less productive? So Lahoti took a proactive approach and now has two massage therapists set up their chairs in his office every Thursday. Each employee (and whoever else happens to be in the office) gets a 15-minute massage, which costs Lahoti $20 a pop, or about $1,000 a year per employee. But don't call it a cost. "It's an investment," he says. "Each Thursday, you can see the ease fall over the office. There's such a great vibe."

Another "investment" that Lahoti makes: free lunch (up to $10) at the deli next door for his staff. Sure, it's generous, but there's a bottom-line component to this perk as well. OnlineGURU's office is situated in a building that's somewhat isolated from other dining options, forcing employees to drive to lunch. This often meant more time away from the office and, Lahoti reckons, lots of unhealthy fast food. Since he started the deli perk in the fall of 2008, Lahoti says that employees "now take 40-minute lunches, and they're talking to each other about work when they're eating. They're also creating personal relationships with

> "I'll make more money by taking care of my people. I will have greater employee retention and attract more qualified employees."
>
> —Raj Lahoti, OnlineGURU

their coworkers." The deli owner, who keeps Lahoti's credit card on file, gives him a 10 percent rebate every month if he spends at least $1,800. Based on the success of the program, Lahoti now offers his employees a $5 breakfast perk at the same deli. The catch: It's only available 8:00 to 8:45 a.m. "It's an incentive to get people to come in early, to congregate and do their huddle" before the workday officially starts, says Lahoti. "The investment is low, and the return is high. I'll make more money by taking care of my people."

UPSTARTS PLAYLIST

Track 7: Redefine Work

1. **Scrap the old hierarchy.** While longevity, seniority, and loyalty are still to be commended, performance is what drives business growth and should be the key factor to consider when you're rewarding and promoting employees. At TerraCycle, CEO Tom Szaky makes it very clear that he expects results and that even young, newly hired employees can rise through the ranks quickly if they deliver. And remember that traditional notions of "promotion" are often meaningless to younger employees. It's not necessarily a new title or even a raise that they crave, but the opportunity to take on new responsibilities and see their ideas come to fruition.

2. **Be flexible.** In a competitive 24/7 business environment, it becomes increasingly difficult to compartmentalize our lives. Should we even be trying? Work/life flexibility expert Cali Williams Yost cautions companies against the word *balance* because, she says "work and life are no longer two separate things. It's all part of a whole, and there are many different ways to handle that." You don't have to let your employees go skiing or to the beach in the middle of the day, but you need to be more flexible about how and when work gets done. "Too much rigidity and too much linear thinking don't allow for innovation and creativity around being flexible, and what we're seeing is that everyone wants flexibility," says Yost.

3. **Integrate training and continuous learning into your company.** Even if your company has only a few employees, it makes sense to devise a system of formal training for your staff, whether they're hourly workers or salaried professionals. Formal training sends employees the message that you're invested in their success and also provides you and them with a blueprint for training future employees consistently as you ramp up your operation. Like Talia Mashiach, CEO of Eved Services, you might even consider launching your own corporate university to give all employees a highly transparent roadmap of the skills they'll need in their current jobs, as

well as for future advancement. Remember that younger employees particularly appreciate companies that continuously teach them new skills that are portable.

4. **Give frequent feedback.** Even GenY CEOs concede that their young employees seem to need far more frequent feedback than their older counterparts. Blame it on parental hovering or the video-game culture, but don't ignore this need. A monthly or bimonthly review of goals and progress can keep employees on track and save everyone time and effort in the long run. Consider setting short-term goals and motivating employees to reach them with the promise of a reward for all. This is how Undercurrent encourages employees to rustle up repeat business from existing clients. To keep things interesting, there's a new reward every quarter.

5. **Go virtual.** Most virtual companies seem to evolve that way out of a confluence of necessity and circumstance. A key employee moves, another wants to work at home, or the company expands by partnering with or hiring people in different geographic locations. A virtual office can reduce your fixed costs considerably, not to mention your company's overall carbon footprint. But be careful. Companies with highly successful virtual operations have the technology tools in place to allow their remote employees to communicate and collaborate as if they were poking their heads into one another's offices. Rachael Herrscher, CEO of TodaysMama, uses collaboration software called Basecamp to manage her virtual workforce. Workers also use conference calls, iChat, Facebook, and Twitter to stay in touch. But perhaps most important, Herrscher gets everyone together in person for an annual meeting that includes strategy and training sessions because face time is still invaluable.

6. **Rethink your workspace.** The design of your workspace can have a huge impact on the well-being of your employees and hence their productivity. An open work environment may not be appropriate for every company, but Dilbert-style cubicle farms are deadly. Consider a design that allows for plenty of employee interaction, but take care to provide private spaces as well. Remember that your workspace is a reflection of your company's culture and its brand: Furniture, art,

music, lighting, and the toys around the office all send signals to employees and visiting customers. Cindy Sugra of Studio 7 Media created a soundproof music room at her company using her own collection of instruments and recording equipment—a great creative outlet for both her and her staff. And the environment tells customers like Microsoft that they're dealing with a cool, creative company.

CHAPTER

8

Morph
Masters

Knowing How to Morph,
Scale, and Grow Up

I t's one thing to start a company when you're young and relatively inexperienced. Shepherding and sustaining it over the ever-shifting terrain of
growth is altogether a different kettle of fish. Markets change, cash runs
low, partners disagree, and the skills that were so crucial to those chaotic
and exhilarating startup days become less important than the ability to manage a growing staff and a more complex organization. If running a business
were easy, we'd all be filthy rich because everyone would do it. But it's not
easy, and the statistics on small-business failure bear this out: 66 percent of
businesses survive more than two years, 44 percent are still around after four
years, and only 31 percent make it to their seventh year. And a mere 5 percent of all companies ever grow beyond $1 million in revenue. Growing a
business always has been tougher than starting one. So is this reality any different for Upstarts than it is for their entrepreneurial elders? I think so.

In many ways, young entrepreneurs are ideally positioned for the challenges that come with sustaining and growing a business in an economic
downturn. Many are unburdened by the financial obligations of adulthood,
and some still enjoy a parental safety net; the childhood room or the base-

ment will do in a pinch. At the very least, they're not averse to living on Top Ramen and mac-and-cheese for a while. Unfazed by the rapid pace of change in today's business environment, they typically react quickly to market changes or shifts. Their mastery of new technology makes their companies lean and efficient, and their highly collaborative nature puts abundant resources at their fingertips. They know how to make their companies stand out from the pack, and they understand what it takes to engage and motivate an increasingly younger workforce. In short, a good number of the qualities I've discussed in previous chapters help Upstarts to make the leap to what's commonly known as the "next level."

But this is rarely painless. As Luke Skurman at College Prowler discovered, the partners with whom you launch are not always the ones best suited to help you grow. Ten Minute Media's Brendan Ciecko realized that if he wanted to grow his business, he'd need to diversify, whereas Rachel Hennig of Catalyst Search needed to specialize in order to save her company from bankruptcy. Marcus Adolfsson of Smartphone Experts and Ben Kauffman at Kluster shifted their business models to avoid commoditization, and Tom Szaky expanded his TerraCycle brand in a way that can only be described as brilliant. Rob Kalin at Etsy realized that the only way to create a company that could realize his lofty goals was to bring on heavy-hitting investors. The cofounders of PopCap learned that sometimes the best way to grow is to give up control; Caleb Sima did the same by selling his company, SPI Dynamics, to Hewlett-Packard. Were all of them successful? You decide.

The Right Team

Launching a startup is heady stuff. You partner with your best friend, your roommate, or maybe a coworker who is equally dissatisfied with working for "the man," and together you prepare to set the world on fire. In the beginning, the business is all about getting things done, and it's a 24/7 proposition that allows little time for introspection. But that's okay because you just assume that everyone wants the same thing and that you're in it together as equal partners. Or are you? You heard Casey Golden, now the CEO of Golden Rule Technologies, talk about his nightmare partnership issues in Chapter 1. While flying lattes typically don't play a big role in most partner disputes, things nonetheless can get messy.

Luke Skurman at College Prowler (see Chapter 1) found out the hard way that a partnership can function extremely well at the startup stage and then turn sour as a company matures. Skurman launched College Prowler when he was a sophomore at Carnegie Mellon in 2000. Initially, it was a publisher of student-written college guidebooks but then evolved into a website that offers digitized content to paid subscribers. Skurman signed on two partners and incorporated in 2002. There were three primary shareholders (with Skurman holding the most shares by a minimal amount) plus two original employees and an advisor who also had a small amount of equity.

Things started to fall apart at the end of 2002, when one of the partners decided to move to New York to pursue an MFA. The plan: He'd go to school and work for College Prowler remotely. But the arrangement caused stress and feelings of resentment that the absent partner was not pulling his weight. They parted ways in 2003. Then two of the original employees left in 2006, shortly after Skurman landed a $550,000 round of financing. This time, there was a different conflict.

The company had been operating on a shoestring budget, and while pay was minimal, the collegial spirit ran high. Skurman and his team worked hard during the day and socialized together after hours, frequently making their way from the office to one of the local haunts for dinner and drinks. No one felt like there was a boss. The investment finally allowed Skurman to pay decent salaries and offer health insurance, but it also made him feel that he had a responsibility to "professionalize my leadership" because "I wanted to be looked at in a different light." So he put some distance between himself and his friends, trying to keep up the team spirit in the office but begging off the socializing. "It was hard for them to understand," he says, "and the relationships deteriorated."

> "Starting a company is like a race, and the people you start the race with are not necessarily the people who you finish with. But the CEO's job is to get to the finish line."
>
> —Luke Skurman, College Prowler

Of the original partners, only Skurman remains at the company. And with each departure, equity positions were renegotiated. While Skurman won't share all the details, he says that he also learned something about how to structure partnerships. "If I were to start another venture, I'd require everyone looking for equity to vest in four years," he says.

Skurman says that now he has "the strongest team I've ever had." There's no emotional baggage, and Skurman is clearly the CEO. "One of my professors once told me that starting a company is like a race, and the people you start the race with are not necessarily the people who you finish with," he says. "But the CEO's job is to get to the finish line."

Standing Firm on Shaky Ground

Sometimes the finish line is a moving target. Things may be going along swimmingly, and then, without warning, the ground shifts beneath you. Your competition does an end run, the industry you serve tanks, or your product or service becomes commoditized. It used to be that you could see the big changes coming, but no more. We're all on Internet time now, and your market can change in the time it takes for your Web page to load. If you don't react immediately, you're dead in the water.

Upstarts thrive on change. Part of the excitement of business for them is that it's dynamic and often demands smart improvisation rather than deliberate planning. They are accustomed to receiving and processing information from multiple sources, and they expect communication to be instantaneous and decisive. They tend to launch their businesses quickly and imperfectly, fully expecting to tweak their products and processes to meet their customers' demands. This is a generation that's uniquely suited to doing business in a rapidly changing environment.

Take Marcus Adolfsson (see Chapter 2), whose $14.7 million company, Smartphone Experts, started out in 2002 by developing online community forums for various brands of smartphones, such as the Treo and BlackBerry. Adolfsson made money by selling phones and accessories on the sites. "For the first couple of years, we were the first kids on the block," says Adolfsson. "But the market became commoditized." U.S. carriers started selling more phones on their own websites and expanded their retail presence. At the same time, Adolfsson was being squeezed by high inventory costs, low margins, and a high percentage of customer returns. So he stopped selling phone on the forums in 2004 but began contract manufacturing his own accessories in China and South America to vastly improve his margins.

In 2005, however, the playing field began to change again. There had been tremendous growth in blogs and community sites, and Adolfsson suddenly found himself with some stiff competition in the form of new smartphone sites that seemed to be getting better and better search-engine rankings. He responded in a rather unpredictable way: Rather than try to compete by building new community sites, he decided to partner with the successful ones, offering to create custom e-commerce stores for them. Adolfsson would provide inventory, fulfillment, customer service, and all the back-end support for the e-stores; the host sites simply would sell the products under their own brand and take a generous commission from Smartphone Experts. "Some of those guys were making $30,000 to $50,000 a month from us, and they had no expenses," says Adolfsson. Today, he has 25 such partnerships. If you do a Google search for, say, a Treo case,

> "For the first couple of years, we were the first kids on the block. But the market became commoditized."
>
> —Marcus Adolfsson, Smartphone Experts

chances are that whatever site you click through to, your order ultimately will go to Smartphone Experts. Had Adolfsson taken a typical competitive approach and gone head to head with the popular community sites rather than finding a way to partner with them, it's unlikely he'd be so successful.

The smartphone market is growing, led by BlackBerry and iPhone, and Adolfsson constantly has his finger on the pulse of what's new so that "we can keep jumping into new niches and ride the wave." He spends a lot of time browsing the Web for clues and talking to his 22 employees who monitor the smartphone community blogs and forums. "And every time I speak at schools," he says, "I ask the students what's hot."

Diversifying for Growth

Brendan Ciecko's primary customer base could not be any hotter. The founder of Ten Minute Media (see Chapter 2), a Web design and marketing firm, cut his teeth in an industry that has many young entrepreneurs salivating—the music business. By building websites for Mick Jagger, Katy Perry, Lenny Kravitz, and many other recording artists, he earned a reputation as a boy wonder. So you could probably forgive him for settling into this seductive niche. But that's not how he views the future of his company.

"A lot of these projects are stepping stones to the next stage of my business," says Ciecko, whose company is in Holyoke, MA, close to where he grew up. He knew that the music industry was in turmoil, and as much fun as he was having, he understood that if he wanted to build a sustainable company, he'd need to look at other markets to hedge his bets. So he decided to become a little more familiar with businesses on his home turf in western Massachusetts. It wasn't as sexy as designing websites for rock stars, but he felt that his creative talents might be even more appreciated in the corporate world than they were in the ever-demanding music industry. It was time, he thought, to let his light shine in his own community.

Ciecko joined the Ad Club of Western Massachusetts, where he did a presentation on the websites he had created for major record labels. "They put it on in a nightclub, and the feedback was crazy," he says. "A month after that, I was on the front page of *Business West*, the business journal of western Massachusetts." He also had entered five of his websites in a regional advertising industry competition and won an ADDY Award—the highest award in the industry—in every category he entered, including best of show. It may seems like a minor accomplishment for someone who had rubbed elbows with Mick Jagger, but the coverage resulted in several leads and convinced Ciecko that doing business on his home turf was the path not only to sustainability but also to scalability. He's landed several corporate clients, and the segment now accounts for 25 percent of his revenue.

Ciecko finds that his corporate work is satisfying in a way that's fundamentally different from the charge he gets from his music-industry projects. "Many times the new corporate clients are sick of the old and traditional and are very interested in the more creative, innovative, freshly stylized edge I can contribute to their project or Web presence," he says. "To me, that is a very exciting position to be in. Helping corporations achieve something even remotely creative is a huge step for them."

In line with his desire to create a local footprint and to help revitalize the flagging business climate in his hometown, Ciecko also bought a 15,000-square-foot building in Holyoke last year with the intention of renovating it and transforming it into a mixed-use creative space. He wants it to house a small-business incubator because "I didn't have any business mentors until after high school, and it's clear that mentors can have a big impact on young businesses, especially in a tough city like Holyoke."

But even as he moves into the corporate market, Ciecko knows that he must exercise some caution. He's aware that his two very different client bases make very different demands on his company, so he's working on creating a separate brand for the corporate sector; grungy rock stars next to clean corporate clients on his client roster just might alienate both types of clients. Ciecko's big challenge will be to keep both markets happy while maintaining his Ten Minute Media brand integrity and building a corporate practice that's also authentic.

The Niche Advantage

Rachel Hennig, age 29, took a different approach to redefining her market. While Ciecko is diversifying his customer base, Hennig, CEO of the Denver-based information technology (IT) recruiting and consulting company Catalyst Search, has narrowed hers. It was a strategy that saved her company. Hennig defines her business in terms of two distinct time frames: before and after 9/11. Like Joel Erb at IMN Marketing (see Introduction and Chapter 7), Hennig almost lost her business after the terrorist attacks.

She had started Catalyst in 1999 after learning about the industry while working at an "older generation" recruiting company run by command-and-control owners. "It was the most aggressive, horrible work environment," she recalls. "Nine months into working for them, I realized I was bringing in most of the clients and the candidates. So I thought, 'Why not start my own business?' I was on straight commission, so I had nothing to lose." Hennig was just 19, but her company grew rapidly to 15 employees and a steady stable of clients. All that changed after 9/11.

"Our industry tanked," she says. "We were relying on a small portfolio of customers, and we definitely had all our eggs in a small basket." Revenues were about $600,000, and Hennig was $300,000 in the hole. So she cut her staff to just one other person and "went back to the basics to claw my way out of debt." For six months, there was no business, and bankruptcy loomed as a very real possibility. Hennig, then age 23, frequently hunted for change on the floor of her car to afford Taco Bell for dinner. And then she was thrown a lifeline.

In the spring of 2003, Hennig pitched a large national insurance company and landed the business. That client ultimately transformed her business. The health-care industry has very specialized technology systems, and Hennig decided to rebuild her business around them because the market seemed so promising. The population was aging, there was talk of health-care reform, and the industry was woefully behind in terms of IT know-how. She planned to leverage her experience with her first client to pursue similar ones. So she educated herself on the intricacies of claims infrastructure and clinical information systems and filled her stable of consultants with candidates who had experience serving health-care providers and payer organizations.

> "Our industry tanked. We were relying on a small portfolio of customers, and we definitely had all our eggs in a small basket."
>
> —Rachel Hennig, Catalyst Search

Catalyst's reinvention, necessitated by disaster but driven by persistence, has paid off handsomely. With just under $8 million in revenue, the company has 20 full-time employees and deploys 80 consultants to 60 clients, all in the health-care industry. Hennig has opened up regional offices in New Jersey and California and says that 2009 started with "the strongest numbers we've ever seen." She's expecting that to continue throughout the year, given President Obama's stimulus plan and his commitment to funding health-care IT systems. "A lot of general recruiting firms are looking to get into this area," she says. "But they don't have the database that we have or the industry knowledge. There are really only two or three other companies that do what we do nationally."

 ## Morphing the Model

Your customers love your product, you're a darling in the press, and there's nothing but blue sky ahead. And then something happens. Or doesn't happen, as the case may be. You hit a wall, and revenue won't budge; you can't get more customers to drink the Kool Aid; or maybe the competition puts the squeeze on you. The trick to not getting steamrolled is understanding what really differentiates you from the pack and leveraging that value. Sometimes that means morphing your business model.

This is a familiar scenario for Ben Kaufman, CEO of Kluster (see Chapter 1). His first company, Mophie, designed iPod accessories in Burlington, VT, and Kaufman successfully differentiated the company by drawing in a community of consumers to help him design new products. Mophie's highly original brand story drove revenue up to $250,000 a month, but margins and cash flow were terrible. "We thought it would be a branded business, but we were wrong," says Bo Peabody, Kaufman's investor and a managing general partner at Village Ventures. "It was a commodity business. We saw the writing on the wall; we could have done a million a month, and it would still be a bad business."

So Kaufman sold Mophie in fall of 2007, but he took with him what he always thought was the most valuable part of the company: the process for collaborative creativity, idea generation, and product development. He built a technology platform around the process, renamed his company Kluster, and moved the entire operation to Manhattan, where he could be closer to potential clients. He now has seven advertising agencies that pay him $10,000 to $20,000 a month to license the software, which facilitates idea sharing among employees. He's also using the technology for his own projects, such as a website called "NameThis," where customer pay $99 to have an online community come up with clever name for their new companies or projects. With just under $1 million in revenue, Kaufman expects Kluster to break even in 2009.

> "I like seeing my stuff in peoples' hands. So I want to take the Mophie concept and Kluster and put them together in a very fluid way."
>
> — Ben Kaufman, Kluster

Perennially restless and dissatisfied, Kaufman is now itching to use the Kluster platform to start doing development for new products. "I like seeing my stuff in peoples' hands," he says. "So I want to take the Mophie concept and Kluster and put them together in a very fluid way." The idea: a new venture called Quirky which will call upon Kluster's community to come up with new-product ideas, which will be validated (or not) by their peers. Kaufman says the winning ideas will be developed until they're ready to be produced, at which point he'll feature them on an e-commerce store. As soon as enough orders are generated so that the product at least breaks even,

Kaufman will put it into production. The inventor, community members who helped to develop the idea, and Kluster, of course, all will share in the revenue. His goal: two new products a week. Pie in the sky? Maybe. But Kaufman, at the impossibly young age of 22, has been around the track enough times with different iterations of his business model that he figures he'll hit pay dirt at some point. And if he hits a wall again? He'll extract what worked, decide what's of value, discard the rest, and try again.

A Different Revenue Stream

Like Kaufman, Luke Skurman at College Prowler has fiddled with his business model more than once, and he's at it again. In March 2007, Skurman digitized 50,000 pages of content from his college guidebooks and made them available online through a $39.95 annual subscription fee. His assumption: Sales of books, plus the additional revenue stream of Web subscriptions, would give sales a good boost. But it didn't happen. "Revenue was neutral," says Skurman. "We tried changing the website, changing the price point, but it all came down to one thing: There's a small percentage of the market that will purchase content, but the majority won't." More sophisticated college websites and scrappy Internet competitors like Unigo (see Chapter 3), which offers student-created college information, just exacerbated the problem.

So early in 2009, Skurman realized that he would need to find a way to offer his valuable content to users for free. But how would he monetize the site? Advertising and strategic partnerships were obvious solutions, and he had made some inroads there. Wachovia Bank (now owed by Wells Fargo), for instance, has a six-figure contract with College Prowler. But it was at an industry trade show, held by the National Association for College Admissions Counselors (NACAC), that Skurman's wheels began to turn.

At the NACAC trade show, he noticed that a substantial number of exhibitors were companies that were in the business of selling leads to colleges. "It felt like the biggest revenue stream at the show," says Skurman. "And almost everyone was selling leads to for-profit universities. Every incremental applicant is profit to them, so they're willing to pay for an applicant." Skurman began to think that he may be sitting on a gold mine. If he could offer free content to his users and, with their permission, pass along their contact information to colleges and universities that would pay him a lead-generation fee, that might amount to a tidy revenue stream for College Prowler.

So he's now talking with five colleges and universities about the possibility of doing business. His biggest hurdle: His prospective clients typically buy all their leads from the industry's 800-pound gorilla, College Board, which sells the names of SAT takers to colleges for 30 cents a pop. He thinks that he may need to give away some leads initially to prove his point, but he's willing to make that investment. He's confident that he can beat College Board in terms of lead conversion—that is, the number of students who actually apply to a college. "In this economy," he says, "everyone wants measured results, and I believe that if we're portraying colleges accurately on our site, our leads will convert the best." If he's right, he may just see the revenue increase that he hoped for when he first digitized College Prowler's content.

Spreading Your Wings

Say you've got a good thing going. Revenues are steady, and cash flow is good. You've got the respect of the market, and your customers are loyal. Your internal systems and processes are in place, and you've got the right team to make them work. Everything is feeling, well, comfortable. For some people, this is a nice place to be. But not for most entrepreneurs. "I don't like being content," grouses Rob Kalin, CEO of Etsy, the online marketplace for handmade goods (see Chapter 5). "If I'm content with everything, I get the hell out." He's not alone. Entrepreneurs view their companies as works in progress, and if it's a classic characteristic that they're easily bored, that's even truer for Upstarts. Blame it on the impatience of youth or that they may have been overscheduled as kids, but this generation of entrepreneurs appears ever eager to take their companies to new levels.

TerraCycle (see Chapter 6), for instance, might have done very nicely had it remained focused on its core business—organic "worm poop" fertilizer packaged in plastic bottles headed for the recycling plant. But CEO Tom Szaky had bigger plans. He suspected that his original product represented only a portion of his company's value; he had a hunch that the "upcycling" concept behind his packaging not only had serious market potential but also might be the path to bringing the green revolution to the masses.

Could he create a business that would make new, branded products out of materials that otherwise would be discarded?

With characteristic chutzpah, Szaky approached some of biggest consumer brands in the country to help him collect trash. The concept was similar to the "Bottle Brigade" system he used to collect used bottles for fertilizer: Outsource the collection of specific types of packaging to schools or not-for-profit organizations, and get companies to sponsor the programs by footing the bill for logistics and donating a few cents per collected item to the not-for-profits. The payoff for the companies: Their packaging—Capri Sun and Honest Tea juice pouches, Oreo and Chips Ahoy! packages, Clif Bar wrappers, and Bear Naked Granola bags—would be turned into cool products such as tote bags, umbrellas, shower curtains, and pencil cases. The result: increased brand exposure combined with a surefire way to communicate to customers that the companies cared about the environment.

Nailing down strategic partnerships like these is every entrepreneur's dream, of course, but Szaky makes it sound easy. "If you create something unique that solves a big problem that these companies have, they'll open the door and make it happen," he says. "It's a totally different paradigm of looking at a way to do business. No one ever came up with a solution like this— I haven't gotten a 'no' yet."

In 2008, TerraCycle started partnering with Nabisco, Kraft, and Kellogg, which now sponsor collection brigades at more than 20,000 organizations. TerraCycle then sends the trash to factories in Mexico, where it's fashioned into new products. The most successful collection brigade, says Szaky, has been Capri Sun juice pouches. "So far, we've turned 35 million juice pouches into half a million units of finished goods," he says. These include backpacks, tote bags, pencil cases, and homework folders that are sold through retail distribution channels that are as impressive as TerraCycle's upcycling partners: Target, Wal-Mart, Whole Foods, OfficeMax, CVS, and Walgreen's are all greening up their operations and their public images by carrying the products. Szaky kicked off his partnership with Target in a campaign that can only be described as true marketing genius. He convinced the giant retailer to buy the front and back covers of the April 14, 2008, issue of *Newsweek*. The ad was designed as a prepaid envelope that readers could tape together, fill with their plastic bags from Target, and send to TerraCycle, which would have them "upcycled" into tote bags to be sold at Target. The reward: Everyone who sent in bags would get a coupon for a free tote. There were 47,000 takers. More important, TerraCycle was featured in *Newsweek*, and it didn't cost the company a dime.

All of this is not exactly what Szaky could have predicted when he started his company in 2002. Then again, he has some pretty ambitious goals. He wants to grow TerraCycle to $1 billion in sales "as soon as possible," and he probably can't do that by selling plant fertilizer. Instead, he has essentially helped to create a new industry—"upcycling"—that he believes will be as big as recycling in 10 years. He's doing it by throwing in his lot with exactly the types of companies that most environmentalists and green entrepreneurs abhor. But it's tough to argue with the rationale: "Tom knows that if you're going to make a difference and affect the buying habits of Americans, you have to do it selling to Target and Wal-Mart," says his vice president of media relations, Albe Zakes. "You won't make a difference selling to co-ops."

In 2008, TerraCycle produced approximately 3 million "upcycled products" from garbage that yielded $100,000 in donations to the not-for-profit organizations that helped collect it. Revenues were $7 million in 2008, and Szaky was predicting $17 million for 2009. This is an ambitious goal, but given Szaky's cachet with some of the largest retailers and consumer brands in the world, it doesn't seem unrealistic. "It's helping us strategically," says Jeff Chahley, senior director of sustainability at Kraft Foods, which sponsors over 6,000 drink-pouch brigades. Kraft's partnership with TerraCycle helps the company reduce the amount of its packaging that ends up in landfills, but, says Chahley, "We're also connecting with moms and reinforcing that the brands their kids love are also environmentally responsible." The program also gives Kraft props with individual and institutional investors who scrutinize companies' commitment to sustainability. It's a big win for all concerned, but especially for TerraCycle.

Financing the Next Level

A big idea often requires big money, but that's not something that Etsy's Rob Kalin sought out initially. Kalin was a classics major on his sixth college (NYU) when he was hired to help redesign a website called "Getcrafty." This is when he got the idea for Etsy (see Chapter 5), an online marketplace where individual craftspeople would sell their handmade goods. With the help of three friends, Chris Maguire, Haim Schoppik, and Jared Tarbell, and an angel investor named Spencer Ain, who gave him $50,000, Kalin built Etsy, and the site went live in June 2004.

Kalin soon realized that he needed help and more cash, so he wrote an impassioned fan letter to two highly successful Web entrepreneurs whom he greatly admired: Caterina Fake and Stuart Butterfield, the cofounders of Flickr. "I told them, 'What you built with Flickr was amazing; here's something I built,'" recalls Kalin. "To my great amazement, they responded right away, and they invited me out to San Francisco." He hung out with Butterfield and Fake for a month in the spring of 2006, and the two introduced him to several venture capitalists. Those connections could have landed him millions, but Kalin made it clear that he wasn't interested in giving up 20 percent of the company for a boatload of cash; he only wanted what he needed at the time. "Staying hungry is something that's really important," he said in a 2007 video interview with *Wallstrip*. Ultimately, he got exactly what he needed and wanted: $650,000 in seed capital from Butterfield; Fake, del.i.cious founder Joshua Schachter, who they had introduced to Kalin; and Fred Wilson, from Union Square Ventures.

Two years later, Etsy had hit its stride and was almost at breakeven, but increased traffic and a burgeoning number of stored images meant that the company would need to spend $5 million on software and hosting within the next two years. Plus, Kalin had some ambitious expansion plans. He wanted the site to be globally accessible, and that meant doing business in other languages and currencies. He wanted to build an in-house payment system so that every buyer wouldn't have to pay every seller individually at checkout time, and he wanted to provide sellers with statistics on their stores. To do all this, he'd need more employees, and he'd need to pay them good salaries and full benefits. But most of all, he realized that while he had created a company that seemed to be succeeding in its lofty mission to help create sustainable businesses for independent crafters, it all could fall to pieces without money in the bank. Suddenly, he needed what the venture community tried to give him back in 2006.

And that's precisely what he got early in 2008, when two of his original investors were joined by Jim Breyer at Accel Parnters in a $27 million capital raise for Etsy. It was a huge departure for Kalin, who had always raised small amounts of money to get the company through the next six months. Now, he's thinking seriously about an initial public offering (IPO) and is in the process of professionalizing the company's management team. In the spring of 2008, he hired an experienced chief operating officer (COO), Maria Thomas, who had worked with Amazon.com and NPR.org, and then named her CEO in July 2008. To introduce her, Kalin produced a video of Thomas playing the drums and talking about her background and her passion for Etsy's community. He posted it on Etsy's blog, "The Storque," so that his community of buyers and sellers could see exactly who was taking his place in the CEO's seat: a folksy, accessible, and reassuring woman who smiles easily, has professional gravitas without the corporate attitude, and looks as if she'd be as comfortable holding a pair of knitting needles as a set of drumsticks.

Did Kalin get pressure from his investors to step down as CEO? He says no. Creating processes and putting systems in place are not his strength. He's now chief creative officer, a role that he says is better suited to his temperament. He'll also devote time to launching a new not-for-profit organization, Parachutes.org, that will focus on educating crafters on how to make a living by making things. But now that he's got venture money and two big investors on his board, the most important role that Kalin will play is one that he has always seemed to relish. "I want to keep people slightly off balance," he says. "I'm the canary in the coal mine against this place becoming too corporate."

Growing Up

Like Kalin—and most entrepreneurs in general—Upstarts inevitably reach the point of desperately needing professional management. It's no big secret that entrepreneurs who thrive on the startup process are often very befuddled when it comes to the day-to-day nuts and bolts of running a company. They're frequently too busy thinking big thoughts about the company's future, or perhaps they simply get bored. Countless entrepreneurs dig themselves into holes because they wait too long to ask for help, either by hiring a good COO or even replacing themselves with a CEO. And so their businesses grow, but they never grow up. I've seen it more times than I can count, and it's almost always a disaster. Upstarts, however, seem to know when it's time to call in the reinforcements. Maybe it's their collaborative nature, their impatience with mundane tasks, or their eagerness to learn from people who know more than they do, but these young entrepreneurs are astute when it comes to understanding their own limitations.

Jordan Goldman, CEO of Unigo (see Chapter 3), frequently calls on his chief financial officer (CFO), 45 year-old Paul Dietz, for advice. "I'm soliciting input at every turn," he says. "I'll go to Paul and say, 'I don't know how to put together a three-year plan. Give me some docs and spreadsheets that I can look at. Show me how to do it right.'" Nick Thomley, CEO of Pinnacle Services (see Chapter 6), hired his COO, Jill Cihlar, in 2007 when the company was struggling with rapid growth. "It was probably a bit premature in terms of where the company was in size," says Thomley. "But since bringing her on board, the operations have been better and smoother than ever. Jill complements me in all of the areas where I'm deficient." Sometimes, though, the best thing you can do is replace yourself altogether. That's what the founders of PopCap did.

"It probably just hit us last year that we're a real company," says John Vechey, the 30-year-old cofounder of the $43 million Seattle-based developer of casual video games. He's exaggerating, of course. PopCap has been a "real company" virtually since he started it nine years ago with Brian Fiete, age 31, and Jason Kapalka, age 37. The company's popular and unassuming games, such as *Bejeweled, Chuzzle,* and *Peggle,* have won a slew of awards and have been downloaded more than a billion times. *Bejeweled,* Pop Cap's first game, has sold 25 million units. The games, which originally were available only online through PopCap's website and from partners such as MSN, AOL, and Shockwave, are now sold through retailers such as Wal-Mart and have been tweaked for mobile devices and game systems such as Xbox LIVE. With steady profits and a consistent 50 percent annual revenue growth rate, the company has been an attractive acquisition target for years, but Vechey, Fiete, and Kapalka have resisted. The first substantial offer they turned down was a bid by Microsoft for $4 million in 2002, says Vechey.

But growth has not been easy for the partners. "I was the only person doing business development and being the CEO, and I was getting more and more frustrated," recalls Vechey. "I didn't have the support structure, and I didn't understand my limitations." The partners' relationships became strained, and Vechey actually left the company at "varying times" between

2003 and 2005 but always seemed to make his way back. Like so many young CEOs, he was feeling the strain of competing responsibilities: The business had taken on a life of his own, drawing his attention further and further away from the game-development projects that he loved.

Then, in 2005, the company received another acquisition offer. This time it was for $70 million—a seriously tempting deal from a buyer the partners won't name at this time. "It was attractive, but we felt we had a lot of upside still left," says Vechey, who feels strongly that the PopCap brand is worth "hundreds of millions." Indeed, even though PopCap's games are far removed from the Halos and Maddens

> "It probably just hit us last year that we're a real company."
>
> —John Vechey, PopCap

of the gaming world, their enormous popularity with people who play games online (primarily women) has made the company an under-the-radar industry darling. That last offer was a wakeup call to PopCap's founders. "If we walked away from that deal, that came with some responsibility to take the business side of the company more seriously," says Vechey. "And we needed someone who would help us." So Vechey and his partners made a decision that they knew would have a major impact on the company: They would hire a seasoned CEO to help them grow so that when it came time for an acquisition or an IPO, there would no question as to PopCap's value.

Enter Dave Roberts, age 47, who had sold his stock photography company and was casting about for a new project. Some of his former employees had landed at PopCap, and when Roberts took a look at the company, he "became enamored. It was a fun business with a relaxed but get-things-done culture," says Roberts. In April 2005, he agreed to a trial six-month period as CEO and has been there ever since. "The biggest challenge came when I tried to expand the business," says Roberts. "There was trepidation; people were thinking, 'What if we become this big horrible company?'"

But expand they did. Roberts hired a full-time lawyer, a human resources (HR) director, and a senior business-development executive who "wore suits and had good hair"; he negotiated some key acquisitions, including a company in Dublin; and he insisted on monthly board meetings and convinced the founders to bring on an outside director. While Roberts helped to professionalize the company's systems, though, he left the culture alone. PopCap still has a kitchen well stocked with free food and drinks and a large game room with a Foosball table, plasma television, and arcade games, and the postman frequently plays *Robotron* at lunch. Roberts' dachshund, Noni, wanders the office, leaving a trail of chewed-up dog toys, and several employees work in an open area under a parachute that hangs from the ceiling. And the HR director, Ellen Marett, plans parties, organizes community volunteer days, stocks the kitchen with "a crazy amount of food," and generally makes sure that the company doesn't become big and horrible.

> "I learned that it's okay to do what I love and let someone else do the rest."
>
> —Brian Fiete, PopCap

"I think we all got really lucky," says Roberts, who now has equity in the company. PopCap's founders agree. With Roberts managing the business, Fiete, who says he "had a little trouble when we became 25 percent games and 75 percent business," can concentrate on simply being PopCap's chief technology officer (CTO). "I learned that it's okay to do what I love and let someone else do the rest," he says. For his part, Vechey spent a year in charge of the PC online division of the business but says, "I didn't get the results I wanted." For that, he blames himself. "I could have gotten more done if I had been more heavy-handed, but that's not my nature." So a few months ago he moved back over to the game studio, where he'll be managing a team of eight. He'll even have a boss, which he's looking forward to, even though "it's weird to know that I'm my boss's boss's boss." The role he's playing now is curiously similar to the one he played when the company was young, so he has come full circle. "Without Dave and the staff he's hired, I would never be able to move about like this," he says. "To be an entrepreneur in my own company is pretty cool."

 ## The Big Payoff

The entrepreneurial race has many finish lines. For some, the end goal is a sustainable business that offers a comfortable means of support and freedom from punching someone else's time clock. Others are serial entrepreneurs, bouncing from startup to startup like an ADHD kid who's off his or her meds. Sill others long to expand their reach nationally or internationally or to build companies that make the world a better place. And, of course, there are those big brass rings: the IPO and the acquisition. The latter turned out to be Caleb Sima's very lucrative finish line.

Last January, Sima traveled from his company's headquarters in Alpharetta, GA, to San Jose, CA, to sit down with the some top executives at a very large company to show them exactly what he could do for them. Or *to* them, rather. Sima, who is 29 years old but looks 19, opened his laptop, typed the name of the company into his Web browser, and then proceeded to hack into the firm's administrative systems where, if had he wanted to, he might have read private e-mails, accessed databases, viewed registration forms, or even injected malware. The executives—a chief information officer and a few key members of his staff—were stunned by their company's vulnerability. But Sima was not.

When he does that kind of presentation (and he does them often), he spends a few minutes before the meeting trying to find a way to hack into the company's website. On the off chance that he can't find a way in, he will do another demo for his audience: He'll hack into Hewlett-Packard's (HP's) website, go straight to the expense-reporting system, and start approving expenses using the identity of a top HP executive. It's okay, though, because Sima's stunt has been approved by HP; he works for them now and has ever since they bought his company, SPI Dynamics, for $100+ million in August 2007.

This is not where Sima thought he would end up. As a teenager, he got kicked out of four high schools in one year, ran away from home, and was "a nightmare to my parents." To say he was technologically precocious is a vast understatement; his favorite pastime was "phone phreaking"—the art of manipulating audio frequencies to hack into a phone system. If you knew how to do it, you could hide in the bushes at McDonald's and screw up people's orders, taunt security guards at shopping malls, or interrupt a couple's conversation with "Hey, baby, who are you talking to?" or, better yet, fart noises. Sima did it all.

Happily, he grew up and decided to use his technology and hacking skills for good rather than mischief. He dropped out of school, got his GED at age 17, and then started working at various companies on Internet security projects. At one company, his job was to hack into clients' websites and then fix their vulnerabilities. "I was so cocky," he says. " I could hack into almost any company through its website, and I was doing it so easily." He went to his boss with a suggestion: Automate the fix so that people could find the holes on their own and repair them. As it turned out, Sima decided to do that on his own and set himself up as a consultant in 2000. But his timing was terrible. "I was a kid making $130,000," he says, " and then the Internet bubble started to pop, and I dropped to about $15,000. I sold my car, put a lot of debt on my credit card, and ate Ramen."

He tried desperately to get venture capital funding, but he was continually frustrated by the investment community's ignorance of Internet security. "Finally, with one venture capital firm I did a break-in right in front of them," he says. "I got into a major online retailer's site, and I showed them how I could manage accounts and stop transactions." At another firm, Sima broke into the company's site (with their permission) and "read their attorney's e-mail right in front of them. So they got it, and our solution made sense to them. My biggest thing was 'evangelism'—showing people that your antivirus and your firewall don't protect your website." On the power of his demos, he landed $2 million in funding in 2003, and SPI Dynamics became "a real company"; three more subsequent rounds totaled $10 million.

Sima's first acquisition offer came at the end of 2004, and he rejected it, along with other offers that seemed to double in price every year. "Stop lowballing us, and we can talk," he told them. Finally, HP stepped up, offering Sima golden handcuffs for two years and the opportunity to be integrated into the company's software group, which, Sima says, "is like a startup," at least compared with its hardware-heavy parent. Still, he closed the deal with some trepidation. "I was stressed over employees, the culture clash, how our processes would change," he says. "The company went through tremendous changes, and it was pretty painful."

> "Now, I'm getting in front of CIOs and CEOs of Fortune 50 companies. HP has given me a totally different perspective."
>
> —Caleb Sima, founder of SPI Dynamics

The first point of pain: HP wanted to move Atlanta-based SPI 30 minutes north to Hewlett-Packard's offices in Alpharetta. "There were cubicles everywhere, and it was dreary and dismal," recalls Sima. "We looked at it, and we said, 'Hell, no.' We wanted couches and beanbags and poker tables, and they said, 'No, no, no.' I knew people would leave and that the value they brought would disappear." Sima stood firm and asked the facilities people at HP to give him the floor diagram for the SPI workspace. They agreed, and Sima and his staff modified it, opening up the space, using fewer materials, and staying within the original budget. "They pushed back and pushed back, and we kept saying, 'No, we won't move unless you allow us to do this.'"

All this over office space? It may seem like a superficial battle, but it was Sima's opening skirmish, and he knew that his 140 employees were taking careful note. How far would their boss go for them? In the end, Sima got his way right down to the poker table. And after a brief period of scuffling, when the facilities staff took down the Bob Marley posters at night and Sima's staff put them back up in the morning, things seemed to settle down. "These were minor things, when you think about it," says Sima, "but they're major for the company because they help us maintain the spirit and retain employees." In the long run, says Jonathan Rende, Sima's boss at HP Software, "it wasn't easy for the facilities people, but they saw the light. When it was all done, they took pictures of the place. They wanted to make that [design] a part of how they integrate small companies in the future."

> "There were cubicles everywhere, and it was dreary and dismal. We looked at it, and we said, 'Hell, no.'"
>
> —Caleb Sima, founder of SPI Dynamics

There's more to integration than just office space, of course. Eighteen months after the acquisition, Sima had lost "a couple of top performers," but retention was looking pretty good. "When you're a startup and you want to do something like change a website, you just do it. Now, we go to legal, then to the marketing people to approve the material, and then to the people who get it on the server. For us, that learning process was very painful, and I think we lost a lot of productivity during that first year because of the things we had to fight for." But Sima has no regrets. "As a startup, you're always selling from the bottom up. Now I'm getting in front of CIOs and CEOs of Fortune 50 companies. HP has given me a totally different perspective."

Sima's golden handcuffs come off in August 2009. He says that he's in no hurry to leave HP or to start another company. "I'm going to take my time and enjoy my education here and learn from it," he says. "I don't want to start another company just to start another company. I'll do it when I find something that I'm passionate about." Sima pauses and then adds, tentatively, "I'm starting to see opportunities that make sense to me." I'll give him six months. Tops.

 **UPSTARTS PLAYLIST**

Track 8: Morph, Scale, and Grow Up

1. **Assemble the right team.** A great staff can help your company soar, but the wrong team can keep it hopelessly grounded. Like Luke Skurman at College Prowler, You may need to let go of the people who helped you in the startup phase and hire new employees who can help you move forward. You'll also need to come to grips with your own limitations. Nick Thomley at Pinnacle Resources brought on a COO to manage day-to-day operations during a period of intense growth; and Jordan Goldman at Unigo relies on his CFO to watch the company's bottom line and to help him become more financially savvy. Don't let revenue growth outpace the capabilities of your team.

2. **Diversify your business.** Brendan Ciecko at Ten Minute Media loved creating websites for rock stars, but with the music industry in flux, he knew that he needed to diversify. Now he summons the same creativity energy he used for Mick Jagger to do innovative work for companies that are sick of their stodgy websites. While he continues to do lots of work for recording artists, the corporate sector gives him stability and flexibility, and it allows him to create a local footprint for his company.

3. **Identify value.** What is your company's true value proposition? It isn't always obvious. Ben Kaufman was making cool iPod accessories using community-based innovation. But he realized that his process and the software program he built to manage it were actually more valuable than the products he was selling. Now he licenses his software to large advertising agencies and uses it to launch his own Web-based and product-development companies. Likewise, Tom Szaky at TerraCycle realized that the used plastic bottles in which he was packaging his organic fertilizer were the springboard for an entirely new business—one that turned trash like candy wrappers and juice boxes into new "upcycled" products.

4. **Read the tea leaves.** Rachel Hennig's IT recruiting company nearly tanked after 9/11. Then she noticed that health-care IT was booming, so she repositioned her company to capture that market. Now her business, Catalyst Search, is thriving. When Marcus Adolfsson at Smartphone Experts realized that an increasing number of smartphone forums were competing with his own sites and often getting better search engine rankings, he saw the writing on the wall. But rather than go head-to-head with his competitors, he started working with them to create e-commerce stores for their sites. Since Smartphone Experts takes a cut of whatever is sold on those sites, increased traffic for competitors now means more revenue for Smartphone.

5. **Stay true to your mission.** Companies grow and change. Rob Kalin at Etsy eschewed big investors for years, but recently took $27 million so that he could beef up infrastructure and better serve customers. Caleb Sima sold his company, SPI Dynamics, to Hewlett Packard. And Tom Szaky at TerraCycle began partnering with the kinds of large retailers and consumer goods companies that most small environmentally conscious companies shun. In each case, the CEO took care to make sure that these big changes took place without compromising the companies' values, mission, or corporate culture.

6. **Don't be afraid to step away.** Not everyone can—or wants to be—a CEO. The best thing you can do for your company is to immerse yourself in what you're good at. Developing software? Drumming up new business? Product innovation? Just do it. Like Brian Fiete at PopCap, understand that "it's okay to do what I love and let someone else do the rest." You may want to choose someone internally or hire someone from outside. In any case, be aware that this is probably the most important hire you will ever make. You need to preserve your culture, reassure employees that the change isn't threatening, and make sure that your suppliers and customers know about and are comfortable with the change.

CHAPTER

9

The Future
of Upstarts

s this book was going to press, our country was in midst of what
President Obama has referred to as "the worst financial crisis since the
Great Depression." To say that the economy changed radically while I
was in the process of writing is a vast understatement. At the beginning of
2009, consumers weren't buying, banks weren't lending, the stock market
had been decimated, and our jobless rate had hit a 14-year high. Small-
business owners, beleaguered by it all, were still uncertain about how the
$787 billion stimulus plan might affect them. So it seems reasonable to ask
if the future of entrepreneurship for this generation of Upstarts is now in
peril. To find out, I went straight to the source.

As I mentioned in the Introduction, I did my research on GenY entrepreneurs partly on Facebook, where I set up a private page so that I could easily communicate with my sources (and they with each other) via discussion
boards and group messages. Over the course of a year or so, I asked them many,
many questions, the answers to which helped to shape the content of this book.
One of my last questions to them involved the economy and how they thought
the recession would affect not only their own companies but also the startup
ambitions of their peers. In this last chapter, I'm including some of their
responses in sidebars because, as it turns out, they're a pretty optimistic group,
and I wanted them to be able to tell you in their own words why they are.

"Entrepreneurs, especially of our generation, are going to play a significant role in leading the country out of the recession. My plan during these tough economic times is to run a leaner organization, diversify our services by entering different markets, and innovate. I am optimistic that we'll emerge with a stronger organization. Entrepreneurs set the tempo for their companies, and optimism is important."

—Nick Thomley, age 29, CEO of Pinnacle Services,
a social services company in Minneapolis

I'm optimistic as well, and with good reason I think. According to data compiled by the Small Business Administration's (SBA's) Office of Advocacy, the last two recessions (1990–1992 and 2001–2003) saw marked increases in small-business creation and declines in small-business deaths after the first year of each downturn. When unemployment is high—and at this writing, it's 9.4 percent—more people seek out entrepreneurial alternatives. No surprise there. Economic hardship can do you in, but it also breeds creativity and innovation, and it demands frugality, discipline, and good, old-fashioned tough-mindedness. This is a pretty good recipe for entrepreneurial success.

In fact, some of the biggest, most recognizable, and successful brands were launched during recessions: Hewlett-Packard, Microsoft, Trader Joe's, Lexis-Nexis, FedEx, MTV, CNN, Clif Bar, RF Micro Devices, and Wikipedia are just a few of the wildly successful businesses that got their start in tough economic times. Niels Bosma, research director at the Global Entrepreneurship Monitor (GEM), says that "recession can be a good time to start a business. Resources tend to be cheaper and, bank loans aside, more available. Many new innovations, such as the supermarket, took off during recessions, while large competitors were weakened and focused on survival. When we look back on this time, we may well find that the economic landscape was changed by entrepreneurs who started in this time."

"To be in probably the worst downturn when you are young gives you the chance to learn the most and see the greatest opportunities. If you can be challenged and survive this, then you can survive anything that is ahead of you. This will shape our leadership, our risk level, the way we leverage our companies in the future and probably enable all of us to build better and stronger companies for the long term. It's better to experience this in the beginning of your company and apply what you learned than to learn the lessons later on when you may not be able to start over. Maybe this is truly a gift for all the young entrepreneurs out there."

—Talia Mashiach, age 32, CEO of Eved Services, which outsources event services to hotels in Chicago

While there's no doubt in my mind that the current recession will force many small businesses to close their doors for good, I believe that it also will be a breeding ground for entrepreneurial greatness. Plenty of entrepreneurs actually will thrive in this environment, and in fact, I predict that we'll see a bigger bump in startups than we have in past recessions. GenY entrepreneurs will launch a significant number of these new companies. According to GEM, 9.15 percent of 18- to 24-year-olds and 12.12 percent of 25- to 34-year-olds started businesses in 2007. Even if those percentages merely remain steady, GenY's sheer numbers—approximately 77 million—would indicate an influx of several million Upstarts into the entrepreneurial arena over the next several years. But I believe their numbers will be even greater than historical data suggest.

The push of high unemployment and corporate meltdowns combined with the pull of lower startup costs will drive GenY to start companies in record numbers. The widespread availability of broadband connections, free and low-cost Wi-Fi networks, smartphones, and cloud computing makes staring a company infinitely cheaper than it was in previous recessions. When your data and software applications can live on the Internet and communicate seamlessly with your desktop, your laptop, your mobile device, and your employees—whether they're down the hall or on a different continent—it's easy to do business in your dorm room or your parents' basement. Yes, that's true for everyone, not just for GenY, but for this generation, there's no learning curve: Technology is like the air they breathe.

"We are feeling the pinch just like everyone else. In these tough times, only the most agile companies will make it through the storm. We are going back to the basics of what made us successful in the first place. When we first started the business, it was just me and my business partner with one truck. Our motto was "Hustle and Grow." We are now motivating all our franchise partners to get out there and hustle every day. These are times when small fish can become big fish, and vice versa. But only the hustlers will survive."

—Omar Soliman, age 27, cofounder of College Hunks Hauling Junk, a junk-removal franchise company based in Tampa, FL

These nascent entrepreneurs will have an excellent group of role models in many of the Upstarts featured in this book. Surviving, let alone thriving, in a recession is no cakewalk, but I believe that Upstarts are well positioned for the challenge for the following reasons:

1. **Upstarts know how to be frugal.** Many have bootstrapped their companies and are accustomed to operating and living on a shoe-string. They're less likely to be burdened with the financial demands of adulthood, such as mortgages and tuition, and may be better able to cut expenses and hang tough until the economy improves. If they can do that while their competitors are closing up shop, they'll capture market share and be ready to rock when the recovery starts.

2. **Technology will help them cuts costs.** Upstarts will continue to use their mastery of new technology and the Internet to operate their businesses more efficiently. It seems to me that the most promising cost savings will be realized in two areas: Upstarts typically eschew traditional marketing and advertising for guerilla and/or Web-based marketing via clever search engine optimizing (SEO) and social networking sites, and they also are extremely comfortable using mobile technology to work remotely and virtually, which allows them to reduce the fixed costs that come with office space.

3. **Nonfinancial resources are plentiful.** Parents, professors, peers, and mentors are willing to be tapped for advice and counsel, which is often even more valuable than cash. This collaborative generation of entrepreneurs will survive by reaching out to give and receive support during tough times. They'll draw upon their vast networks—their "tribes," as Seth Godin says—to find everything from employees (and there are plenty of good ones on the market during a recession) to strategic alliances to creative funding sources.

4. **Upstarts are innovators.** Many of their innovative ideas are borne out of a desire to serve the unmet needs of their own generation, and GenY is a very large and relatively affluent demographic. Their particular needs, along with those of their Baby-Boomer parents, will have an impact on the market for goods and services for decades to come. Companies that establish themselves as responsive to GenY, particularly at a time when tight-fisted consumers approach every purchase with intense scrutiny, have a clear competitive advantage going forward.

5. **Upstarts are agile and flexible.** Most Upstarts don't spend a lot of time on business plans, preferring instead to "just do it" and reinvent themselves as the market dictates. Their paths to success are more often winding than straight; chaos and uncertainty don't seem to faze them. They're unburdened by preconceived notions of how business should be done, preferring instead to build their own models. This extends to their workplace cultures as well, and they tend to create companies where the work-life interplay is fun, fluid, and flexible. This appeals to and engenders loyalty among young employees, who just may be a company's most important asset during a recession when stress and work demands run high.

"I welcome the rough times with open arms, as I'm certain that I'll learn some valuable lessons. The sinking of the economic *Titanic* is pushing me to become more efficient, creative, and fast on my feet. Our generation, having seen the collapse of major banks and household-name corporations, knows that there is no such thing as 'job security' or any type of security for that matter. That is both scary and exciting. It's forcing more GenYers to consider becoming entrepreneurs."

—Brendan Ciecko, age 21, CEO of Ten Minute Media, a Web design and marketing company in Holyoke, MA

For those who not only embrace the lessons of a shattered economy but also take advantage of the current economic situation to build stronger companies, I believe that the recession actually may be a blessing. Some of the Upstarts you've read about are already reaping the benefits. Firms such as First Global Xpress (see Chapter 3), Grasshopper—formerly GotVMail—(see Chapter 1), and Eved Services (see Chapter 3) are in the business of providing other companies with essential services such as voice mail, shipping, and event planning, and they do so in ways that help their customers operate more economically and creatively. TerraCycle (see Chapter 6), Happy Baby Food (see Chapter 5), and OneHope Wine (see Chapter 6) make products that are clearly linked to a social mission, giving consumers a way to feel good about spending when money is tight. Still others, such as Borrego Power (see Chapter 6), Shape Up The Nation (see Chapter 2), Catalyst Search (see Chapter 8), and Brass Media (see Chapter 1), are poised to profit from economic-stimulus dollars targeted toward alternative energy, health care, and education.

But whatever industry they're in, most Upstarts are now experiencing a dramatically different business climate than when they first launched their companies. Although more than you might think have been in business long enough to remember the dark days of the dot-com bust, this recession is far deeper and longer lasting, and its psychological impact is fundamentally different. This time, it's not overvalued, high-flying technology companies and foreign terrorists that have sent our economy into a tailspin; it's our own trusted institutions that are largely to blame. We're now watching companies that were "too big to fail" do exactly that. It's an unsettling time, but a time ripe with possibility. When I started writing this book, it was clear to me that GenY would emerge as the most entrepreneurial generation in history and that its members would change the business landscape for all of us. I believe this now more than ever. As we all struggle to understand what landed us in the fix we're in, one thing is for certain: Business as usual is a recipe for disaster. Upstarts just may have the secret sauce for success.

"If I had to summarize my feelings towards my generation, the current economy, and the future, I would use two words not being used much these days: thankful and excited.

"I am thankful for multiple reasons. We would all rather be starting and growing businesses in a stronger economy, we are the masters of our own destinies. I am thankful to be experiencing this economic climate at a young age. I am not married and do not have children, so I am not forced to choose between investing in my business or meeting my family's needs.

"I am excited and optimistic. I truly believe my generation's approach to entrepreneurship is the future of business. Many of my peers have watched their parents work at large companies, earning stock options and planning for retirement, only to see all of that flipped upside down. So our perception of risk has changed. When an interesting business idea is developed, my generation is far more inclined to think, 'How can I afford to not try this?' instead of 'How can I afford to try this?' That shift in mind-set leaves me incredibly excited and optimistic about our future."

—**Anderson Schoenrock, age 29, CEO of ScanDigital,**
a photo-scanning company in El Segundo, CA

Upstarts Survey

Y ou've just read the stories of 63 amazing Upstart entrepreneurs, but the structure of this book evolved after more than 150 interviews with young CEOs from just about every corner of the United States and in a huge variety of industries. In the spring of 2009, I checked back in with many of them and asked them to take a short survey so that I could give my readers a data-driven portrait of the people who helped me develop the architecture of *Upstarts!* It also seemed like a good time to ask them about the effect of the recession on their companies, and to get their thoughts on how the Obama administration's policies might impact them.

The survey, which I ran on Zoomerang.com, got 66 responses. The median age of the respondents was 27, and, collectively, they had started 168 companies! I think you'll find the rest of the results fascinating and sometimes surprising. Here they are:

1. What is your gender?

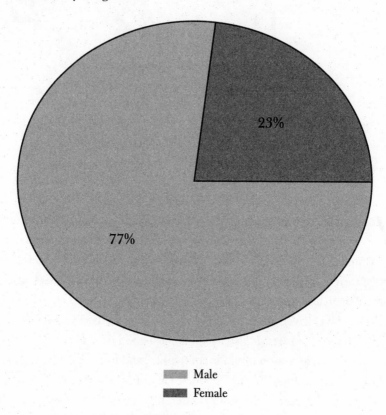

23%

77%

Male
Female

2. How many companies have you started?

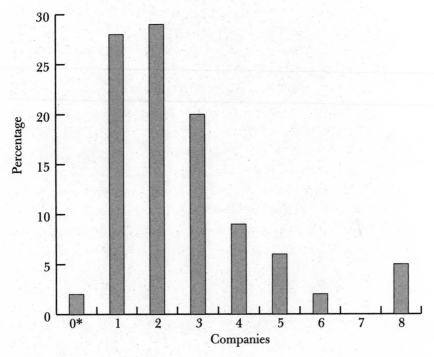

* Now running a family business

3. Did you start your company with a partner or partners?

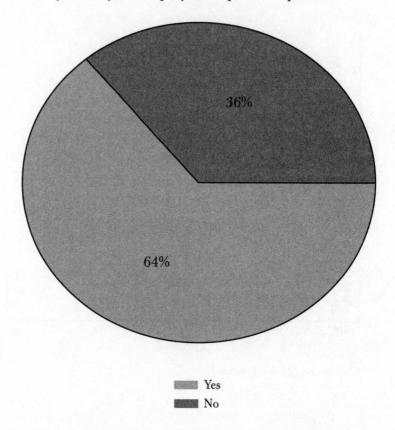

36%

64%

Yes
No

Male entrepreneurs were more likely to have started businesses with partners (67 percent) than were their female counterparts (53 percent).

4. Were either of your parents entrepreneurs?

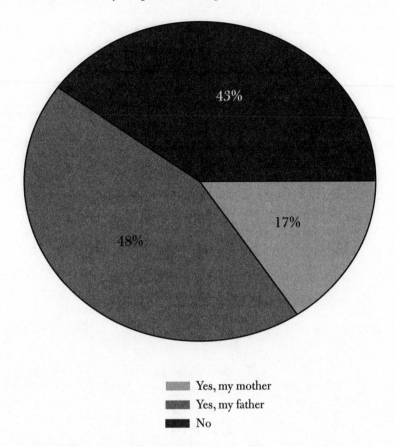

Yes, my mother
Yes, my father
No

*Totals exceed 100 percent, as participants were invited to check all that applied.

5. How old were you when you started your first company?

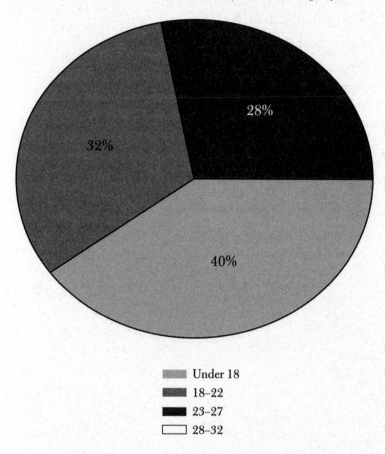

While nearly 50 percent of male respondents said they started their first company before age 18, only 14 percent of females got such an early start; 64 percent of female respondents started their first company between the ages of 23 and 27.

6. How would you describe your workday as compared to your peers who don't have their own companies?

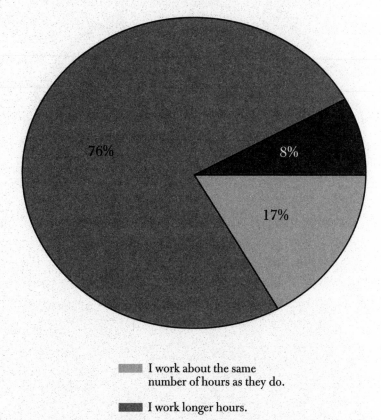

I work about the same
number of hours as they do.

I work longer hours.

I don't work as many hours
as they do.

7. What is the highest level of education you have completed?

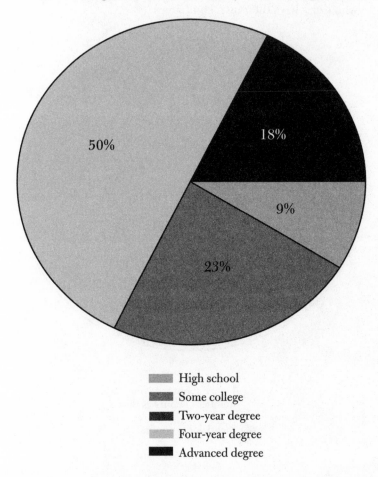

While 68 percent of respondents had a four-year or an advanced degree, education level seemed to have no relationship to either revenues or profits. Those with a high school education or some college were just as likely to have profitable companies exceeding $1 million in revenue as those with degrees.

8. Have you ever taken an entrepreneurship class in college?

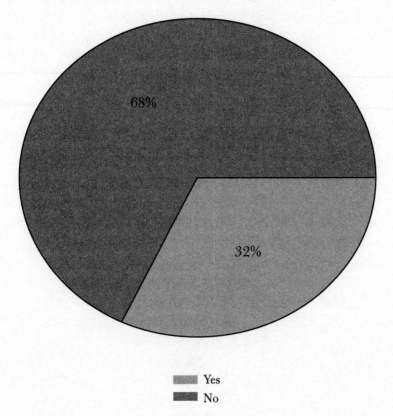

Of the 32 percent of respondents who had taken an entrepreneur-ship class, 48 percent had started their first company prior to age 18.

9. How old is your current company?

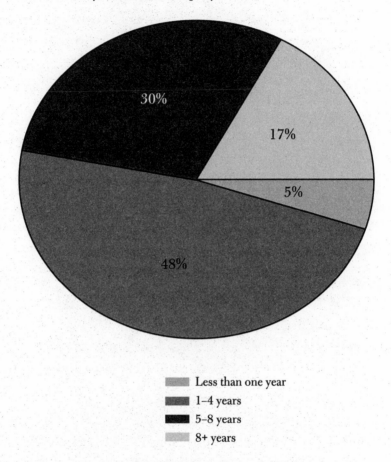

Less than one year
1–4 years
5–8 years
8+ years

Older companies had higher revenues: of the 29 percent of respondents who reported revenues of more than $5 million, 95 percent were more than five years old.

10. How many full-time employees do you have?

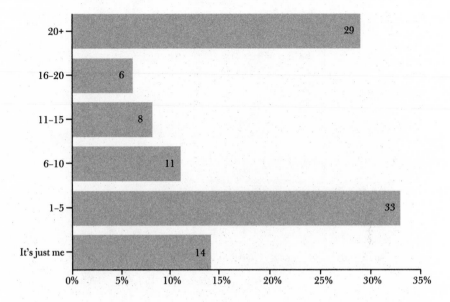

11.   What were your company's 2008 revenues?

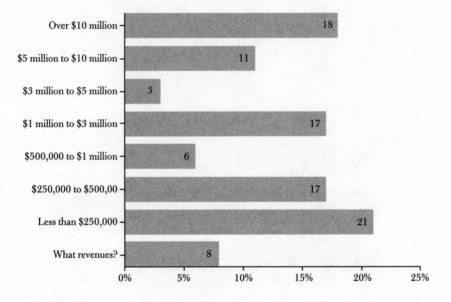

12.   Is your company profitable?

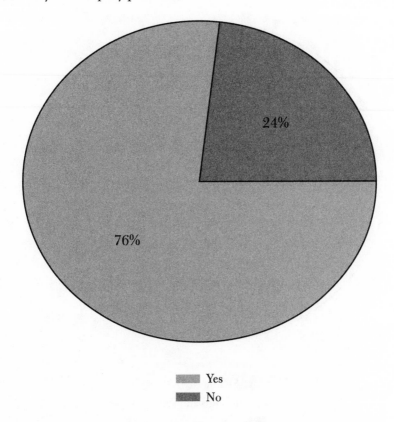

While revenue size doesn't always correlate with profitability, for
this group, it did. Of the 76 percent who said they were profitable,
62 percent of them had revenues in excess of $1 million. Female-
owned companies were slightly more likely to be profitable (80
percent) than their male counterparts (73 percent).

13. How is your company funded?

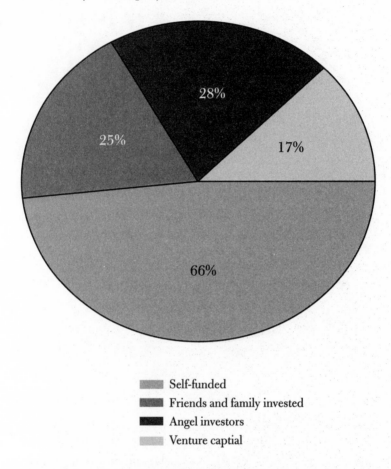

Self-funded
Friends and family invested
Angel investors
Venture captial

Approximately half of the companies that had received angel or venture capital financing were profitable, while nearly 80 percent of self-funded companies were in the black.

*Totals exceed 100 percent, as participants were invited to check all that applied.

14. Would you describe your company as having a social mission?

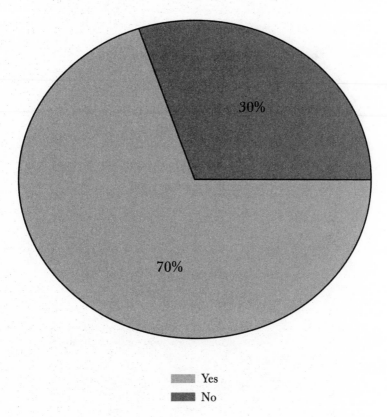

30%

70%

▭ Yes
▬ No

Companies with less than $1 million and those with more than $10 million were most likely to have a social mission. Female entrepreneurs were more likely to say they had a social mission (80 percent) than their male counterparts (67 percent).

15. How has the recession impacted your company?

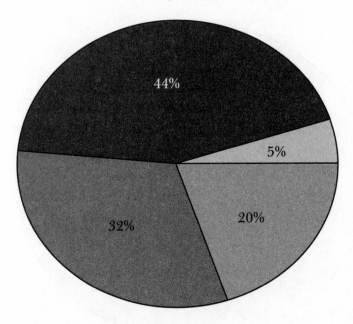

- ░░ The recession has actually been good for our company.
- ▓▓ We've felt very little impact.
- ██ Revenues will be lower than expected for 2009, but we're stable.
- ▒▒ We'e taken a big hit and are just barely hanging on.

Approximately half of the respondents said the recession has been good for, or has had little impact on, their company; 62 percent of that group had revenues under $1 million. Of the companies that said they were stable but predicted lower revenues for 2009, 66 percent had more than $1 million in revenue.

16. What kind of impact do you think President Obama's administration will have on your company?

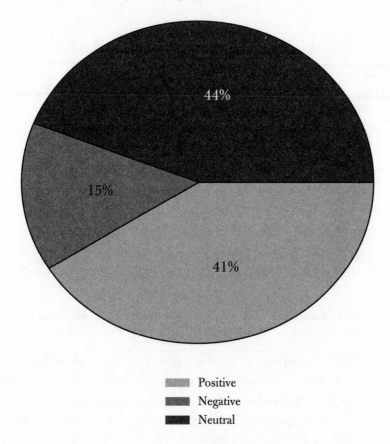

Positive
Negative
Neutral

17. On a scale of 1 to 10, with 10 being "most likely," how likely are you to …

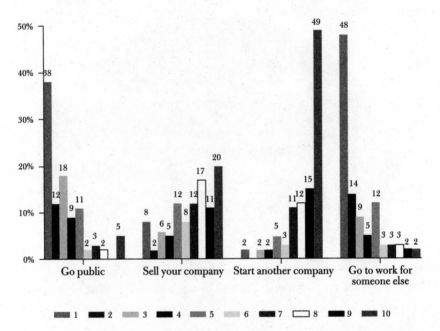

This is a generation of serial entrepreneurs, although significantly more male respondents (85 percent) than females (53 percent) said they were highly likely to start another company. In the entire population of respondents, the median number of companies already started was 2.

Expert Advice B
for Upstarts
from Rock Star
Entrepreneurs

They're the first generation to grow up with entrepreneurial heroes. Bill Gates, Steve Jobs, Richard Branson, and dozens of other rock star entrepreneurs showed GenY that starting a business is not just a way to make a living but also a way to change the world—and a very cool way, at that. As they blaze their own entrepreneurial trails, Upstarts look for guidance and inspiration to those who set the gold standard for excellence. To find out who they most admire, I messaged several of my interviewees in our private Facebook group and asked them to name names. Then I did my best to contact as many of those role models as I could, and I asked them to share some entrepreneurial words of wisdom. Here they are:

Advice for GenY

Don Tapscott, author of *Wikinomics* and *Grown Up Digital*

1. **Go to college.** It's way more interesting than high school, and you'll need more than a high school diploma to succeed in a knowledge economy. Besides, you'll need to continue to learn throughout the course of your life anyway. Read books of fiction and you will be enriched. Hone your writing skills, and your grammar. And don't use netspeak or slang at school or at work. It doesn't belong there.

2. **Be patient at work**, especially when you see old, outdated technology and bureaucratic ways of doing things. Instead of bolting right away, hang around for a while and fight for change. You're worth it: your knowledge about collaboration will drive innovation and success this century. Boomers might be your best allies. They have kids like you and are more likely to understand you and your use of technology. And you're right about the idea of the work-life dichotomy. It shouldn't be an oxymoron.

3. **Consider being an entrepreneur.** Small companies can have all the capability of large companies without all the liabilities—like deadening bureaucracy, legacy cultures, and technology.

4. **Don't discount experience.** You are an authority on something important—but you're not an authority on everything. As you enter adult institutions, you have much to teach, but much to learn. Your experience will make you a better entrepreneur, activist, teacher, or whatever you choose to be.

5. **Aspire to live "a principled life of consequence."*** You have one life—make it count. You're right to say that money isn't everything. By all means aspire to be prosperous. But the future needs more from you. Think about the world your kids will inherit and do

---

*Adapted from the Amherst College charter: "Amherst College educates men and women of exceptional potential from all backgrounds so that they may seek, value, and advance knowledge, engage the world around them, and lead principled lives of consequence."

what you can to make it a better one. Work in your community. Get engaged politically. Do the right thing.

6. **Don't give up.** When adults criticize your generation, don't take it personally. You are the smartest generation—really. You are the first global generation. You have a better world within your grasp. Reach out; hold on; make it happen.

Four Rules for Startups

Guy Kawasaki, founder of Alltop and author of *Reality Check*

First, do not listen to naysayers and bozos—not matter how successful or famous they are—when they tell you that "this can't be done."

Second, build a prototype before you create a PowerPoint, Word, or Excel document, because entrepreneurship is about doing, not planning.

Third, never ask your customers to do something that you wouldn't do.

Fourth, focus on sales, not partnerships or business development, because sales fix everything.

Choose the Right Cofounders

David Cohen, cofounder of TechStars

Choosing the right cofounders is clearly a critical element of success. Cofounders of a business typically spend more time together in more pressure-packed situations than married couples do. Through my work as an entrepreneur, angel investor, and my time running TechStars, one thing is abundantly clear: one of the biggest reasons for failure of early-stage companies is simply a failure for the founding team to work well together and truly execute. Cofounders need to have a mutual respect and deep appreciation for each other, but at the same time they always need to challenge each other to be better and move faster. They need to be there for each other so that when one is down, the others can pick her spirits up. Startups are hard enough even with great teams that work incredibly well together. Picking your cofounders wisely will very often make or break your company.

How to Challenge Convention

Seth Godin, author of *Tribes: We Need You to Lead Us*

I'd argue that there are four things to keep in mind when deciding to challenge a convention. You should incur the costs and hassles of inventing a new way to do things when you are prepared to deal with all four:

1. **Notice it.** When you make a new way to do something, people are going to notice it. We'll notice it when the volume knob on the radio doesn't work the way all the other ones do, or when the navigation on your website isn't where it "should" be. Is your creativity about the convention? For example, if you make a stereo that sounds better, it's not clear you should also change the way the volume control works. Noticing the shift in interface doesn't help sell your concept of better sound.

2. **Talk about it.** Often, a new convention leads to conversations. People need to teach other about the ideas in your product or service, or complain about it or debate it. Again, no point changing the convention unless what you want is people to talk about your new convention.

3. **Leverage it.** Does the success of the new convention in the marketplace actually help you? Sure, you could invent a new kind of handshake or a new pricing structure. But if it catches on, do you win? Is it at the core of your business model? Which leads to the last one ...

4. **Protect it.** Once the convention catches on, does the new way of doing things reinforce your position in the marketplace and lead to long-term benefits?

Time it Right

Bo Peabody, Managing General Partner, Village Ventures

Lately, I've found myself telling entrepreneurs two things. First, that being too early and being wrong are indistinguishable. And second, that technology does less in two years and more in 10 years than you think it's going to. These are just different ways of saying the same thing, which is that entrepreneurs can have too much vision. Markets don't often develop quickly because changing customer behavior takes a lot of time and money. If you're too far out in front, you may run out of money before the customers change their behavior. But if you're not far enough in front you won't have anything interesting to sell. Vision is not often compatible with capital efficiency, but capital efficiency is often synonymous with boring. Finding the right balance between vision and reality is the entrepreneur's toughest challenge.

Know How to Fail

Andy Stenzler, founder of five businesses, including Cosi and Kidville

Entrepreneurs need to be able to handle failure and actually thrive on it. Successful entrepreneurs will be the ones who failed at many things along the way but figured out a way to keep the overall business from ending up in the graveyard. If you have failed and live to tell about it, you will be a winner in the end.

Chase the Vision, Not the Money

Tony Hsieh, CEO of Zappos

I've been asked by a lot of entrepreneurs and people thinking of starting their own businesses questions such as "What's a good business to get into where I can make a lot of money?" or "What's a good market opportunity?"

My response has always been the same: don't chase the money. Instead, think about what you would be so passionate about doing that you'd be happy doing it for 10 years even if you didn't make any money from doing it, and that's what you should be doing. Chase the vision, and not the money ... and the ironic thing is that if you do that, the money will actually follow, because employees, customers, and business partners will all feed off your passion for what you're doing.

Make Work Fun

David Kelley, Founder and Chairman, IDEO, and Tom Kelley, General Manager, IDEO

If you are lucky enough to get in on the "ground floor" of a new-to-the-world enterprise, try creating an environment that blurs the line between work and play. Because life is long, and work fills a healthy slice of it. And whether this is good news or bad, GenY is likely to remain in the workforce later into life than any generation of the past century. But if you can find a way to make your work life intrinsically rewarding, if you can find projects that have meaning, if you can find work that you truly *enjoy*, then you won't mind the time you spend on the job. One of the founding principles of IDEO, more than 30 years ago, was to have a place we could work with our friends. As a result of that principle, we've made dozens of choices along the way that—in the short term at least—seemed to put our cultural values ahead of our financial interests: the *heart* ahead of the *dollar*. In the long run however, a funny thing happens: if you can successfully blur work and play, then people have more passion for their work and more fun on the job. They tap into more of their talent and creativity and energy. And—should this be so surprising?—passionate, energized teams *simply do better work* ... which creates the ultimate source of sustainable competitive advantage.

Following are citations for books, articles, research reports, and statistics that are referenced in the book, listed roughly in the order in which they appear. For a full list of the organizations I mention, along with links to the Upstarts' websites, visit the *Upstarts!* website at www.upstartsbook.com.

Introduction

Donna Fenn, *Alpha Dogs: How Your Small Business Can Become a Leader of the Pack*. New York: Collins, 2005.

Institute for the Future for Intuit, "Intuit Future of Small Business Report," Mountain View, CA, 2007–2008; available at http://about.intuit.com/futureofsmallbusiness.

Junior Achievement, "JA Worldwide 2006 Interprise Poll on Teens and Entrepreneurship," Colorado Springs, CO, 2006.

Ewing Marion Kauffman Foundation, "Survey of Endowed Positions in Entrepreneurship and Related Fields in the United States," Kansas City, MO, 2004.

Ewing Marion Kauffman Foundation, "Entrepreneurship in American Higher Education," Kansas City, MO, 2007.

Don Tapscott, *Growing Up Digital: The Rise of the Net Generation*, New York: McGraw-Hill, 1998.

Gallup, "Gallup Youth Survey," 2002, Washington, DC.

Bureau of Labor Statistics, "The Employment Situation Summary: January 2009;" available at www.bls.gov/news.release/empsit.nr0.htm.

"Generation Y Earns $211 Billion and Spends $172 Million Annually," Harris Interactive YouthPulse Study, Rochester, NY, September 2003.

Sydney Jones and Susannah Fox, "Generations Online in 2009," Pew Internet & American Life Project. Washington, DC, 2009.

"2006 Cone Cause Millennial Study. The Millennial Generation: Pro-Social and Empowered to Change the World." Cone, Inc., and AMP Insights, 2006.

University of California at Los Angeles Higher Education Research Institute, "The American Freshman: National Norms for Fall 2005," Los Angeles, CA, 2006.

Chapter 1

"Thomas Edison Invention Factory," National Trust for Historic Preservation, http://www.saveamericastreasures.org/profiles/edison .htm, June 1999.

Samir Husni, *Launch Your Own Magazine: A Guide for Succeeding*. Nashville, TN: Hamblett House, 1998.

Sharon Jayson, "GenY Makes its Mark and its Imprint is Entrepreneurship," *USA Today*, December 8, 2006.

Don Tapscott, *Wikinomics: How Mass Collaboration Changes Everything*. New York: Portfolio, 2006.

Max Chafkin, "The Customer Is the Company," *Inc.*, June 2008.

Chapter 2

Bruce Tulgan, *Not Everyone Gets a Trophy: How to Manage Generation Y*. San Francisco: Jossey-Bass, 2009.

Don Tapscott, *Grown Up Digital: How the Net Generation Is Changing the World*. New York: McGraw-Hill, 2008.

"Bill Gates demos Xobni, the new plugin for Microsoft Outlook," YouTube, http://www.youtube.com/watch?v=Mr5zOxG7wbU, 2008.

Erick Schonfeld, "Xobni Walks Away From a Microsoft Deal," TechCrunch, http://www.techcrunch.com/2008/04/30/xobni-walks-away-from-a-microsoft-deal/, April 30, 2008.

Paul Graham, "A Student's Guide to Startups," http://www.paulgraham .com/mit.html, October 2006.

"U.S. Deploys 'Zsa Zsa Saddam'," CNN.com, http://www.cnn.com/2003/WORLD/meast/08/18/saddam.pictures, April 18, 2003.

"Enterprise Value of Online Communities Yet to Be Fully Realized," Highlights from Deloitte's Tribalization of Business Study, New York, 2008.

Jeff Jarvis, "Hey Starbucks, How About Coffee Cubes?" *BusinessWeek*, http://www.businessweek.com/magazine/content/08_17/ b4081000030457.htm, April 15, 2008.

Chapter 3

To read more about Unigo, see Jonathan Dee, "The Tell All Campus Tour," *The New York Times Magazine*, September 18, 2008.

To read more about FGX, see Nitasha Tiki, "The Leadership Makeover," *Inc.*, March 2008.

"American Family Business Survey," Massachusetts Mutual Life Insurance Company, Springfield, MA, 2007.

Chapter 4

"2008 Alloy College Explorer Study," Alloy Media + Marketing, powered by Harris Interactive. New York, 2008.

The Crimson Staff, "Maid for Harvard? Students Should be Wary of Dormaid's Divisive Implications," *The Harvard Crimson*, March 10, 2005.

To hear Rush Limbaugh's segment on DormAid and to view the DormAid segment on *The Daily Show*, go to www.dormaid.com/press.

For demographic data on Match.com and eHarmony.com, go to www.quantcast.com.

To read more about about "Wal-Marting Across America," see Pallavi Gogoi, "Wal-Mart's Jim and Laura: The Real Story," *BusinessWeek*, October 9, 2006.

Elissa Moses, *The 100 Billion Dollar Allowance: How to Get Your Share of the Global Teen Market*. New York: Wiley, 2000.

To watch *The Ramp*, go to www.rampenfest.com.

Chapter 5

Seth Godin, *Tribes: We Need You to Lead Us*, New York: Portfolio, 2008.

Rob Walker, *Buying In: The Secret Dialogue Between What We Buy and Who We Are*. New York: Random House, 2008.

"Childhood Overweight and Obesity," Centers for Disease Control and Prevention, http://www.cdc.gov/nccdphp/dnpa/obesity/childhood/index.htm.

For growth statistics on the organic food and beverage industry, visit the Organic Trade Association at www.ota.com/organic/mt/business.html.

B.E. Hamilton, J.A. Martin, S.J. Ventura, Births: Preliminary data for 2006. *National vital statistics reports; vol 56 no 7*. Hyattsville, MD: National Center for Health Statistics, 2007.

Chapter 6

To learn more about IdeaBlob, go to www.ideablob.com.

Cone, Inc., "Past. Present. Future. The 25th Anniversary of Cause Marketing," Boston, MA, 2008.

Deloitte, Inc., "2007 Deloitte Volunteer IMPACT Survey of Gen Y (18- to 26-Year Olds)," New York, 2007.

To read more about TerraCycle, see Bo Burlingham, "The Coolest Little Start-Up in America," *Inc.*, July 2006.

Note: Direct links to the not-for-profit organizations mentioned in this chapter can be found at www.upstartsbook.com.

Chapter 7

"Employer Firm Births and Deaths by Employment Size of Firm, 1989–2005," Office of Advocacy, U.S. Small Business Administration, from data provided by the U.S. Bureau of the Census, *Statistics of U.S. Business*, Washington, DC.

Randstad North America, "2008 World of Work," Atlanta, GA, 2008.

"Smashing the Clock: Inside Best Buy's Radical Reshaping of the Workplace," *BusinessWeek*, December 11, 2006.

Bureau of Labor Statistics, "Labor Force Statistics from the Current Population Survey," Washington, DC, 2008.

To read more about Zingerman's, see Bo Burlingham, "The Coolest Small Company in America," *Inc.*, January 2003.

Chapter 8

Amy E. Knaup and Merissa C. Piazza, "Business Employment Dynamics Data: Survival and Longevity, Part II," *Monthly Labor Review* 30(9): 3–10, 2007.

"Introducing Maria Thomas," The Storque, http://www.etsy.com/storque/ etsy-news/introducing-maria-thomas-1660/, July 22, 2008.

Chapter 9

Ryan McCarthy, Nadine Heintz, and Bo Burlingham, "Starting Up in a Down Economy," *Inc.*, May 2008.

Niels Bosma, Zoltan J. Acs, Erkko Autio, Alicia Coduras, Jonathan Levie, "Global Entrepreneurship Monitor Report," *2008 Executive Report*, Babson Park, MA.